PRICING THE PLANET'S FUTURE

PRICING THE PLANET'S FUTURE

The Economics of Discounting
in an Uncertain World

CHRISTIAN GOLLIER

Princeton University Press
Princeton and Oxford

press.princeton.edu

Jacket Photograph: The 800-mile Alyeska oil pipeline crossing
the tundra near the Brooks Range in interior Alaska.
© Ken Graham / AccentAlaska.com

Library of Congress Cataloging-in-Publication Data

Gollier, Christian.
Pricing the planet's future : the economics of discounting
in an uncertain world / Christian Gollier.
p. cm.
Includes bibliographical references and index.
ISBN 978-0-691-14876-2 (hbk. : alk. paper) 1. Discount.
2. Investments—Social aspects. I. Title.
HG1651.G65 2013
332.8'4—dc23
2012017060

British Library Cataloging-in-Publication Data is available

This book has been composed in Times LT Std and Trade Gothic LT Std

Printed on acid-free paper. ∞

Printed in the United States of America

1 3 5 7 9 10 8 6 4 2

Contents

Preface

Nearly fifty years ago, in 1968, William Baumol[1] commented that "few topics in our discipline rival the social rate of discount as a subject exhibiting simultaneously a very considerable degree of knowledge and a very substantial level of ignorance." This book aims to reduce the level of ignorance about the social discount rate, presenting recent advances in the field. Ultimately, the objective is to help build a consensus around the way society should value the future.

Many people have contributed to the development of this book. I am grateful to my co-authors on various papers related to this book: Louis Eeckhoudt, Miles Kimball, John Pratt, Jean-Charles Rochet, Ed Schlee, Harris Schlesinger, Nicolas Treich, Marty Weitzman, and Richard Zeckhauser. I also thank Dominique Bureau, Christoph Heinzel, Jim Hammitt, and Stéphane Gallon for their very detailed comments. My graduate students at the University of Toulouse also provided useful remarks and suggestions. I am particularly grateful to Steve Elderkin for his superb research assistance, with respect to both diligence and talent.

My debt to Jacques Drèze goes back to the 1980s when, as a student at CORE in Louvain, I attended his enthusiastic and profound lectures on the economics of uncertainty. Although my intellectual interest in discount rates came later, I can trace it back to the IDEI lecture about the economics of climate change given by Kenneth Arrow in 1995. Since then, my curiosity about discounting and sustainable development has grown, reinforced by my interaction with many public and private institutions which have struggled with these complex questions. In the public sphere, let me mention the Centre d'Analyse Stratégique, the Conseil Economique du

[1] W. J. Baumol (1968), On the social rate of discount, *American Economic Review* (58), 788–802.

Développement Durable, the French Ministry of Ecology, and more recently the U.S. Environmental Protection Agency. I have also benefitted from frequent enquiries and interactions with economists from Electricité de France (EDF), AREVA, and Réseau de Transport d'Electricité (RTE), among others.

This book would not have been possible without the exceptional environment in my life. In addition to the members of my own family, I want to thank my colleagues at the Toulouse School of Economics (TSE) for the quality of the scientific atmosphere that I have enjoyed throughout the last twenty years. Working on a long-term project such as writing a book is a risky activity that requires self-belief to be maintained. This would not have been possible without the friendly encouragement of Jean Tirole, with whom I have shared the burden and honor of creating and managing TSE since 2007.

Finally, I acknowledge the continuing financial support of various institutions at crucial times in the writing of the book. The research has received funding from the European Research Council under the European Community's Seventh Framework Programme (FP7/2007–2013) Grant Agreement no. 230589. This project was also supported by various partners of TSE and IDEI, in particular the Financière de la Cité, the partners of the Chair "Sustainable Finance and Responsible Investment," and the French reinsurance company SCOR, which funded the Chair "Risk Markets and Value Creation" at IDEI.

Chapter 3 is derived in part from "On the Underestimation of the Precautionary Effect in Discounting," *Geneva Risk and Insurance Review*, 36 (2011): 95–111.

Chapters 5 and 6 are derived in part from "Discounting with Fat-Tailed Economic Growth," *Journal of Risk and Uncertainty*, 37 (2008): 171–186.

Chapter 7 is derived in part from "Maximizing the Expected Net Future Value as an Alternative Strategy to Gamma Discounting," *Finance Research Letters*, 1 (2004): 85–89, and C. Gollier and M. L. Weitzman, "How Should the Distant Future Be Discounted when Discount Rates Are Uncertain?" *Economic Letters*, 107 (3) (2010): 350–353.

Chapter 8 is derived in part from "The Consumption-Based Determinants of the Term Structure of Discount Rates," *Mathematics and Financial Economics*, 1 (2) (2007): 81–102.

Chapter 9 is derived in part from "Wealth Inequality and Asset Pricing," *Review of Economic Studies*, 68 (2001): 181–203.

Chapter 10 is derived in part from "Ecological Discounting," *Journal of Economic Theory*, 145 (2010): 812–829.

Chapter 11 is derived in part from "Discounting an Uncertain Future," *Journal of Public Economics*, 85 (2002): 149–166.

Chapter 14 is derived in part from "Discounting and Risk Adjusting Non-marginal Investment Projects," *European Review of Agricultural Economics*, 38 (3) (2011): 297–324.

PRICING THE PLANET'S FUTURE

Introduction

Many books have described how civilizations rise, blossom, and then fall. Underlying this observed dynamic are a myriad of individual and collective investment decisions affecting the accumulation of capital, the level of education, the preservation of the environment, infrastructure quality, legal systems, and the protection of property rights. This vast literature, from Adam Smith's *Wealth of Nations* through Gregory Clark's *Farewell to Alms* to Jared Diamond's *Collapse*, is retrospective and positive, examining the link between past actions and the actual collective destiny. In contrast, this book takes a prospective and normative view, analyzing the problem of investment project selection. Which projects should be implemented to maximize intergenerational welfare? The solution to this problem relies heavily on our understanding and beliefs about the dynamics of civilizations.

FUTURE GENERATIONS IN THE PUBLIC DEBATE

Life is full of investment decisions, trading off current sacrifices for a better future. In this book, I examine the economic tools which are used to evaluate actions that entail costs and benefits that are scattered through time. These tools are useful to optimize the impacts of our investments both at the individual and collective levels.

The publication in 1972 of "The Limits to Growth" by the Club of Rome marked the emergence of public awareness about collective perils associated with unsustainable development. Since then, citizens and politicians have been confronted by a growing list of environmental problems, including the disposal of nuclear waste, exhaustion of natural resources, loss of biodiversity, and polluted land, air, and water. For example, there is particular concern regarding one form of air pollution. The increased concentration of greenhouse gases in the atmosphere owing to deforestation and the combustion of fossil fuels is likely to affect our environment for many centuries. My fellow experts from the Intergovernmental Panel on Climate Change tell us that this could cause rising sea levels, increase the frequency of extreme climatic events such as droughts and cyclones, as well as an increase of 5°C or more in the average temperature of the earth if the remaining stocks of coal, petrol, and natural gas are burned (IPCC 2007). All of these environmental problems raise the crucial challenge of determining what we should and should not do for future generations. The challenge has wider relevance beyond the environment. It is also central to other policy debates, including, for example, the appropriate level of public debt, investment in public infrastructure, investment in education, and the level of funding for research and development. Many U.S. states still discount their pension liabilities at an 8% rate, which I believe implies a huge underestimation of the public pension debt to future retirees.

Public decision makers are not the only ones who must deal with complex choices in the face of long-term environmental risks. Some firms and altruistic citizens want to contribute to a more sustainable development. Financial markets are often criticized for being short-termist. However, financial markets offer specific "socially responsible" investments (SRI), which claim that they will restore a desirable level of long-term thinking in their rules for evaluating assets and their portfolio strategy. New institutions have been created to supply extra-financial analyses to measure companies' performance in the field of sustainable development. To say the least, these institutions together with managers of SRI funds face difficulties agreeing upon a definition of sustainable development, and creating a methodology to translate these concepts into operational rules for asset pricing. The absence of methodological transparency clearly limits the development of these products. Social scientists, in particular economists, should contribute to a coherent development of these markets and instruments.

Today, the judge, the citizen, the politician, and the entrepreneur are concerned by the sustainability of our development, but they don't have a strong scientific basis for the evaluation of their actions and their decision-making. The objective of this book is to provide a simple framework to organize the debate on *what should we do for the future?*

WHAT DO WE ALREADY DO FOR THE FUTURE?

For many thousands of years, since homo sapiens emerged as the dominant species on earth, almost all of their consumption was determined by what they collected or produced over the seasonal cycle. Pressured by Malthus' Law, humanity remained at a subsistence level for thousands of generations. The absence of the notion of private property, or the inadequacy of a legal system to guarantee that what an individual saves belongs to him, was a strong incentive to consume everything that was produced year after year.

It is clear that human beings, contrary to most other species, are conscious of their own future. At the individual level, a trade-off is made between immediate needs and aspirations for a better future. Individual investments can take many forms. When young, individuals invest in their human capital. Later on, they save for their retirement. They invest in their health by engaging in sports, brushing their teeth, eating healthy food. They plan their own future and those of their offspring to whom they can bequest the capital they have accumulated. In short, individuals sacrifice some of their immediate pleasures for future benefits. Once individual property rights on assets were guaranteed by strong enough governments and institutions, the potential of individual investments was unlocked. At the collective level they have generated the enormous accumulation of physical and intellectual capital that the western world has experienced over the last three centuries. New institutions, like corporations, banks, and financial markets, have been created for the governance of these investments. Taken together, this has been a powerful engine for economic growth and prosperity. With a real growth rate of GDP per capita around 2% per year, we now consume fifty times more goods and services than we did two hundred years ago.

States and governments also intervened in this process. They invested in public infrastructures like roads, schools, and hospitals. They heavily invested in public research whose scientific discoveries quickly diffused in the economy. At the collective level, these public investments diverted some of the wealth produced in the economy away from the immediate consumption of non-durable goods.

In this book, I want to address the difficult question of whether the allocation and the intensity of these sacrifices in favor of the future are socially efficient or not. There are indeed many ways to improve the future. It could be achieved through investments in the productive capital of the economy, which in itself contains a multitude of options. However, future prosperity is not determined solely by the level of productive capital that has been accumulated. For example, the future can also be improved by limiting the extraction of exhaustible resources, by preserving the environment, by limiting emissions of greenhouse gases, or by improving the educational system. It is crucial that we allocate our present sacrifices for the future in the way that maximizes the increase in welfare of future generations. In other words, it is crucial to be able to prioritize across the set of investment opportunities. This looks like "mission impossible."

COST-BENEFIT ANALYSIS

Economists have developed a relatively simple and transparent toolkit to address this challenge. Cost-benefit analysis (CBA) is a set of valuation techniques that enables priorities to be put on the set of investment opportunities to be compatible with maximizing intertemporal welfare. Acting in favor of the future generally entails multiple effects. For example, investment in climate change mitigation will probably cause, among many other effects, reduced flooding, an improvement in agricultural productivity, an increase in life expectancy, and a better protection of biodiversity. When evaluating the effectiveness of climate change mitigation for improving intertemporal welfare, CBA experts evaluate all these costs and benefits by valuing non-monetary impacts. There are techniques for putting values on non-monetary impacts, like biodiversity or statistical life-years saved, but it is a complex and controversial matter that will not be discussed in this book. The focus instead is on how to compare temporally distributed valuations of different projects' impacts, once these valuations have been made.

One key ingredient in the CBA toolkit is the discount rate, which can be interpreted as the minimum rate of return required from a safe investment project to make it socially desirable to implement. This discount rate may be a function of the duration of the project, but it is absolutely crucial that the same discount rate is used to evaluate safe projects with the same duration. By a simple arbitrage argument, this discount rate must be equal to the interest rate observed in financial markets. Indeed, rather than investing in the safe project under scrutiny, one can alternatively invest in a risk-free bond with the same maturity. If one is interested in maximizing the benefit of our actions for the future, the bond should be invested in if the interest rate it generates is greater than the internal rate of return of the project. This justifies using the market interest rate as the required minimum rate of return for safe investment projects. Stated differently, an investor should always compare the return of his or her investment project to the opportunity cost of capital, which is the return on the alternative strategy of investing in the productive capital in the economy.

It is often suggested that a zero discount rate is more appropriate if one is really interested in improving the welfare of future generations. This is a classic mistake. Consider for example investing some of our collective wealth in a long-term safe project that yields a rate of return of 1% when the rate of return of productive capital is 4%. This goes against the interest of future generations, since it diverts capital from higher to lower return investments. Implementing such a project, with a rate of return smaller than the market interest rate, destroys—rather than creates—social value.

The discount rate puts a price on time. With a discount rate of 4%, one kilogram of rice delivered next year has a value of only $1000/1.04 = 962$ grams of rice delivered today. This is the present (or discounted) value of one kilogram of rice next year. The decision rule comparing the internal rate of return and the discount rate can be restated equivalently as the one based on the comparison of the present value of the benefits and the present value of the cost. If the difference, which is called the net present value (NPV), is positive, then the investment project is socially desirable. For example, a project that reduces my consumption of rice this year by 950 grams, but increases my consumption of rice next year by 1 kilogram, has a NPV of $962 - 950 = 12$ grams of rice. Because the NPV is positive, this action should be implemented, and the NPV measures the value creation of the investment. The NPV jargon is an alternative way to state the principle of requiring an investment project to have an internal rate of return larger than the discount rate.

THE LEVEL OF THE DISCOUNT RATE

This book specifically addresses the question of the value of time as expressed by the level of the real discount rate. A high discount rate implies that few investment projects will successfully pass the test of a positive NPV. At the collective level, the outcome will be a low level of investments and savings. Natural resources will be quickly extracted because of the low NPV of the strategy of extracting them later. Emissions of CO2 will not be abated because of the low present value of the climate change damages that they will generate in the distant future. On the contrary, a reduction of the discount rate enlarges the set of NPV positive investment opportunities. This means that a larger share of the wealth of nations will be invested rather than consumed. The level of the discount rate therefore plays the key role of determining the best allocation of resources between the present and the future.

This point can be illustrated by considering the case of climate change once more. Nordhaus (2008) claims that a real discount rate of 5% is socially efficient. Using an integrated assessment model, he estimated that the net present value of the future damages generated by one more tonne of CO_2 emitted today is 8 dollars. This means that none of the big technical projects to curb our emissions, such as carbon sequestration, wind generation, solar power, or biofuel technologies, are currently socially desirable, because they all reduce emissions at a cost which is much larger than 8 dollars per tonne of CO_2. The NPV of these abatement investments is negative because the present value of the costs is greater than the present value of the benefits (avoided damages from climate change). Nordhaus concludes that the efficient response to climate change would, in the near term, be dominated by investment in green research and development with a slow ramp-up in abatement effort over time as technology costs fall and damages rise. On the other hand, Stern (2007) implicitly used a smaller real discount rate of 1.4%. He ended up with a NPV of future damages around 85 dollars per tonne of CO_2. With this value of carbon, it is efficient to invest in significant levels of abatement now. We should immediately implement at least some of the green technologies which are already available, such as wind turbines. This means a massive reallocation of capital in the economy: old technologies—in particular in the energy sector—will become obsolete faster; consumers should replace their old cars and appliances as soon as possible, and they should spend money on insulating their house rather than on vacations. The higher estimate of the present value of damages from emissions drives greener growth but requires greater sacrifice from current generations.

In 2004, a Danish statistician named Bjorn Lomborg asked a prestigious group of economists, including some Nobel laureates, to evaluate a set of big international projects for the benefit of humanity. The "Copenhagen Consensus" (Lomborg 2004) that came out of this process put as its top priority public programs yielding immediate benefits (fighting malaria and AIDS, improving water supply, among others), and recommended that environmental projects (climate change mitigation) should be implemented only after all these other projects are fully funded. Driving this conclusion were the use of a relatively large discount rate, together with the recognition that for many living in the early twenty-first century, some of the most basic needs for a decent life are still not satisfied.

THE CASE OF THE DISTANT FUTURE

Suppose that the rate of return r of safe productive capital in the economy is constant. The continuously reinvested value of 1 dollar over t years in the productive capital of the economy is $\exp(rt)$. The exponential nature of compounded interest comes from the fact that the interest obtained in the short run will itself generate interest in the future. Reversing the argument, this means that the present value of 1 dollar in t years must be equal to $\exp(-rt)$. As was said earlier, if the interest rate is 4%, the present value of 1000 grams of rice next year is approximately 962 grams of rice. However, the net present value of 1000 grams of rice in 200 years is an extremely small 0.3 gram of rice. This means that one should not be ready to sacrifice more than 0.3 gram of ricetoday for an investment project that yields one kilogram of rice in 200 years. This example illustrates the origin of a long-standing disagreement between economists and ecologists. Standard CBA tools generate an almost uniform policy recommendation: Ignore the very long-term impacts of one's actions! Only the short-term costs and benefits influence the social desirability of an investment. In other words, CBA, and more generally economic theory, drives short-term thinking in our society, and goes against the sustainability of our development.

Economists have recently been working on two questions related to this disagreement. First, a discount rate of 4% may be too high to evaluate safe investment projects.[1] To examine this point, it is necessary to think about the determinants of the discount rate, which is the main objective of this book. The weight placed on impacts in the distant future is highly sensitive to the discount rate used. For instance, using a 2% discount rate, the value of 1 kilogram of rice in 200 years' time is 18 grams of rice—approximately fifty times higher than the 4 cents' valuation obtained when using a 4% discount rate. Second, it could be socially efficient to use a rate of 4% to discount safe cash flows occurring in the short run, and only 2% to discount safe cash flows occurring in the distant future. In other words, there is no a priori reason to use the same discount rate for different time horizons. This book also addresses the question of the term structure of the discount rate.

RECENT CHANGES IN THE DISCOUNT RATE AROUND THE WORLD

The level of the discount rate to be used to evaluate public investment projects was hotly debated in the 1960s and 1970s in most developed countries. In the United States, the debate originated in the water resources sector during the 1950s (Krutilla and Eckstein 1958), but it quickly spread to other public policy debates, most notably energy, transportation, and environmental protection. During the Nixon administration, the Office of Management and Budget tried to standardize the widely varying discounting assumptions made by different agencies and issued a directive requiring the use of a 10% rate (U.S. Office of Management and Budget, OMB 1972). In 1992, this rate was revised downward to 7%. It was argued at that occasion that the "*7% is an estimate of the average before-tax rate of return to private capital in the U.S. economy*" (OMB 2003). In 2003, the OMB also recommended the use of a discount rate of 3%, in addition to the 7% already mentioned as a sensitivity test. This new rate of 3% was justified by the "*social rate of time preference. This simply means the rate at which society discounts future consumption flows to their present value. If we take the rate that the average saver uses to discount future consumption as our measure of the social rate of time preference, then the*

---

[1] All rates are expressed in real terms in this book.

real rate of return on long-term government debt may provide a fair approximation" (OMB 2003). The 3% corresponds to the average real rate of return of ten-year Treasury notes between 1973 and 2003. In another field, guidelines established by the Government Accounting Standards Board (GASB) recommend that state and local governments discount their pension liabilities at expected returns on their plan assets, which is usually estimated around 8%.

In the United Kingdom, the HM Treasury (2003) issued general guidelines to evaluate public policies in the Green Book. It recommends the use of a discount rate of 3.5%, a rate that is justified by the Ramsey rule which we will examine in chapter 2. This discount rate is reduced to 3% for cash flows accruing more than thirty years into the future, 2% for cash flows accruing more than 125 years into the future, and even to 1% for more than 200 years. This reduction of the discount rate for the distant future is justified by the high degree of uncertainty surrounding the distant future. This justification is examined in chapters 4–8 of this book.

From 1985 to 2005, France used a discount rate of 8% to evaluate public investments, which implied that most public investments had a negative net present value. As a consequence, lobbyists put pressure on those evaluating public policy to not rely too heavily on the use of CBA and had a tendency to inflate the future social benefits of investment projects. In fact, the choice of the 8% was itself in part justified by this intrinsic optimism bias. In 2004, the French government commissioned Daniel Lebègue, then a high-level civil servant, to produce a report on the discount rate. The outcome was the Lebègue Report (2005) written by Luc Baumstark. This report recommended the use of a real discount rate of 4%. Moreover, on the basis of recent developments in the scientific literature, it also recommended that the discount rate should reduce to only 2% for cash flows occurring after more than thirty years.

International institutions have also addressed the question of the discount rate. For example, the World Bank traditionally uses a discount rate in the range of 10–12%. It is justified "*as a notional figure for evaluating Bank-financed projects. This notional figure is not necessarily the opportunity cost of capital in borrower countries, but is more properly viewed as a rationing device for World Bank funds*" (Operational Core Services Network Learning and Leadership Center 1998).

RELEVANT LITERATURE

For most of the twentieth century, a single reference existed to drive the economic theory of the discount rate. Ramsey (1928) discovered a formula that links the growth of the economy and some psychological traits of consumers to the socially efficient discount rate. This "Ramsey rule," which is quite simple and intuitive, played a crucial role in the shaping of the rules used to evaluate public investments. Alternatively, the simple arbitrage argument, evoked above, suggests the use of the observed interest rate on financial markets as the socially efficient discount rate. Combining the two approaches yielded the well-known neoclassical theory of economic growth first explored by Solow (1956).

The modern theory of finance has also investigated the level of the equilibrium interest rate and the shape of its term structure. Hundreds of articles have been published on this term structure. Despite using sophisticated mathematical tools, these theories rely on simple arbitrage arguments based on exogenous stochastic dynamics of the short-term interest rate. Given the limited economic ingredients contained in those financial theories, not much space is devoted to presenting them in this book. Note, however, that the theory of finance contains many puzzles. One of them is the "risk-free rate puzzle"; theory predicts an equilibrium interest rate which is much larger than the one that has been observed on markets during the last century (Weil 1989).

An intense debate emerged at the end of the 1990s about whether it is socially efficient to use a discount rate for the distant future that is different from the one used to discount cash flows occurring within the next few years. The root of this literature, which has generated much controversy, is Weitzman (1998a), which argued for a declining term structure. I believe that much of this controversy is now resolved, which in part justifies the writing of this book.

Weitzman (1998b) sent a simple questionnaire to around 2,800 Ph.D.-level economists in which he asked the following question:

> Taking all relevant considerations into account, what real interest rate do you think should be used to discount over time the (expected) benefits and the (expected) costs of projects being proposed to mitigate the possible effects of global climate change?

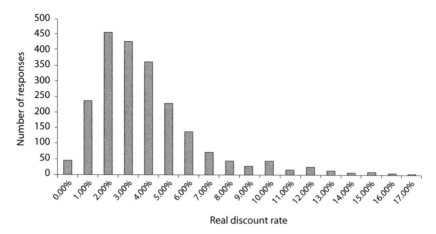

Figure I.1. Histogram of individual estimates of the discount rate among 2,160 Ph.D.-level economists. Source: Weitzman (1998b)

The number of responses was 2,160. The frequency of responses is depicted as a histogram in figure I.1. The sample mean is 3.96%, with a standard deviation of 2.94%. A striking feature of this exercise is the large diversity of answers. This clearly shows that, at least in 1998, there was no consensus on what level of discount rate should be used to evaluate investments for a better future. This was confirmed by a second survey collected by Weitzman (1998b), who focused on fifty distinguished economists from Ken Arrow to Robert Merton and Jean-Jacques Laffont. This "balanced blue-ribbon panel" of expert opinion exhibited the same diversity, with a mean 4.09% and standard deviation 3.07%. The significant disagreement about the efficient discount rate in the economic profession is another motivation for this book.

EVALUATION OF RISKY PROJECTS

Part of the misunderstanding about the discount rate comes from the fact that different people define it in different ways. In this book, I define the discount rate as the minimum internal rate of return to implement a *safe* investment project. But most investments are risky. Thus, this leaves the question of how to value them opened. The vast literature of finance, and in particular the Capital Asset Pricing Models (CAPM), is in favor of using different discount rates to value different investments projects as a function of their degree of riskiness. Among practitioners, this idea supported the practice of using the Weighted-Average Cost of Capital (WACC) as a firm-specific discount rate. Because of risk and risk aversion, this WACC can differ from the safe interest rate by a wide margin.

This approach, consisting of taking account of the riskiness of a project by adapting the discount rate, has the advantage of simplicity. Yet it is not always consistent with the theory, as explained in the last part of the book. Moreover, measuring risk of projects requires much energy and skill, and is rarely consensual. Empiricism in this dimension is not always satisfactory. General methods (Monte Carlo and econometric estimation of betas, for example) exist but are rarely used to evaluate private and collective projects, as explained in a recent report (Gollier 2011) that I wrote for the French prime minister. The consequence is that most evaluators around the world use a universal discount rate to value best estimates of cash flows, independent of their degree of uncertainty. This of course yields an inefficient allocation of capital in our economies. Taking account of risk remains a challenge. Consider for example the case of climate change. It is still true that there is a lot of uncertainty associated with the long-term impact of emitting CO_2 in the atmosphere. A crucial element of risk evaluation is the beta of reducing emissions, that is, the elasticity of monetarized damages to the world GDP. My own discussions with specialists in the field tell me that we don't even agree about whether the beta of reducing emissions is negative, between 0 and 1, or larger than 1, in other words, about whether the role of uncertainty reduces or increases the discount rate used in the evaluation of projects associated to climate change!

STRUCTURE OF THE BOOK

This book has four parts. Part I is devoted to the basic theory of the discount rate, yielding the extended Ramsey rule. In part II, various arguments are explored in favor of using a smaller discount rate for more distant cash flows. Extensions are discussed in art III, including wealth inequalities, non-monetary cash flows, and alternative decision criteria. Finally, the problem of how to evaluate risky projects is examined in part IV.

REFERENCES

Gollier, C. (2011), *Le calcul du risque dans les investissements publics*, Centre d'Analyse Stratégique, Rapports & Documents n°36, La Documentation Française.

HM Treasury (2003), The Green Book—Appraisal and evaluation in central government, London.

IPCC (2007), Contribution of Working Groups I, II and III to the Fourth Assessment Report of the Intergovernmental Panel on Climate Change, Core Writing Team, R. K. Pachauri and A. Reisinger (eds.), IPCC, Geneva, Switzerland. p. 104.

Krutilla, J. V. and O. Eckstein (1958), *Multiple Purpose River Development*, Baltimore, MD: Johns Hopkins University Press.

Lebègue, D. (2005), *Révision du taux d'actualisation des investissements publics*, Commissariat Général au Plan, http://www.plan.gouv.fr/intranet/upload/actualite/Rapport %20Lebegue%20Taux%20actualisation%2024-01-05.pdf.

Lomborg, B. (2004), *Global Crises, Global Solutions*, Cambridge: Cambridge University Press.

Nordhaus, W. D. (2008), *A Question of Balance: Weighing the Options on Global Warming Policies*, New Haven, CT: Yale University Press.

Operational Core Services Network Learning and Leadership Center (1998), *Handbook on Economic Analysis of Investment Operations*, Washington, DC: World Bank.

Ramsey, F. P. (1928), A mathematical theory of savings, *Economic Journal*, 38, 543–559.

Solow, R. M. (1956), A contribution to the theory of economic growth, *Quarterly Journal of Economics*, 70(1), 65–94.

Stern, N. (2007), *The Economics of Climate Change: The Stern Review*, Cambridge: Cambridge University Press.

U.S. Office of Management and Budget (1972), Circular N. A-94 (Revised) To the Heads of Executive Department Establishments, Subject: Discount Rates to be Used in Evaluating Time Distributed Costs and Benefits. Washington, DC: Executive Office of the President.

U.S. Office of Management and Budget (2003), Circular N. A-4 To the Heads of Executive Department Establishments, Subject: Regulatory Analysis. Washington, DC: Executive Office of the President.

Weil, P. (1989), The equity premium puzzle and the risk-free rate puzzle, *Journal of Monetary Economics*, 24, 401–421.

Weitzman, M. L. (1998a), Why the far-distant future should be discounted at its lowest possible rate, *Journal of Environmental Economics and Management*, 36 (3), 201–208.

Weitzman, M. L. (1998b), Gamma discounting, *American Economic Review* 91, 260–271.

PART I

---◄o►---

THE SIMPLE ECONOMICS OF DISCOUNTING

1

Three Ways to Determine the Discount Rate

In this chapter, we present the simple two-period model that is used in classical economics textbooks to examine the problem of consumption, saving, and investment in a competitive economy. This model reminds us of the key role of the interest rate for the determination of economic growth. Its equilibrium level balances the demand and the supply of liquidity, which are themselves characterized by time preferences and investment opportunities. From a simple arbitrage argument, any new investment opportunity in the economy should be evaluated by using the interest rate as the rate at which the future benefits of the project should be discounted.

DESCRIPTION OF THE ECONOMY

Let us consider a simple economy composed of several identical individuals who live for two periods, "today" and "the future." These periods are indexed respectively by 0 and t. At the beginning of the first period, each agent is endowed with a quantity w of the single consumption good. Let us call this good "rice." Rice can be consumed immediately, or it can be planted to produce a crop in the future. This means that rice is also an asset, a form of capital yielding a benefit for the future. Let us assume that planting k units of rice today yields $f(k)$ units of grain in the future. We assume that function f is increasing and concave, and that $f(0) = 0$. The derivative of f is the marginal productivity of capital, which is thus assumed to be positive and decreasing.

How should these individuals allocate their initial endowment of rice between immediate consumption and saving/investment for the future? In order to answer this question, it is necessary to first determine the consumers' lifetime objective. At this stage, the general view is taken that they evaluate their lifetime utility as $U(c_0,c_t)$, where c_0 and c_t are the level of consumption of rice today and in the future respectively. The bivariate utility function U is assumed to be increasing in its two arguments. Increasing consumption increases welfare. It is also assumed to be concave. This implies in particular that the marginal utility of rice in periods 0 or t is decreasing. The effect on welfare of one more grain of rice is larger when the consumption level is low than when it is high. The concavity of U also implies that there is a preference for consumption smoothing over time. If the two consumption plans $(c_0,c_t) = (1,3)$ and $(3,1)$ are equaly preferred, then the consumption plan $(2,2)$ is certainly preferred to either of them.

OPTIMAL CONSUMPTION PLAN

It is possible to use the standard graphical representation of this problem. In figure 1.1, the set of feasible consumption plans has been drawn in a Fisher diagram. It is represented by the grey area whose upper frontier is represented as the locus of consumption plans $(w - k, f(k))$: When k is saved from the initial endowment w of rice, one can consume $c_0 = w - k$ in the first period, and $c_t = f(k)$ in the second period. Because of decreasing marginal productivity of capital, this feasibility frontier is concave. Also represented is the indifference curve defined by equation $U(c_0, c_t) = U_A$ that is tangent to this feasibility frontier. Because U is concave, indifference curves are convex. All plans represented by points above this curve yield an intertemporal welfare that is larger than U_A. It clearly appears that the preferred consumption plan in the feasible set is consumption plan A, which yields an intertemporal welfare U_A. There is no feasible consumption plan that generates a level of intertemporal welfare larger than that.

The optimal consumption plan A is characterized by the tangency of the feasibility frontier and the indifference curve. Technically, it is written as

$$f'(k) = \frac{U_0(c_0, c_t)}{U_t(c_0, c_t)}, \tag{1.1}$$

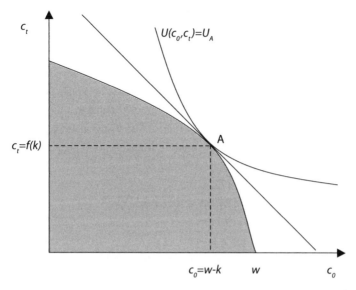

Figure 1.1. The optimal consumption plan in a Fisher diagram

where U_i is the partial derivative of U with respect to c_i. Condition (1.1) is the first order condition of the problem of maximizing $U(w - k, f(k))$ with respect to k. The left-hand side of equation (1.1) is the marginal productivity of capital or the increase in future consumption when one more unit of rice is invested today in the productive capital of the economy. It measures the (absolute value of the) slope of the feasibility frontier, evaluated at A. The right-hand side of this equality is the marginal rate of substitution between current and future consumption, or the welfare-preserving return on saving. This intertemporal marginal rate of substitution tells us by how much future consumption must be increased to compensate for the sacrifice of one unit of current consumption. It measures the (absolute value of the) slope of the indifference curve at A.

Condition (1.1) has a simple economic intuition. It states that at the optimum, one additional grain of rice planted today yields an increase $f'(k)$ in the future consumption of rice which is just sufficient to compensate for the marginal sacrifice of this grain of rice not consumed today. If another plan on the feasibility frontier to the southeast of A were selected, where k is smaller, the same sacrifice today yields a future benefit that more than compensates for the initial sacrifice. This is because the smaller k implies at the same time a larger marginal productivity of capital and a smaller marginal rate of substitution. The latter arises from the fact that to the southeast of A, consumption is very unequal over time, which implies that one is ready to sacrifice more for the future. Symmetrically, in the northwest section of the feasibility frontier where k is larger than at A, the marginal productivity is small, and the marginal rate of substitution is large. It implies that a reduction of k yields an increase in intertemporal welfare.

THE INTEREST RATE

Because all individuals are assumed to have the same initial endowment and the same intertemporal preferences, they will all select consumption plan A in autarky. Suppose that a frictionless credit market opens, in which agents can exchange one unit of rice today against the commitment to deliver R units of rice in the future, where t is the number of years between the present and the future. In the absence of any solvency problem,[1] one can interpret R as the gross interest rate in the economy. Because agents have the possibility to transfer wealth by investing in their own rice technology, a simple arbitrage argument leads to the conclusion that

$$R = f'(k). \tag{1.2}$$

To show this, suppose that this equality did not hold and that R was larger than the marginal productivity of capital. This would imply that all agents would be willing to reduce their investment in their own rice technology to invest in the credit market that yields a larger return. This would induce an excess supply of credit on financial markets. This cannot be an equilibrium. The interest rate would go down. Symmetrically, if R was smaller than the marginal productivity of capital, all agents would like to get a loan to invest in rice production. This cannot be an equilibrium either. Thus, condition (1.2) characterizes the unique equilibrium on

---

[1] The existence of a really risk-free asset in the economy may be questioned. Most sovereign debts contain a default risk. Moreover, their returns are rarely indexed on inflation, so that an inflation risk should be included in the picture. See chapter 7.

credit market. We conclude that the competitive equilibrium on financial markets is such that the interest rate equals the rate of return of productive capital in the economy.

The existence of a credit market transforms the individual feasibility condition represented by the grey area in figure 1.1 by a budget constraint corresponding to the straight line in the same figure. Its slope equals $-R$. By construction, this transformation of the constraint faced by each consumer in the economy does not change their optimal consumption plan.

THE DISCOUNT RATE

Let us now consider the crucial question this book addresses. Suppose that an entrepreneur, the government, or a consumer is contemplating a new collective investment project. This project has an initial cost ε unit of rice per capita, and it will yield a sure benefit εR_i unit of rice per capita in the future. Variable R_i can be recognized as the internal gross rate of return of the project. In our framework, in which the single consumption good is rice, this investment project could be using a fraction of the initial endowment in rice to manipulate some of the rice's genes, yielding an improved rice production technology. However, this section can be applied more generally to investment projects in a more complex economy. How should projects such as new transportation infrastructure, investments in education, or fighting climate change be valued?

What is the minimum rate of return of the project under scrutiny that would make it desirable from the collective point of view? The answer to this question is usually referred to as the efficient discount rate. Is it necessary to know how the initial cost of an investment will be financed to characterize it? Does it matter whether the initial cost of the project will be financed by a corresponding reduction in the level of current consumption or by a corresponding reduction in everyone's investment in their own rice production technology?

Suppose first that the initial cost is financed by a reduction in the level of initial consumption. How does this collective investment modify the people's intertemporal welfare? Because we assume that ε is small, one can use standard differential calculus to obtain

$$\Delta U = -\varepsilon U_0(c_0, c_t) + \varepsilon R_i U_t(c_0, c_t). \tag{1.3}$$

To get the minimum rate of return that makes the project socially desirable, one should equalize ΔU to zero. This implies that the socially efficient discount rate R_i is such that

$$R_i = \frac{U_0(c_0, c_t)}{U_t(c_0, c_t)} \tag{1.4}$$

This means that the efficient discount rate is equal to the welfare-preserving return on saving.

Suppose alternatively that the collective investment project is financed by a corresponding reduction in the productive capital in the economy. Trivially, the project is socially desirable only if its internal rate of return is larger than the marginal return of productive capital in the economy. This seemingly innocuous observation is important and is deep-rooted in the brain of most economists: evaluations must also be made by comparisons, and one should take into account the opportunity cost of funds. This means that the discount rate must equal the rate of return of capital: $R_i = f'(k)$. This condition guarantees that the marginal investment project is socially at least as good as investing in the productive capital in the economy. Requiring that the Net Present Value (NPV) of a project is positive is equivalent to checking that this project does better for the future than all other unfunded projects available in the economy.

Because consumption plans are optimized, we know that $f'(k) = U_0/U_t$. When calculating the socially efficient discount rate, it is in fact irrelevant whether the initial cost is financed by a reduction in consumption or in other productive investments. To sum up, it has been shown that

$$R_i = R = f'(k) = \frac{U_0(c_0, c_t)}{U_t(c_0, c_t)}. \tag{1.5}$$

Notice that we could have gone straight to the point that the efficient discount rate must be equal to the interest rate by observing that any agent can finance the initial cost ε by borrowing it today on the credit market. This will yield a reimbursement at date t equaling εR, where R is the interest rate. Obviously, the project is efficient if its benefit at date t net of this reimbursement—which is referred to as the Net Future Value (NFV)—is non-negative. The critical internal rate of return is thus defined as yielding a zero NFV:

$$NFV = \varepsilon R_i - \varepsilon R = 0. \tag{1.6}$$

This rule is better known as the NPV rule by dividing the above equality by R:

$$NPV = -\varepsilon + \frac{\varepsilon R_i}{R} = 0, \tag{1.7}$$

which holds if and only if $R_i = R$. This is a very natural approach for any specific economic agent. When assessing a project, she does not need to know whether the investment will crowd out other investments, or whether it will reduce aggregate consumption in the economy.

CONTINUOUSLY COMPOUNDED RATES

In this chapter, as in most of this book, we consider discrete-time models. However, we will hereafter use continuously compounded interest rates and rates of return. For example, consider as previously stated a credit contract in which the borrower must repay R units of rice in t years per unit of rice borrowed today. At which rate ρ does the debt grow over time from 1 to R between dates 0 and t? If one wants this rate to be constant, it must be defined by $\exp(\rho t) = R$, or

$$\rho = \frac{1}{t} \ln R. \tag{1.8}$$

Notice that ρ is the continuously compounded interest rate, whereas R is the gross interest rate between 0 and t. In the same fashion, we can define respectively the (continuously compounded) rate of return of capital at the margin and the welfare-preserving rate of return of saving as follows:

$$\rho_k = t^{-1} \ln f'(k) \quad \text{and} \quad \rho_u = t^{-1} \ln \frac{U_0(c_0, c_t)}{U_t(c_0, c_t)}. \tag{1.9}$$

Parameter ρ_u characterizes the minimum *rate* of return on an investment of duration t to at least maintain intertemporal welfare. In this chapter, we have shown that the discount rate must be equal to $\rho = \rho_k = \rho_u$.

AN INTERGENERATIONAL PERSPECTIVE

Earlier in this chapter, we implicitly considered private investment projects without externalities. Consider alternatively collective projects that have impacts over several generations of consumers. In this context, we can identify c_0 as the consumption level of the current generation, and c_t as the one of the future generation living in period t. When generations' lifetimes do not overlap, credit markets will not be operational. There is just no way for future generations to compensate current ones for the sacrifices that the later could be requested to make. Some forms of exchange can be organized on credit markets among different generations that overlap with each other, but it is intuitive that the equilibrium observed in this economy will not be efficient. Overlapping Generations (OLG) models were first examined by Allais (1947), Samuelson (1958), and Diamond (1965). The existence of OLG implies that consumption plans are not socially efficient, and that the interest rate observed on financial markets should not be used as a driver to evaluate public policies impacting several generations.

When different generations bear the costs and the benefits of the investment under scrutiny, the utility function U considered in the chapter should be reinterpreted as the social welfare function. This tranforms our descriptive approach into a prescriptive one. In this framework, U characterizes the collective preferences toward the allocation of consumption across generations. It should be used to evaluate collective investment projects. Consumption plan A in figure 1.1 represents the socially efficient solution, but is generally not a competitive equilibrium.

SUMMARY

This chapter has shown that the socially efficient discount rate can be estimated in three different ways:

1. The discount rate is the interest rate observed on financial markets. This interest rate reveals important information about society's willingness to transfer wealth to the future.

2. The discount rate is the rate of return on marginal productive capital in the economy. Indeed, one should invest in a new project only if its rate of return is larger than alternative opportunities to invest in productive capital.

3. The discount rate is the welfare-preserving rate of return on savings. Investment reduces current consumption and therefore has a negative impact on welfare. However, the investment will increase consumption and therefore has a positive impact on intertemporal welfare. One should invest in a new project only if the reduction in welfare due to the immediate sacrifice is more than compensated for by the increase in welfare due to the future benefit.

It has also been shown that these three definitions of the discount rate are fully compatible with each other when consumption plans are optimized and credit markets are frictionless.

REFERENCES

Allais, M. (1947), *Economie et intérêt*, Imprimerie Nationale et Librairie des Publications Officielles, Paris.

Diamond, P. (1965), National debt in a neoclassical growth model, *American Economic Review*, 55, 1126–1150.

Samuelson, P. A. (1958), An exact consumption-loan model of interest with or without the social contrivance of money, *Journal of Political Economy* 66(6), 467–482.

2

---◄○►---

The Ramsey Rule

In this chapter, we present the main argument in favor of a positive discount rate. In a growing economy, future generations will consume more goods and services than we do. In this context, investing for the future is equivalent to asking poor consumers to sacrifice more of their consumption for the benefit for wealthier people. Because of inequality aversion, one would be ready to do so only if the rate of return of these investment projects is large enough to compensate for the increased intertemporal inequalities that these projects would generate. The Ramsey rule quantifies this wealth effect.

WHY DO WE NEED A MODEL?

The most obvious way to determine the efficient discount rate is to make it equal to the rate of return on risk-free capital, as explained in chapter 1. This is referred to as the interest rate, which measures the opportunity cost of funds in the economy. This is certainly a good reference when the cash flows to be discounted occur in the next few months or years. However, in order to use financial markets to estimate the discount rate, it is necessary to observe the real rate of return for truly risk-free assets.

Most corporations and public institutions use as their discount rate the rate at which they can borrow on financial markets, or their Weighted Average Cost of Capital (WACC). Normally this rate contains a risk premium because their investment projects are risky, with cash flows that are correlated with systematic risk in the economy (see part IV of this book). It is often suggested that corporations and their shareholders use a rate of around 15% to evaluate their investment projects. This rate contains a risk premium. Therefore it is not what is referred to in this book as the discount rate, which is instead the rate at which a *sure* future benefit must be discounted to measure its present value.

The safest assets on the planet are bonds issued by governments in the western world. Those issued by the United States are the safest, but the recent crisis on sovereign debts reminds us that this safest asset is not risk-free, in particular for long maturities. However, the probability of default of U.S. Treasury bonds remains small, because of the extensive ability to tax U.S. citizens' incomes. The nominal opportunity cost of risk-free capital is revealed by the rate of return on these bonds. Combined with an almost deterministic short-term inflation rate it is straightforward to calculate the real rate of return for short-term maturities. This provides a clever basis to fix the short-term discount rate.

In the longer term, the rate of return on government bonds with longer maturities provides a noisier signal about the cost of borrowing for a risk-free agent. There are increasing uncertainties surrounding inflation and the probability of default. These uncertainties imply that empirical data from financial markets are tainted with frictions, inefficiencies, and bubbles. In turn this implies a role for economic models which can be used to construct a scientific basis for the discount rate.

There is a further limitation to using rates of return on government bonds in the longer term. There does not exist, in any significant quantity on sufficiently liquid markets, bonds with maturities longer than thirty or fifty years. Moreover, as is well-known from the overlapping-generation models of the theory of growth, future generations cannot trade on present credit markets, which makes them intrinsically dynamically inefficient (Diamond 1977). Therefore, there isn't any clear benchmark from financial markets to help determine the rate at which distant cash flows should be discounted. As a consequence, two of the three ways proposed in chapter 1 to estimate the discount rate are invalid for long time horizons.

In the following, an approach based on the welfare-preserving rate of return of saving is used, which will produce the famous Ramsey rule. This approach is sustained by the assumption that the investment project to be evaluated will be financed by a reduction of aggregate consumption rather than by a substitution from other investments, so that the discount rate is related to the marginal rate of substitution between current and future consumption. This can also be interpreted as an attempt to predict what the equilibrium interest rate should be in an economy with perfect financial markets and paternalistic investors. In other words, our aim is to price risk-free assets according to a welfare-compatible interpretation of the notion of sustainable development.

ADDITIVE TIME PREFERENCES

The previous chapter examined a simple sure investment project yielding only two cash flows—a cost today and a benefit at some specific date t. It was seen that the minimum (continuously compounded) rate of return that makes this project socially desirable is:

$$r = \frac{1}{t} \ln \frac{U_0(c_0, c_t)}{U_t(c_0, c_t)}. \tag{2.1}$$

In the absence of financial market failures, this socially efficient discount rate is also the equilibrium yield to maturity of a zero-coupon bond with maturity t. In this chapter, this simple equation is calibrated. Two ingredients are required; the shape of the intertemporal utility function U, and the economic growth from c_0 to $c_t \geq c_0$.

An important simplifying assumption is that U is additive with respect to time. Namely, it is assumed that there exist two functions, u and v, from $\mathbb{R}$ to $\mathbb{R}$ such that

$$U(c_0, c_t) = u(c_0) + v_t(c_t). \tag{2.2}$$

Equation (2.2) can be interpreted as follows: agents evaluate their intertemporal welfare by adding their immediate utility $u(c_0)$, generated by consuming c_0, to the anticipated utility $v_t(c_t)$, generated by consuming c_t in the future. This anticipated utility is independent of past consumption: the level of initial consumption c_0 has no effect on the utility of consumption at date t. This precludes the formation of consumption habits, any anticipatory feelings, or any emotional hysteresis. This assumption is important because it allows the two dates 0 and t to be isolated in the evaluation of the welfare-preserving rate of return on saving related to a benefit occurring at t. If there were some formation of consumption habits, the entire consumption plan between 0 and t would have an effect on the marginal value of consumption at date t. Similarly, if we would allow for anticipatory feelings, consumption levels after time t would matter to determine the utility associated with date t. The origin of the additively separable discounted utility function can be traced back to Samuelson (1937). Its axiomatic foundation was provided by Koopmans (1960).

EXPONENTIAL PSYCHOLOGICAL DISCOUNTING

Since Ramsey (1928), economists have made the assumption that agents are impatient. They value their future utility less than current utility. An immediate pleasure is preferred to an identical one that is experienced in the future. This impatience is modelled by assuming that there is a single function u that links the level of instantaneous consumption to the level of instantaneous felicity, and that lifetime utility is a discounted flow of current and future felicities. In other words, the additive specification (2.2) is considered in the special case with $v_t(c) = \exp(-\delta t)u(c)$ for all c. More generally with more than two periods, the intertemporal welfare function is assumed to be a weighted sum of the flow of future felicities, the weight associated to any maturity t being exponentially decreasing at a constant rate δ.

Parameter δ is the rate of pure time preference, or the rate of impatience. Some economists refer to it as the "discount rate," which is a source of misunderstanding. Indeed, it is a discount rate, since it is used to discount the flow of future *utility*. However, it is not the discount rate in the usual sense, which is the rate used by economists to discount future *cash flows*. Of course, as is shown next, there is a link between the psychological discount rate δ and the monetary discount rate that is denoted by r in this book.

The choice of the exponentially decreasing function, $f(t) = \exp(-\delta t)$, for the utility discount factor relies on a simple argument of time consistency. Consider the same investment problem as in the previous chapter, with an initial cost to be incurred at date 0 and a benefit at date t. However, rather than examining the value of the project at date 0, suppose that it is examined at some date $-\tau < 0$, before its implementation. Suppose that no new information about the quality of the project and about the environment of the investor is expected between $-\tau$ and 0. Time consistency requires that if it is optimal at date $-\tau$ to plan to invest at date 0, it is indeed optimal to invest when date 0 comes. Planning is rational. From the initial date $-\tau$, the duration of time before enjoying utility $u(c_0)$ is τ years, so that a discount factor $\exp(-\delta\tau)$ must be attached to utility occurring at date 0. Similarly, the duration of time before enjoying utility at date t is $\tau + t$ years, so that a discount factor $\exp(-\delta(\tau + t))$ should be used to discount utility from consumption at date t, $u(c_t)$. It can be concluded that the intertemporal welfare function at date $-\tau$ can be written as

$$e^{-\delta\tau}u(c_0) + e^{-\delta(\tau + t)}u(c_t) = e^{-\delta\tau}(u(c_0) + e^{-\delta t}u(c_t)) = e^{-\delta\tau}U(c_0, c_t). \quad (2.3)$$

It can be observed that the objective function at date $-\tau$ is the product of a constant independent of the characteristics of the project, and of the objective function at date 0. Therefore, any project that raises the welfare $U(c_0, c_t)$ as evaluated at date 0 also raises welfare when evaluated at date $-\tau$. This guarantees time consistency. The exponential nature of the discount factor in the intertemporal welfare function guarantees that the relative "exchange rate" of utility for any pair of dates is insensitive to the passing of time. Other specifications for the utility discount factor, such as the hyperbolic one with $f(t) = (1 + at)^{-1}$, induce time inconsistent behaviors. Strotz (1956) and Laibson (1997) provide interesting insights about the saving behavior of time-inconsistent consumers.

RATE OF IMPATIENCE

There is a simple way to estimate the rate of impatience δ. Suppose you believe that your income in the future will be the same as this year, and that you currently have no savings. What is the minimum interest rate that would induce you to save some of your current income? The answer to this question is called your welfare-preserving rate of return, which is defined by equation (2.1). Under the previous assumptions with $c_0 = c_t$, we obtain that $U_0/U_t = \exp(\delta t)$, so that $r = \delta$. The rate of impatience is equal to the minimum interest rate that induces people to save when their income profile is flat.

There is no convergence among experts toward an agreed, or unique, rate of impatience. Frederick, Loewenstein, and O'Donoghue (2002) conducted a meta-analysis of the literature on the estimation of the rate of impatience. Rates differ dramatically across studies and within studies across individuals. For example, Warner and Pleeter (2001), who examined actual households' decisions between an immediate down payment and a rental payment, found that individual discount rates vary between 0% and 70% per year! Thus, the calibration of δ is problematic if the objective is positive, that is, if one wants to explain real behaviors.

As long as consumption at date 0 and t concerns a given person, impatience is a psychological trait that economists should take as given. However, many experts in the field have questioned, from a normative perspective, the appropriateness of impatience for the evaluation of social welfare. Arrow (1999) cites various classical authors on this matter. The most well-known citation is from Ramsey (1928) himself: "It is assumed that we do not discount later enjoyments in comparison with earlier ones, a practice which is ethically indefensible and arises merely from the weakness of the imagination." Many other distinguished economists can also be cited: Sidgwick (1890): "It seems . . . clear that the time at which a man exists cannot affect the value of his happiness from a universal point of view; and that the interests of posterity must concern a Utilitarian as much as those of his contemporaries"; or Harrod (1948): "Pure time preference [is] a polite expression for rapacity and the conquest of reason by passion." Koopmans: "[I have] an ethical preference for neutrality as between the welfare of different generations." Solow (1974): "In solemn conclave assembled, so to speak, we ought to act as if the social rate of pure time preference were zero."

The general view is that a small or zero discount rate should be used when the flow of utility over time is related to different generations. The fact that I discount my own felicity next year by 2% does not mean that I should discount my children's felicity next year by 2%. In fact, there is no moral reason to value the utility of future generations less than the utility of the current ones. As explained by Broome (1992), good at one time should not be treated differently from good at another, and the impartiality about time is a universal point of view. The normative doctrine is that the rate of time preference is zero. In later sections, this book takes a *normative* stand to set δ at zero. This is justified because the dominant role of the discount rate over the longer term is to allocate utility across different generations rather than within an individual's lifetime. If one treats different generations equally, the only argument in favor of a positive rate of pure preference for the present is the possibility of extinction. For example, Stern (2007) uses a δ of 0.1% per year that is justified by the quite arbitrary assumption that there is a 0.1% probability per annum that humanity will disappear within the next twelve months.

A classical argument against a zero discount rate goes as follows. Consider the standard utilitarian social welfare function

$$\sum_{t=0}^{T} e^{-\delta t} u(c_t) \tag{2.4}$$

where the time horizon T of the social planner tends to infinity. If δ is zero, this social welfare function will be unbounded. Economists would find that problematic. For example, consider the problem of the optimal rate of extraction of a non-renewable resource. Because the objective function is unbounded, this problem could not be solved, or has multiple solutions. Macroeconomists and growth theorists would face a similar challenge. However, the problem of the discount rate does not require maximizing anything. The discount rate is the price of time that is compatible with a given consumption plan. It tells us what the changes in consumption are that improve intertemporal welfare, independent of whether the initial consumption plan is dynamically optimal or not. Thus, this argument of an undoubted social welfare function when $\delta = 0$ and T tends to infinity is irrelevant for our purpose in this book.

AVERSION TO INTERTEMPORAL INEQUALITY OF CONSUMPTION

It was shown in the previous chapter that the concavity of the intertemporal welfare function U characterizes a preference for the smoothing of consumption over time. In the additive case examined here, this is translated into the concavity of the utility function u.[1] The local measure of the degree of concavity of the utility function u is defined:

---

[1] Zuber and Asheim (2011) propose a non-additive social welfare function where the aversion to intertemporal inequalities has two dimensions: the concavity of u and a rank-dependent

$$R(c) = -\frac{cu''(c)}{u'(c)}. \tag{2.5}$$

This index is hereafter referred to as the relative aversion to intertemporal inequality of consumption. To illustrate why, suppose that an individual's consumption plan, (c_0, c_t), is unequally distributed over time. Suppose more particularly that future consumption is larger than current consumption: $c_t > c_0$. How much would the individual be ready to pay today to increase consumption by one unit in the future? This should be less than one unit for two reasons: impatience and aversion to consumption inequality. In the absence of both of these effects, the individual would be prepared to exchange one for one, as explained in the previous section. Let k be the maximum reduction in current consumption that is compatible with the unit increase in future consumption. It must satisfy the following indifference condition:

$$ku'(c_0) = e^{-\delta t} u'(c_t). \tag{2.6}$$

Assume that $t = 1$, and that δ and $c_1 - c_0$ are small. Using a first-degree Taylor approximation of $u'(c_1)$ around c_0 and using the approximation $\exp(-\delta) \simeq 1 - \delta$ implies that:

$$ku'(c_0) \simeq (1 - \delta)\left(u'(c_0) + \frac{c_1 - c_0}{c_0} c_0 u''(c_0)\right). \tag{2.7}$$

This can in turn be rewritten as:

$$k \simeq (1 - \delta)\left(1 - \frac{c_1 - c_0}{c_0} R(c_0)\right). \tag{2.8}$$

This equation can be used to estimate your relative aversion to intertemporal inequality $R(c_0)$. Suppose that your rate of impatience is $\delta = 0$, and that you anticipate an increase in future consumption of 10%. In spite of this increase, you are considering a sure investment which will transfer consumption to the future. What is the maximum reduction k of current consumption that you are ready to sacrifice, or invest, to increase future consumption by 1 dollar? The answer to this question gives us an

---

discounting scheme. More precisely, these authors propose that the discount factor associated with a specific date depends upon the rank of the consumption in the intertemporal consumption plan, a larger consumption being associated with a smaller discount factor.

estimation of your relative aversion to intertemporal inequality, since by (2.8), $R(c_0) \simeq 10 - 10k$. For example, answering 90 cents to the question yields a relative aversion $R = 1$, whereas an answer of 80 cents yields a relative aversion $R = 2$.

There is no consensus on the intensity of relative aversion to intertemporal inequality. Using estimates of demand systems, Stern (1977) found a concentration of estimates of R around 2 with a range of roughly 0–10. Hall (1988) found an R around 10, whereas Epstein and Zin (1991) found a value ranging from 1.25 to 5. Pearce and Ulph (1995) estimate a range from 0.7 to 1.5. Following Stern (1977) and the author's own introspection, we will hereafter consider $R = 2$ as a reasonable value.

When different generations are concerned by the investment project to be evaluated, the choice of the discount rate entails interpersonal comparisons of utility. In that case, function U is interpreted as a social welfare function, and the concavity of u characterizes collective aversion to interpersonal inequality. Is the level of R affected by this shift in analysis? In this literature, it is generally assumed that our normative attitude toward consumption inequalities should not depend upon the nature of the comparisons of consumption levels. Under the common paternalistic view, one should evaluate the impact on social welfare of an intertemporal inequality of consumption exactly as if it would be an interpersonal inequality. The social evaluation should be impartial. It is claimed that the two problems are equivalent by nature. From a normative point of view, if one is ready to pay up to 80 cents to increase one's own consumption by one dollar next year, in spite of an anticipated 10% increase in consumption, society should also be ready to sacrifice 80 cents of person A's consumption in order to increase consumption by one dollar for person B, who is 10% wealthier than person A. Thus, it is maintained that $R = 2$ is a sensible level of relative aversion to inequality even in the intergenerational context.

THE POWER UTILITY

Economists and econometricians often limit their analysis by using a specific utility function in their model. They usually favor exponential, quadratic, logarithmic, or power utility functions. In this book, as in the

modern theory of finance, the special case of the power utility function will
be used most frequently:

$$u(c) = \frac{c^{1-\gamma}}{1-\gamma}. \tag{2.9}$$

Parameter γ is positive and different from 1. When $\gamma = 1$, we take $u(c)$
$= \ln(c)$, since it can be verified that the limit of (2.9) when γ tends to 1 is
the logarithmic utility function. These utility functions are increasing and
concave because $u'(c) = c^{-\gamma}$. Moreover, the index R of relative aversion to
intertemporal inequality is a constant independent of c, and is equal to γ.

Using this utility function, we can re-examine the degree of realism of
our assumption $R = \gamma = 2$ without relying on Taylor approximations as in
the previous section. Consider an agent with utility function $u(c) = -c - 1$
and with $\delta = 0$. Suppose that this person expects to double his consumption in the future. This implies that this person will be ready to give up as
much as $u'(c_t)/u'(c_0) = (c_t/c_0)^{-2} = 0.25$ dollar today to increase consumption
by one dollar in the future. In the context of the reduction of inequalities,
consider a society in which half of the population consumes twice as much
goods and services than the other half of the population. If we assume
a utilitarian social welfare function with this power utility function, one
would find socially desirable to sacrifice as much as one dollar for each
rich to increase consumption by 25 cents for each poor. If one would have
considered a calibration with $R = \gamma = 1$, the ratio 1:4 should be replaced by
a ratio 1:2. Readers can decide for themselves about the "right" level of γ
from this type of introspective exercise.

The use of a power utility function is not an innocuous assumption. The
constancy of the relative aversion means in particular that the answer k to
the earlier question depends not on the initial absolute level of consumption, but only upon its growth rate. This implication can be challenged, in
particular given the fact that there must be some positive minimum level
of subsistence. If current income is at or above this minimum subsistence
level, an individual would be entirely unwilling to transfer consumption
to a future period, independent of the growth rate of consumption. This
is not the case with function (2.9). In addition, this power utility function implies that the marginal utility tends to infinity when consumption
tends to zero. Consider a future state of nature where consumption tends

to zero. Specification (2.9) implies that one would be ready to sacrifice almost 100% of one's current wealth in order to increase wealth in this future state by one dollar. This is not realistic. It is therefore necessary to be quite cautious in the use of the classical power utility model when there is the possibility of Armageddon scenarios.

THE RAMSEY RULE

It is time to bring together the different pieces discussed so far in this chapter. Rewriting equation (2.1), the efficient discount rate must be equal to

$$r = \frac{1}{t} \ln \frac{u'(c_0)}{e^{-\delta t} u'(c_t)} = \delta - \frac{1}{t} \ln \frac{u'(c_t)}{u'(c_0)}. \tag{2.10}$$

A Taylor expansion of $u'(c_t)$ around c_0 yields

$$r \simeq \delta + \frac{c_t - c_0}{t c_0} R(c_0). \tag{2.11}$$

Equations (2.10) and (2.11) show that the socially efficient discount rate has two components. It is the sum of the rate of impatience and a wealth effect. The wealth effect is positive when people expect a positive growth in their consumption. It is approximately equal to the product of the annualized growth rate of consumption and of the relative aversion to intertemporal inequality. This approximation is exact in the special case of the power utility function. Indeed, plugging $c_t = c_0 \exp(gt)$ and $u'(c) = c^{-\gamma}$ in equation (2.10) yields

$$r = \delta + \gamma g, \tag{2.12}$$

where g is the yearly growth rate of consumption between dates 0 and t. This is the well-known Ramsey rule, which links the efficient discount rate to two "taste" parameters (the rate of impatience, δ, and the relative aversion to intertemporal inequality, γ), and the growth rate g of the economy. This equation is the cornerstone of this book.

When people expect that the economy will grow fast in the future, their aversion to intertemporal inequality makes them reluctant to sacrifice present income to further improve the already better future. They will be willing to do so only if the rate of return on their investment is large enough to compensate for the induced increase in intertemporal inequality and for their pure preference for the present. This behavior can be observed in financial markets. When households have better expectations about their future income, say, at the end of a recession, they reduce their savings, which in turn implies an increase in the equilibrium interest rate. In contrast, the expectation of a recession induces them to save more, which implies a reduction in the equilibrium interest rate. In short, the interest rate varies pro-cyclically, and the Ramsey rule quantifies this effect.

WHAT ARE THE QUANTITATIVE IMPLICATIONS OF THIS APPROACH?

Several experts have used the Ramsey rule (2.12) to make recommendations on the choice of the discount rate to evaluate public policies, in particular toward climate change. The easiest proposal to memorize is from Weitzman (2007), who recommended the use of a trio of twos:

$$\delta = 2\%, g = 2\% \quad \text{and} \quad \gamma = 2. \tag{2.13}$$

We share the view of Weitzman that "these numbers at least pass the laugh test." They yield a discount rate of 6%. Nordhaus (2008) uses 5%, the lower rate arising from a choice of a rate of impatience $\delta = 1\%$.

Stern (2007) has often been criticized for using a much smaller discount rate of approximately $r = 1.4\%$. In fact, because the impacts of global warming cannot be considered as marginal, the standard evaluation technique based on the net present value cannot be used. This is why Stern (2007) did not actually use any specific discount rate. Rather, he measured the monetary equivalent of the impact of climate change on the intertemporal welfare function. However, this intertemporal welfare function used the following trio of parameter values:

$$\delta = 0.1\%, g = 1.3\% \quad \text{and} \quad \gamma = 1. \tag{2.14}$$

The choice of the rate of time preference at 0.1% comes from the moral stand of time impartiality—each to count for one, and none for more than one—and from the possibility of extinction (for which, as mentioned previously, Stern set the probability of occurrence at 0.1% per year). Observe also that Stern assumes a logarithmic utility function, whose relative risk aversion ($\gamma = 1$) is at the lower bound of estimates for R in the wider literature. Trio (2.14) plugged into the Ramsey rule (2.12) yields a discount rate $r = 1.4\%$, which is considered as a radical position by a majority of economists. It drives the conclusion of the Stern Review urging governments around the world to act immediately and strongly to reduce emissions of greenhouse gases.

Following the publication of the Green Book (2003), the UK recommends a discount rate of 3.5% for cash flows with a maturity of less than thirty years based on the following calibration of the Ramsey rule:

$$\delta = 1.5\%, g = 2.0\% \quad \text{and} \quad \gamma = 1. \tag{2.15}$$

For periods longer than thirty years, a declining forward discount rate is recommended. For cash flows maturing between 31 and 75 years, 3% is used. This declines to 2.5% for maturities of 76 to 125 years, 2% for 126 to 200 years, 1.5% for 201 to 300 years, and finally the discount rate reaches its minimum value of 1% for maturity beyond 301 years. This declining rate is justified by uncertainty over future economic growth—a justification that will be explored further in this book.

In France, the Rapport Lebègue (2005) has been endorsed by the French government, resulting in the adoption of a 4% discount rate for all cash flows with a maturity less than thirty years. This recommendation is based on the following calibration of the Ramsey rule:

$$\delta = 0\%, g = 2\% \quad \text{and} \quad \gamma = 2. \tag{2.16}$$

For time horizons longer than thirty years, a forward discount rate of 2% is used.[2]

SUMMARY OF RESULTS

The discount rate is the maximum rate of return to compensate for the increased intertemporal inequality that investing generates.

---

[2] Thus, the discount factor to be used for a maturity t larger than 30 is $e^{-(0.04*30 + 0.02(t-30))}$.

1. The Ramsey rule $r = \delta + \gamma g$ gives us the efficient discount rate r based on the estimation of the welfare-preserving rate of return of saving. It relies on three parameters: the rate of impatience δ, the relative aversion to intertemporal inequality γ, and the growth rate g of the economy.
2. The collective rate of impatience should be zero. A justification was presented for a normative view that intertemporal preferences, when they concern different people, should be impartial with respect to time.
3. A relative aversion to intertemporal inequality of $\gamma = 2$ has also been advocated.
4. Because the mean growth rate of consumption per capita has been approximately 2% per year in the western world over the last two centuries, the extrapolation of this fact to future growth would justify using a real discount rate of 4%.

However, the calibration of the growth rate g in the Ramsey rule is problematic. There is significant uncertainty surrounding the evolution of economies in the years, decades, and centuries to come. The next chapter explains how to overcome this difficulty.

REFERENCES

Arrow, K. J. (1999), Discounting and intergenerational equity, in Portney and Weyant (eds.), Washington, DC: *Resources for the Future*.

Broome, J. (1992), *Counting the Cost of Global Warming*, Cambridge: White Horse Press.

Diamond, P. (1977), A framework for social security analysis, *Journal of Public Economics*, 8, 275–298.

Epstein, L. G., and S. Zin (1991), Substitution, risk aversion and the temporal behavior of consumption and asset returns: An empirical framework, *Journal of Political Economy*, 99, 263–286.

Frederick, S., G. Loewenstein, and T. O'Donoghue (2002), Time discounting and time preference: A critical review, *Journal of Economic Literature*, 40, 351–401.

Hall, R. E. (1988), Intertemporal substitution of consumption, *Journal of Political Economy*, 96, 221–273.

Harrod, R. F. (1948), *Towards a Dynamic Economics*, London: MacMillan.

HM Treasury (2003), The Green Book—Appraisal and evaluation in central government, London.

Koopmans, T. C. (1960), Stationary ordinal utility and impatience, *Econometrica*, 28, 287–309.

Laibson, D. I. (1997), Golden eggs and hyperbolic discounting, *Quarterly Journal of Economics*, 62, 443–479.

Nordhaus, W. D. (2008), *A Question of Balance: Weighing the Options on Global Warming Policies*, New Haven, CT: Yale University Press.

Pearce, D., and D. Ulph (1995), *A Social Discount Rate For The United Kingdom*, CSERGE Working Paper No 95-01 School of Environmental Studies University of East Anglia Norwich.

Ramsey, F. P. (1928), A mathematical theory of savings, *Economic Journal*, 38, 543–559.

Rapport Lebègue (2005), Révision du taux d'actualisation des investissements publics, Commissariat Général au Plan, Paris. http://www.plan.gouv.fr/intranet/upload/actualite/Rapport%20Lebegue%20Taux%20actualisation%2024-01-05.pdf.

Samuelson, P. A. (1937), A note on measurement of utility, *Review of Economic Studies*, 4, 155–161.

Sidgwick, H. (1890), *The Methods of Ethics*, London: Macmillan.

Solow, R. (1974), The economics of resources or the resources of economics, *American Economic Review Papers and Proceedings* 64 (2), 1–14.

Stern, N. (1977), The marginal valuation of income, in M. Artis and A. Nobay (eds.), *Studies in Modern Economic Analysis*, Oxford: Blackwell.

Stern, N. (2007), *The Economics of Climate Change: The Stern Review*, Cambridge: Cambridge University Press.

Strotz, R. H. (1956), Myopia and inconsistency in dynamic utility maximization, *Review of Economic Studies*, 23 (3), 165–180.

Warner, J. T., and S. Pleeter (2001), The personal discount rate: Evidence from military downsizing programs, *American Economic Review*, 95 (4), 547–580.

Weitzman, M. L. (2007), The Stern review on the economics of climate change, *Journal of Economic Literature*, 45 (3), 703–724.

Zuber, S., and G. B. Asheim (2011), Justifying social discounting: the rank-discounted utilitarian approach, CESifo Working Paper 3192. Forthcoming in *Journal of Economic Theory*.

3

————◄o►————

Extending the Ramsey Rule to an
Uncertain Economic Growth

It is commonly accepted that individuals are ready to sacrifice more in the present for the future when this future becomes more uncertain. Keynes was the first to mention this idea by pointing out the precautionary motive for saving. What is desirable at the individual level is also desirable at the collective one. A society that wants to reinforce the incentive to invest for the future because of its uncertain nature should select a smaller discount rate to evaluate the set of all possible investment projects. We formalize these ideas in this chapter.

A DECISION CRITERION UNDER RISK

Uncertainty is a feature of everyday life. We don't know with certainty today what tomorrow will look like, and for many of us, the more distant future is extremely uncertain. This complicates the dynamic optimization problem of maximizing our lifetime welfare together with the valuation of our investment projects. In particular, determining the optimal level of savings requires an estimate of the future utility gain of this transfer of wealth in a context in which little is known about future incomes. This problem is at the core of the question of what should be done for the future.

When the growth rate of consumption is unknown, the intensity of the wealth effect described in the previous chapter cannot be estimated, and the Ramsey rule (2.12) is unable to produce a precise prescription for the choice of the discount rate. Estimating the growth rate of consumption for the coming year is already a difficult task. Any estimate of growth for the next decade is subject to potentially very large errors. Over a century, estimation errors could be enormous.

The history of the western world before the industrial revolution is full of significant economic slumps, such as those that occurred following the collapse of the Roman Empire in the fifth century, or the Black Death epidemic in the mid-fourteenth century. The recent debate on the concept of sustainable growth is itself an illustration of the degree of uncertainty faced when thinking about the future of society. Some argue that the effects of improvements in information technology have yet to be realized and that the world is entering a period of more rapid growth. By contrast, those who emphasize the effects of natural resource scarcity, or the inability of financial markets to allocate capital efficiently, predict lower growth rates in the future. Some even suggest a negative growth of GDP per head, owing to a deterioration of the environment, population growth, and decreasing returns to scale. The implication of this last position is that the wealth effect on the discount rate is negative rather than positive as supposed in the previous chapter. Under these plausible beliefs, the future is poorer than the present so we should make more sacrifices today to improve the future. We are unable to tell which scenario is right, and which is wrong, in other words, our future is uncertain by nature. Uncertainty over how wealthy the future will be at least casts some doubt on the relevance of the wealth effect to justify the use of a large discount rate.

In order to address the question of the role of uncertainty on the selection of the discount rate, it is necessary to characterize its impact on welfare. From now on the classical approach is followed, relying on the Bernoulli–von Neumann–Morgenstern expected utility theory. More specifically, it is assumed that when the consumption level c_t at date t is uncertain, the ex ante welfare at that date is measured by the expected utility of this uncertain consumption. Thus, seen from date 0, the social welfare in the economy is written as

$$V = u(c_0) + e^{-\delta t} Eu(c_t), \tag{3.1}$$

where the expectation operator E is related to the probability distribution of the random variable c_t. The expected utility criterion relies on an intuitive "independence axiom." Consider three different actions, A, B, and C. A could be to go to see a movie; B could be to go to a restaurant, and C to stay home. Under the independence axiom, if one prefers A with certainty rather than B with certainty, one will also prefer the lottery which yields A with probability p to the lottery which yields B with the same probability, where for both lotteries the alternative is to get C with probability $1 - p$. In other words, if you prefer to go to the movie rather than the restaurant today, this choice will not be altered if you learn that there is a risk that you will have to stay home with some probability p. In spite of its intuitive appeal, the Allais' paradox (Allais 1953) shows that there are circumstances under which some agents violate this axiom. However, the aim of this book is mostly normative. An answer is sought to the question of which discount rate should be used for rational evaluation of public policies. For this purpose, it is reasonable to rely on the very intuitive and normatively appealing independence axiom.

RISK AVERSION

An agent is risk-averse if he always prefers the expected payoff of a lottery to the lottery itself. In the expected utility model, it is well-known that the concavity of the von Neumann–Morgenstern utility function characterizes the aversion to risk of the decision maker. Indeed, by Jensen's inequality, the concavity of u implies that $Eu(c_t)$ is smaller than $u(Ec_t)$. A mean-preserving reduction in risk increases expected utility because marginal utility is decreasing. For example, if future consumption is 80 or 120 with equal probabilities, decreasing marginal utility implies that increasing consumption by 20 in the bad state increases utility more than the reduction of utility from reducing consumption by 20 in the good state. Therefore, eliminating the risk and receiving 100 with certainty is ex ante welfare-improving.

Let $z = Ec_t$ and $\varepsilon_t = (c_t - Ec_t)/Ec_t$ denote respectively the expected consumption and the relative risk at date t. In addition, let π denote the risk premium, which is defined as the maximum price that one is ready to pay for the full elimination of ε_t, expressed as a fraction of expected consumption:

$$u((1 - \pi)Ec_t) = Eu(c_t) = Eu((1 + \varepsilon_t)Ec_t). \qquad (3.2)$$

The level of π measures the degree of aversion to relative risk ε. Case $\pi = 0$ corresponds to risk neutrality, in the sense that risk does not affect welfare in that case. The well-known Arrow–Pratt approximation allows us to link π to the variance σ_t^2 of ε_t and to the index of the concavity of u, which is $R(c) = -cu''(c)/u'(c)$:

$$\pi \simeq 0.5\sigma_t^2 R(z). \qquad (3.3)$$

The relative risk premium is approximately equal to half the product of the variance of the relative risk and of the index of relative risk aversion R. This is obtained through Taylor approximations of the two sides of equation (3.2) around z.

Equation (3.3) gives us a new opportunity to estimate the degree of concavity of u. Suppose that your consumption is subject to an equal chance of an increase or a decrease of 10%. What fraction of consumption are you prepared to pay to eliminate this risk? Since σ_t^2 equals 1% in this case, the answer to this question should approximately be equal to 0.5% of R. For example, when relative risk aversion equals 2, this fifty-fifty chance of a gain or a loss of 10% of consumption is equivalent to a sure loss of $\pi \simeq 1\%$. This test provides further reassurance that $R = 2$ is a reasonable level of concavity of the utility function.

How good is the Arrow–Pratt approximation (3.3)? In general, because it is derived from Taylor approximations, its quality decreases as the size of risk ε_t increases. There is however one special case in which approximation (3.3) is exact, whatever the size of the risk. This special case is used almost universally in the theory of finance, and is applied extensively later in this book. For these reasons it is good to write it as a formal lemma.

Lemma 1: *Suppose that x is normally distributed with finite mean μ and variance σ^2. Consider any scalar $A \in \mathbb{R}$. Then:*

$$Ee^{-Ax} = e^{-A(\mu - 0.5A\sigma^2)}. \qquad (3.4)$$

In other words, the Arrow–Pratt approximation (3.3) is exact when the risk is normally distributed and the utility function is exponential.

A proof of the first part of lemma 1 is provided in the appendix of this chapter. Using (3.4), it is immediate that approximation (3.3) is exact when $u(c) = -e^{-Ac}$ and ε is normally distributed with mean 0 and variance σ^2. The reader will check that $R(z) = Az$ in this case.

It is notable that in the additive model (3.1), which is also referred to as the "Discounted Expected Utility" model, the concavity of u plays two different roles: aversion to intertemporal inequality and aversion to risk. This has often been criticized in the literature because the attitudes toward risk and time are often considered to have different natures. This limits the positive power of the model, to describe how people behave in relation to risk and time. However, from a normative point of view, the use of decreasing marginal utility to explain the two types of aversion is quite appealing. It makes sense to link the resistance to transfer wealth either to a wealthier future or to a wealthier state of nature to the property that marginal utility is decreasing.

PRUDENCE AND PRECAUTIONARY SAVING

The previous section examined the impact of risk on welfare. However, the main question here is quite different. We are interested in determining the impact of uncertainty on willingness to improve the future. Before examining this question at a global level, it is useful to return to the individual level. The most obvious action that we take in favor of our own future is to save. So, it is useful to explore the effect on saving behavior of uncertainty over future income. This provides a helpful insight into how we should collectively behave in the face of an uncertain collective destiny. After all, any collective risk will percolate down into risks that must be borne by individuals. Intuition suggests that uncertainty surrounding the future should raise our willingness to save. This is the concept of precautionary saving introduced by Keynes, which has been revisited since then by Leland (1968), Drèze and Modigliani (1972), and Kimball (1990), among others.

Consider individuals who have a flow of income y_0 at date 0, and y_t at date t. Their optimal level of saving, s, solves the following maximization program:

$$\max_s V(s) = u(y_0 - s) + e^{-\delta t} E u(y_t + e^{rt} s), \tag{3.5}$$

where r is the interest rate. Under the concavity of u, the objective function V is concave in s, and the following first-order condition is necessary and sufficient:

$$V'(s) = -u'(y_0 - s) + e^{(r-\delta)t} E u'(y_t + e^{rt} s) = 0. \tag{3.6}$$

Compare two cases. In the certainty case, y_t equals a constant z with certainty. Without loss of generality, suppose that the optimal saving level is zero in that case. This is true if

$$e^{(r-\delta)t}u'(z) = u'(y_0). \tag{3.7}$$

In the uncertainty case, $y_t = z(1+\varepsilon_t)$, where ε_t is a zero-mean relative risk on future income. Compared to the certainty case, the future risk raises the optimal saving if and only if it raises $V'(0)$. This requires that:

$$e^{(r-\delta)t}Eu'(z(1+\varepsilon_t)) \geq u'(y_0). \tag{3.8}$$

Using condition (3.7), this is equivalent to

$$Eu'(z(1+\varepsilon_t)) \geq u'(z). \tag{3.9}$$

This is the case for all z and for all zero-mean ε_t if and only if u' is convex. In words, marginal utility must be decreasing at a decreasing rate to guarantee that precautionary saving is nonnegative. Using the terminology introduced by Kimball (1990), an agent is called prudent if his marginal utility is convex. Prudence is the necessary and sufficient condition to guarantee that individuals want to save more when the future becomes more uncertain.

Let us define the precautionary premium ψ as the sure relative reduction in future income that has the same effect on saving as the future risk on income:

$$u'((1-\psi)Ec_t) = Eu'(c_t) = Eu'((1+\varepsilon_t)Ec_t). \tag{3.10}$$

We say that $(1-\psi)Ec_t$ is the precautionary equivalent of $c_t = (1+\varepsilon_t)Ec_t$. Comparing equations (3.10) and (3.2), observe that the precautionary premium ψ of u is the risk premium of $-u'$, which is increasing and concave under prudence. By analogy, equation (3.3) can be rewritten as:

$$\psi \simeq 0.5\sigma_t^2 P(z), \tag{3.11}$$

where $P(z) = -zu'''(z)/u''(z)$ is the index of relative prudence (Kimball 1990). Thus, adding a zero-mean relative risk to future consumption has an effect on current saving that is approximately equal to half the product of the variance of this risk and of the index of relative prudence.

There has not been much attempt to estimate individuals' degree of prudence. Usually, researchers use one of a family of utility functions that require the choice of a single parameter which determines both the degree of risk aversion of the decision maker and their degree of relative prudence. In practice, the choice of this parameter is calibrated to the assumed degree of risk aversion. For example, consider the case of the power utility function, with $u'(c) = c^{-\gamma}$, which implies that $u''(c) = -\gamma c^{-\gamma-1} < 0$ and $u'''(c) = \gamma(\gamma+1)c^{-\gamma-2} > 0$. It yields $R(c) = \gamma$ and $P(c) = \gamma + 1$. For power functions, relative prudence equals relative risk aversion plus one. If we take $R = 2$, we obtain $P = 3$. Facing an equal chance of gaining or losing 10% of future income has an effect on current saving that is approximately equivalent to the effect of a sure reduction of future income by 1.5%.

PRUDENCE AND DOWNSIDE RISK AVERSION

Is the convexity of marginal utility a natural assumption to make? It has already been assumed that marginal utility is positive and decreasing. This implies that it must be convex, at least locally, for large consumption levels. Observe also, though this is not a very convincing argument, that all classical utility functions used in economics exhibit a convex marginal utility. This is the case for exponential, power, and logarithmic utility functions. The quadratic utility function has a linear marginal utility.

Two positive arguments are in favor of prudence. The first is that there is empirical evidence that people increase their saving when their future becomes more uncertain. See for example the econometric analysis by Guiso, Jappelli, and Terlizzese (1996). Second, people are downside risk-averse, which is another term for prudence. The meaning of downside risk aversion can be illustrated by the definition proposed by Eeckhoudt and Schlesinger (2006). Suppose that your future consumption is either a low z_l or a high z_h, with equal probabilities. Suppose that you are forced to bear a zero-mean risk in one of these two states. Do you prefer to allocate this risk to the low- or high-consumption state? If you answer that it is better to face the risk in the high-consumption state then you are downside risk-averse. This is true if and only if

$$\frac{1}{2}Eu(z_h + \varepsilon) + \frac{1}{2}u(z_l) \geq \frac{1}{2}u(z_h) + \frac{1}{2}Eu(z_l + \varepsilon), \qquad (3.12)$$

or equivalently:

$$Eu(z_h + \varepsilon) - Eu(z_l + \varepsilon) \geq u(z_h) - u(z_l). \tag{3.13}$$

Rewriting this inequality:

$$\int_{z_l}^{z_h} [Eu'(z + \varepsilon) - u'(z)]dz \geq 0. \tag{3.14}$$

Because z_l and $z_h > z_l$ are arbitrary, this integral is positive if and only if $Eu'(z + \varepsilon) \geq u'(z)$ for all z. It follows that the preference for putting risk in the higher income state requires that marginal utility is convex. Prudence and downside risk aversion are two equivalent concepts.

THE EXTENDED RAMSEY RULE AS AN APPROXIMATION

Uncertainty surrounding the growth of consumption affects the discount rate. Let us consider a marginal investment that has a unit cost today and that yields a sure benefit $R = \exp(rt)$ at date t. It preserves the intertemporal welfare V defined by (3.1) if and only if:

$$-u'(c_0) + e^{-\delta t} e^{rt} Eu'(c_t) = 0. \tag{3.15}$$

This can be rewritten:

$$r = \delta - \frac{1}{t} \ln \frac{Eu'(c_t)}{u'(c_0)}. \tag{3.16}$$

Now, remember that the existence of the relative risk $\varepsilon_t = (c_t - Ec_t)/Ec_t$ on future consumption has an effect on expected marginal utility that is equivalent to a sure relative reduction of consumption by the precautionary premium. Technically, using (3.10), equation (3.16) can be rewritten as:

$$r = \delta - \frac{1}{t} \ln \frac{u'((1 - \psi)Ec_t)}{u'(c_0)}. \tag{3.17}$$

This is a return to the certainty case that was examined in the previous chapter. For example, approximation (2.11) can be rewritten as follows:

$$r \simeq \delta + \frac{(1 - \psi)Ec_t - c_0}{tc_0} R(c_0). \tag{3.18}$$

This is reminiscent of the Ramsey rule with an impatience effect and the wealth effect, but the latter is reduced by risk. This reduction ψ can be approximated by using equation (3.11). Alternatively, a second-degree Taylor approximation of $u'(c_t)$ around c_0 can be used in equation (3.16) to get:

$$r \simeq \delta + t^{-1} E\left(\frac{c_t - c_0}{c_0}\right) R(c_0) - \frac{1}{2} t^{-1} Var\left(\frac{c_t - c_0}{c_0}\right) R(c_0) P(c_0). \quad (3.19)$$

This is the extended Ramsey rule. As in the standard Ramsey rule (2.11), there is an impatience effect and a wealth effect. The third term in the right-hand side of (3.19) is what is called the precautionary effect. It tends to reduce the discount rate. Its intensity is proportional to the product of relative prudence, relative risk aversion, and the annualized variance of the growth rate of consumption between 0 and t.

This confirms the intuition that uncertainty affecting the future tends to raise our willingness to invest for that future. Uncertainty over future economic growth translates into a lower discount rate, lowering the threshold rate of return that a sure investment must achieve to be considered welfare enhancing.

THE EXTENDED RAMSEY RULE IN THE LOGNORMAL CASE

The extended Ramsey rule described by (3.19) can be obtained as an exact solution in an important special case. Let us consider a one-year horizon ($t = 1$). Suppose that

$$c_1 = c_0 e^x, \quad (3.20)$$

where x is the continuously compounded growth rate of consumption, or the increase in the logarithm of consumption. Let us assume that x is normally distributed with mean μ and variance σ^2. Notice that, using lemma 1 and equation (3.4) with $A = -1$, implies that the growth rate of expected consumption (or the change in log expected consumption) between dates 0 and 1 is $g = \ln(Ec_1/c_0) = Ee^x = \mu + 0.5\sigma^2$.

Suppose also that the representative agent in the economy has a power utility function, with $u'(c) = c^{-\gamma}$. This implies that

$$\frac{Eu'(c_1)}{u'(c_0)} = \frac{Ec_0^{-\gamma} e^{-\gamma x}}{c_0^{-\gamma}} = Ee^{-\gamma x}. \tag{3.21}$$

Now, equation (3.4) can be used again to rewrite the right-hand side of equation (3.21) as $\exp(-\gamma(\mu - 0.5\gamma\sigma^2))$. Plugging this into the pricing formula (3.16) yields

$$r = \delta + \gamma\mu - 0.5\gamma^2\sigma^2. \tag{3.22}$$

It is preferable to rewrite this formula using the growth rate g of expected consumption:

$$r = \delta + \gamma g - 0.5\gamma(\gamma + 1)\sigma^2. \tag{3.23}$$

This exact extended Ramsey rule combines the three components of the efficient discount rate: impatience, the wealth effect, and the precautionary effect. As in the Ramsey rule under certainty, the wealth effect is positive and is the product of the expected growth rate of consumption by the relative aversion to intertemporal inequality. The precautionary effect is negative, and is equal in absolute value to half the product of three factors: relative risk aversion γ, relative prudence $\gamma + 1$, and the variance of the growth rate of consumption. This shows that approximation (3.19) is exact in the special case of a power utility function and a log normal distribution of future consumption.

CALIBRATION OF THE EXTENDED RAMSEY RULE USING TIME SERIES DATA

In the previous chapter, in which risk was ignored, a justification was provided for the use of $\delta = 0$, $\gamma = 2$, and $g = 2\%$. In turn, this justified using a discount rate of 4% per year. How much smaller than 4% should the discount rate be to take account of future risk? To answer this question for a one-year horizon, the volatility of the annual growth rate of consumption must be estimated.

Kocherlakota (1996), using U.S. annual data over the period 1889–1978, estimated the standard deviation σ of the growth of consumption per capita to be 3.6% per year. Assuming normality and an expected growth rate of 2%, this means that there is a 95% probability that the actual growth

TABLE **3.1.**
Benchmark calibration of the extended Ramsey rule

μ	σ	δ	γ
2%	3.6%	0%	2

rate of consumption next year will be between -5% and $+9\%$. Using $\sigma^2 = (0.036)^2$ and $\gamma = 2$ as stated in table 3.1 yields a precautionary term in the extended Ramsey rule (3.23) equaling -0.4%. The precautionary effect reduces the efficient rate at which one should discount cash flows occurring next year from 4% to 3.6%.

In Gollier (2011), we have calibrated the extended Ramsey rule for other countries. In this exercise, whose results are described in table 3.2, it is assumed that each country has its own stable trend and volatility for the growth rate of its economy. In order to estimate them, we used a data set of real historical GDP per capita extracted from the Economic Research Service (ERS) International Macroeconomic Data Set provided by the U.S. Department of Agriculture (USDA). This set contains the real GDP/cap expressed in dollars of 2005 for 190 countries for each year from 1969 to 2010. If we limit the analysis to the United States, the first two moments of the growth rate of GDP/cap over the period has been respectively $g = 1.74\%$ and $\sigma = 2.11\%$. With $\delta = 0\%$ and $\gamma = 2$, it yields a wealth effect of 3.48% and a precautionary effect of -0.13%, implying a discount rate of 3.35%.

We obtain the same order of magnitude for the wealth effect and the precautionary effect for other developed countries like France, Germany, and the United Kingdom. For Japan, the mean growth rate and the volatility have been larger, yielding a net positive effect with a discount rate around 4.5%. The picture is quite different for emerging countries, which by definition experienced a much larger growth rate of consumption. The most striking example is China, with a mean annual growth rate of around 7.5% per year, and a relatively large volatility around 4%. The calibration of the extended Ramsey rule (3.23) with these parameter values yields a discount rate as large as 14.82%. If one believes that this growth is sustainable, intertemporal inequality aversion and the associated wealth effect should induce the Chinese authorities to limit their safe investments to projects having a rate of return above this large discount rate.

TABLE 3.2.
**Country-specific discount rate computed from the extended
Ramsey rule using the historical mean g and standard
deviation σ of growth rates of real GDP/cap 1969–2010**

	Country	g (γg)	σ $(-0.5\gamma(1+\gamma)\sigma^2)$	Discount Rate
Developed countries	United States	1.74% *(3.48%)*	2.11% *(−0.13%)*	*3.35%*
	France	1.75% *(3.50%)*	1.57% *(−0.07%)*	*3.43%*
	Germany	1.76% *(3.52%)*	1.83% *(−0.10%)*	*3.42%*
	United Kingdom	1.86% *(3.71%)*	2.18% *(−0.14%)*	*3.57%*
	Japan	2.34% *(4.67%)*	2.61% *(−0.20%)*	*4.47%*
Emerging countries	China	7.60% *(15.20%)*	3.53% *(−0.37%)*	*14.82%*
	South Korea	5.38% *(10.75%)*	3.40% *(−0.35%)*	*10.41%*
	Taiwan	5.41% *(10.82%)*	5.29% *(−0.84%)*	*9.98%*
	India	3.34% *(6.88%)*	3.03% *(−0.28%)*	*6.61%*
	Russia	1.54% *(3.08%)*	5.59% *(−0.94%)*	*2.14%*
Africa	Gabon	1.29% *(2.58%)*	9.63% *(−2.78%)*	*−0.20%*
	Liberia	−1.90% *(−3.79%)*	19.58% *(−11.50%)*	*−15.30%*
	Zaire (RDC)	−2.76% *(−5.53%)*	5.31% *(−0.85%)*	*−6.38%*
	Zambia	−0.69% *(−1.38%)*	4.01% *(−0.48%)*	*−1.86%*
	Zimbabwe	−0.26% *(−0.53%)*	6.50% *(−1.27%)*	*−1.79%*

At the other extreme of the spectrum is the set of countries that have experienced low growth rates. The worst example is Zaire (RDC), with an awful mean growth rate of −2.76% per year over the last four decades. If one believes that this negative growth trend is persistent, a negative discount rate of −6.38% should be used to evaluate safe projects in that country. Liberia provides another example of a country with a negative discount rate. In this country, the volatility of the growth rate has been extremely large, with σ equaling 19.58%. This implies a precautionary effect around −11.5%. Combining that with a wealth effect of −3.8%, we obtain a socially efficient discount rate for Liberia around −15%. These examples clearly show the shortcomings of this calibration exercise. In particular, it is implicitly assumed here that the future will look like the past, and that there is no business cycle. For Sub-Saharan countries, we hope that the future will not look like the past.

The important differences in growth outcomes among the 190 countries present in the ERS/USDA data set over the last four decades make it difficult to draw general conclusions about the discount rate. In table 3.3, we summarize the calibration of the extended Ramsey rule on the basis of the mean wealth and precautionary effects among the 190 countries of the data set.

In figure 3.1, we draw the frequency graph for the wealth effect and the discount rate. It is noteworthy that the precautionary effect tends to be much smaller in developed countries, because of the more efficient stabilizing policies put in place in these countries. This is an important reason for the relatively larger discount rates that are efficient in the western world. Precautionary investment is a substitute to macroeconomic stabilizing policies.

TABLE 3.3.
The mean discount rate among the time series of the 190 countries

Mean wealth effect	3.54% per year
Mean precautionary effect	−1.00% per year
Mean discount rate	2.54% per year

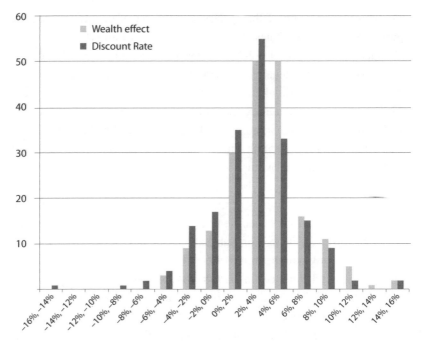

Figure 3.1. Frequency for the wealth effect and the discount rate among the 190 countries, using the extended Ramsey rule

This exercise in which we apply the extended Ramsey rule (3.23) to each individual country relies on the assumption that risks are efficiently shared within each country, so that the volatility of the growth of GDP/cap is the right measure of uncertainty born by all citizens within that country. By the power of imagination, suppose that risks are efficiently shared at the level of the entire world, so that the growth of world GDP/cap would be the right measure of consumption growth of all human beings on the earth. Expectations about the future can be inferred from the first two moments of the growth of world GDP/cap over the last four decades. Using the same data set, we obtain by pure chance that the mean and the volatility of the real growth rate of world GDP/cap are equal to 1.41%. This yields a wealth effect and a precautionary effect of respectively 2.82% and −0.06%, implying a discount rate of 2.76%. Because country-specific risks are washed out through international diversification, the small precautionary effect reflects the low systematic risk at the aggregate level. However, this exercise has no economic meaning because it is clear that credit and risk-sharing markets do not work efficiently at the international level. Even in an integrated economic union like Europe, there is little international solidarity across borders.

To sum up our results in this section based on a time-series analysis of country-specific economic growth, one must admit that the precautionary effect remains a marginal component in the estimation of the socially efficient discount rate. For the western world, the precautionary effect is generally smaller than a quarter of a percent, and is close to 0.1% for countries like the United States, France, the United Kingdom, and Germany. This is because of the low volatility of their economic growth observed during the last four decades. This precautionary effect is marginal compared to the usually much larger wealth effect equaling two times the anticipated growth rate. However, this conclusion of the limited role of uncertainty to determine the intensity of our sacrifices in favor of the future does not hold for developing countries. Many of them have experienced a huge volatility of their growth rate during the same period. This suggests that the discount rate that should be used in these countries should be smaller than in the western world, even in the case of similar expectations on the trend of economic growth.

CALIBRATION OF THE EXTENDED RAMSEY RULE USING CROSS-SECTION DATA

In the previous section, we made the assumption that each country faces its own stochastic growth process characterized by a random walk for the annual growth rate of consumption with known country-specific mean and volatility. If we take a more long-term perspective, one must recognize that growth processes undergo persistent shocks, or that they are subject to long-lasting cycles covering several decades. Contrary to what is implicitly assumed in the previous computations, it is indeed hard to believe that China will be able to stay permanently with a trend of growth around 8% per year, or that Zaire will permanently face an expected growth rate of −2.7% per year. Based on this idea, Gollier (2011) proposes consideration of an alternative modeling of growth risk other than the one that is classically considered in the literature, as illustrated in the previous section.

In the spirit of Kondratiev waves ranging from forty to sixty years in length, let us consider the abstract stochastic growth process in which each country-specific growth rate is reset every forty-one years with resetting dates 1969, 2010, 2051, . . . To be more precise, let us assume that each country-specific change in log consumption x_{41} is drawn from the same worldwide "urn" which is normally distributed with mean $\mu = g - 0.5\sigma^2$ and volatility σ. This allows us to again use equation (3.23) to estimate the socially efficient rate r at which cash flows occurring in forty-one years should be discounted at each resetting date. In this framework, all countries should use the same discount rate ex ante.

The observation of the change in log consumption between 1969 and 2010 in the 190 countries of the ERS/USDA data set allows us to estimate the first two moments of random variable x_{41}. Its mean and its volatility are respectively equal to $\mu = 65.74\%$ and $\sigma = 72.18\%$. It yields a growth rate of expected consumption equaling $g = \mu + 0.5\sigma^2 = 91.79\%$, or 2.24% per year. The calibration of the extended Ramsey rule in this cross-sectional analysis is summarized in table 3.4.

Focusing on the annualized rates, two conclusions should be drawn from these results when tables 3.3 and 3.4 are compared. First, the relatively large growth rate of expected consumption in this model implies a large wealth effect in the Ramsey rule. But the precautionary effect is also large, amounting to almost 4% per year. Remember that the mean level of the precautionary effect that we documented in the previous section was only 1%. This huge difference in the precautionary effect when using a cross-sectional approach rather than the traditional time-series approach comes from the important heterogeneity in the country-specific growth rates observed during the last four decades. In other words, there is more

TABLE 3.4.
The discount rate using the cross-section
approach during period 1969–2010

Wealth effect	183.59%	4.48% per year
Precautionary effect	−156.30%	−3.81% per year
Discount rate	27.29%	0.67% per year

volatility across countries than through time. The bottom line is a small discount rate at 0.67% per year.

SUMMARY OF MAIN RESULTS

1. Under prudence ($u''' \geq 0$), uncertainty about the growth of aggregate consumption induces people to invest more for the future. At the collective level, this is done by reducing the discount rate.
2. Quantitatively, the precautionary effect reduces the discount rate by half the product of three factors: relative risk aversion, relative prudence, and the variance of the growth rate of consumption. Under CRRA, this is equal to $0.5\gamma(\gamma + 1)\sigma^2$.
3. The volatility of the growth rate of the US GDP/cap over the last century is around 3.6%. It justifies reducing the short-term discount rate by 0.4%. In short, taking account of short-term risk, the efficient short-term discount rate should be reduced from 4% to 3.6%.
4. Examining other developed countries and other time periods does not radically transform the message that uncertainty does not have a strong impact on short-term discounting.

In the second part of this book, the question of uncertainty is explored further, by considering risk in the longer term and its implications for discount rates.

APPENDIX

Lemma: *Suppose that x is normally distributed with finite mean μ and variance σ^2. Consider any scalar $A \in \mathbb{R}$. Then, we have that*

$$Ee^{-Ax} = e^{-A(\mu - 0.5A\sigma^2)}. \tag{3.24}$$

Proof: Suppose that $u(c) = -\exp(-Ac)$. If c is normally distributed with mean μ and variance σ^2, we have that:

$$Eu(c) = \frac{-1}{\sigma\sqrt{2\pi}} \int \exp(-Ac)\exp\left(-\frac{(c-\mu)^2}{2\sigma^2}\right)dc.$$

Rearranging the integrant, we obtain:

$$Eu(c) = -\exp\left(-A\left(\mu - \frac{A\sigma^2}{2}\right)\right)\frac{1}{\sigma\sqrt{2\pi}}$$
$$\int \exp\left(-\frac{(c - (\mu - A\sigma^2))^2}{2\sigma^2}\right)dc. \tag{3.25}$$

Observe that:

$$f(c) = \frac{1}{\sigma\sqrt{2\pi}}\exp\left(-\frac{(c - (\mu - A\sigma^2))^2}{2\sigma^2}\right)$$

is the density function of a normally distributed random variable c with mean $\mu - A\sigma^2$ and variance σ^2. Because the integral of a density function equals 1, this implies that we can rewrite (3.25) as follows:

$$Eu(c) = -\exp\left(-A\left(\mu - \frac{A\sigma^2}{2}\right)\right) = u\left(\mu - \frac{A\sigma^2}{2}\right).$$

This concludes the proof of the lemma. $\square$

REFERENCES

Allais, M. (1953), Le comportement de l'homme rationnel devant le risque, Critique des postulats et axiomes de l'école américaine, *Econometrica*, 21, 503–546.

Drèze, J. H., and F. Modigliani (1972), Consumption decisions under uncertainty, *Journal of Economic Theory*, 5, 308–335.

Eeckhoudt, L., and H. Schlesinger (2006), Putting risk in its proper place, *American Economic Review*, 96 (1), 280–289.

Gollier, C. (2011), On the underestimation of the precautionary effect in discounting, *Geneva Risk and Insurance Review*, 36, 95–111.

Guiso, L., T. Jappelli, and D. Terlizzese (1996), Income risk, borrowing constraints, and portfolio choice, *American Economic Review*, 86, 158–172.

Kimball, M. S. (1990), Precautionary saving in the small and in the large, *Econometrica*, 58 (1990), 53–73.

Kocherlakota, N. R. (1996), The equity premium: it's still a puzzle, *Journal of Economic Literature*, 34, 42–71.

Leland, H. E. (1968), Saving and uncertainty: The precautionary demand for saving, *Quarterly Journal of Economics*, 465–473.

PART II

—◄○►—

THE TERM STRUCTURE OF DISCOUNT RATES

4

<hr>

Random Walk and Mean-Reversion

The first part of this book concluded that there is a solid scientific basis to recommend the use of a discount rate around 3.6% in the western world for cash flows occurring in the next few years. Does this imply that the same rate should be used to discount all sure cash flows, irrespective of when they occur? The theoretical answer to this question is, in general, "no." The socially efficient discount rate need not be constant with respect to the time horizon. However, our benchmark result in this chapter is that the discount rate should be independent of the maturity of the cash flow under scrutiny if relative risk aversion is constant and if the aggregate consumption follows a geometric Brownian motion. This is not the case if the growth rate of consumption is mean-reverting, mainly because of the cyclicality of the wealth effect.

THE TERM STRUCTURE OF THE DISCOUNT RATE

Up to this point, for the sake of simple notation, we have referred to r as "the" discount rate. However, if r is maturity varying it should be indexed by the maturity of the cost or benefit to be discounted. In fact, the general pricing formula (3.16) can now be rewritten:

$$r_t = \delta - \frac{1}{t} \ln \frac{Eu'(c_t)}{u'(c_0)}. \tag{4.1}$$

The right-hand side of the equality depends in general upon t; therefore the left-hand side does as well. In fact, the pricing formula (4.1) provides the entire term structure of the discount rate.

Before going into further detail, it is helpful to develop an intuition of the determinants of this term structure. As has been seen before, the discount rate is determined by two competing effects: the wealth effect and the precautionary effect. Over two different time intervals, looking forward from the present to two different points in time, t and $t' > t$, the intensity of each of these two effects may differ. This implies differing discount rates should be applied to cash flows occurring in period t to those occurring in period t'. Changes in the intensity of the wealth effect and the precautionary effect therefore form the shape of the term structure.

A FLAT TERM STRUCTURE

The simplest case arises when the growth rate is a constant g, now and forever. Assuming constant relative risk aversion γ, the pricing formula (4.1) implies that

$$r_t = \delta - \frac{1}{t} \ln \frac{Eu'(c_t)}{u'(c_0)} = \delta - \frac{1}{t} \ln \frac{c_0^{-\gamma} e^{-\gamma g t}}{c_0^{-\gamma}} = \delta + \gamma g. \qquad (4.2)$$

The term structure is completely flat. Consumption increases exponentially with time, which implies that the intertemporal marginal rate of substitution, which is the discount factor $\exp(-r_t t)$, must decrease exponentially. This requires that the discount rate r_t is constant.

THE CASE OF DIMINISHING EXPECTATIONS

Suppose that, as in the simplest case just presented, there is certainty over the evolution of the economy. However, contrary to the previous paragraph, let us assume that the growth rate is not constant over time. Suppose that the growth rate decreases at a constant rate from x_{-1} last year toward $\mu < x_{-1}$ in the long run. More specifically, suppose that there exists a constant $\phi \in [0,1]$ such that

$$\begin{cases} c_{t+1} = c_t e^{x_t} \\ x_t = \mu + \phi(x_{t-1} - \mu). \end{cases} \qquad (4.3)$$

When ϕ equals 0, the growth rate goes immediately to μ in the next period, and remains there forever. When ϕ equals 1, the growth rate remains equal to x_{-1} forever. When $\phi \in]0,1[$, the growth rate converges smoothly to μ. In short, ϕ measures the degree of persistence of the initial shock from $x = \mu$ to $x = x_{-1}$. In any case, we obtain that

$$\ln c_t - \ln c_0 = \mu t + (x_{-1} - \mu)\phi\frac{1-\phi^t}{1-\phi}. \qquad (4.4)$$

In this certainty case with diminishing expectations, and assuming a power utility function, the pricing formula (4.1) can be rewritten as:

$$r_t = \delta + \gamma\frac{\ln c_t - \ln c_0}{t} = \delta + \gamma\left[\mu + (x_{-1} - \mu)\phi\frac{1-\phi^t}{t(1-\phi)}\right]. \qquad (4.5)$$

The first equality in (4.5) tells us that the wealth effect is proportional to the annualized growth of log consumption. This yields the following discount rates in the short and long terms:

$$\begin{cases} r_1 = \delta + \gamma x_0 \\ r_\infty = \delta + \gamma\mu \end{cases}. \qquad (4.6)$$

In between, the efficient discount rate decreases smoothly at a constant rate. When expectations are diminishing, the term structure is downward sloping. This is because the wealth effect is strong for the short term, but reduces for longer time horizons.

There are two ideas that this simple dynamic of diminishing expectations illustrates. In the first story, the economy just faces standard business cycles. In that case, the preceding equations apply for the first few maturities t depending on the position in the cycle, either high ($x_{-1} > \mu$) or low ($x_{-1} < \mu$). Remember, the socially efficient discount rate is also the equilibrium interest rate that one would observe on frictionless capital markets. Our analysis tells us that the shape of the yield curve, the term structure of the market yield to maturity of zero-coupon bonds, is a crucial source of information about what economic agents believe about the future dynamics of economic growth. A downward yield curve suggests people believe that the economy will experience a downturn in the future. On the contrary, an upward sloping yield curve is typical of an economy where growth is expected to accelerate, since the formulas (4.5) and (4.6) apply also when $x_{-1} < \mu$.

The same ideas apply for longer time horizons. In the second story, we may believe that the current level of growth is unsustainable, and that the economy will have to adapt to a lower, sustainable, growth rate μ. If one believes that the growth rate experienced by developed economies during the last two centuries is just unsustainable, this should be taken into account in the evaluation of long-term investment projects. The term structure of the discount rates should be decreasing. This will favor investment projects that have large positive benefits in the distant future in comparison to projects with more immediate benefits. In short, a decreasing term structure of discount rates supports sustainable development.

If the current growth rate of the economy is 2%, but its sustainable growth rate is believed to be only 0.5%, then applying the above pricing formula given, with $\delta = 0$ and $\gamma = 2$, yields discount rates of 4% and 1% respectively for the short and long terms.

Economic growth is subject to business cycles. This should be accounted for when shaping the term structure of discount rates. In particular, discount rates should be revised periodically to take into account any changes in expectations about future growth in the short and medium terms. However, from our point of view, there is no argument which convinces us to believe that growth in the future will *necessarily* be smaller or larger than it is today. We do not side with catastrophists who believe that because of finite natural resources our economic growth is unsustainable. Just as there is a chance that future growth will be smaller than it is today, there is a chance that our society will experience a larger rate of growth—even larger than has been experienced since the beginning of the industrial revolution. This growth could be sustained by technological progress and the increasing de-materialization of economic activity. However, this does not mean that we should be unconcerned with the dynamics of growth into the distant future; quite to the contrary, as the next few chapters show.

DECREASING TERM STRUCTURE AND TIME CONSISTENCY

It is often suggested in the literature that economic agents are time inconsistent if the term structure of the discount rate is decreasing. This is not the case. What is crucial for time consistency is the constancy of the rate of impatience, δ, which is a cornerstone of the classic analysis presented in this book. We have seen that this assumption is compatible with a declining monetary discount rate. Other illustrations of this fact will be presented later on in this book. Let us re-examine this question under the simple framework of diminishing expectations as modeled by the deterministic dynamic process (4.3).

An agent is time consistent if the plan that is optimal at time t remains optimal for all future date $t' > t$. To illustrate, consider an investment that costs one monetary unit at date T and that generates a single benefit k at time $T + \tau$. Evaluating this project from date 0, investing is optimal if and only if its net present value is positive, that is, if:

$$-e^{-r_T T} + ke^{-r_{T+\tau}(T+\tau)} \geq 0. \tag{4.7}$$

This is equivalent to:

$$-1 + ke^{r_T T - r_{T+\tau}(T+\tau)} \geq 0. \tag{4.8}$$

Assume that the agent's consumption dynamics are represented by (4.3). The term structure r_t given by (4.5) should be used at date 0 to discount the cash flows in equation (4.8). Suppose that this condition is satisfied, so that, seen from today, it is optimal to implement the project at date T.

Consider now the decision problem at date T, when the time to invest in the project arrives. To solve this problem, we need to determine the discount rate that should be used at date T to discount the cash flow k occurring τ periods later. Let $r_{T \to T+\tau}$ denote this discount rate. Seen from date T, it is optimal to invest in the project if and only if:

$$-1 + ke^{-r_{T \to T+\tau} \tau} \geq 0. \tag{4.9}$$

The problem of time consistency is about whether conditions (4.8) and (4.9) are equivalent, independent of k. Obviously, this requires that $-r_{T \to T+\tau} \tau = r_T T - r_{T+\tau}(T + \tau)$. At date T, the level of x_T equals:

$$x_T = \mu + \phi^T (x_0 - \mu). \tag{4.10}$$

Duplicating the analysis presented in the previous section to the context of date τ implies that:

$$r_{T \to T+\tau} \tau = \delta\tau + \gamma \left[\mu\tau + (x_T - \mu) \frac{1 - \phi^\tau}{(1 - \phi)} \right]$$

$$= \delta\tau + \gamma \left[\mu\tau + (x_0 - \mu) \frac{\phi^T (1 - \phi^\tau)}{(1 - \phi)} \right].$$

(4.11)

It is straightforward to check that this is equal to $r_T T - r_{T+\tau}(T + \tau)$, which implies that the decision criterion to be used at date T is consistent with the one to be used at date 0. The decision process is thus perfectly time consistent, even though the term structure of discount rates is not flat.

RANDOM WALK

For uncertain future growth rates, the simplest assumption that can be made is that they follow a random walk. This means that the growth rate observed this year does not provide any information about the growth rate that will be experienced in the future. More specifically, suppose that the growth rate of the economy follows an independent and identically distributed (iid) process over time:

$$\begin{cases} c_{t+1} = c_t e^{x_t} \\ x_0, x_1, \dots \text{ iid.} \end{cases}$$

(4.12)

This implies that the pricing formula (4.1) can be rewritten as:

$$r_t = \delta - \frac{1}{t} \ln \frac{Eu'\left(c_0 \prod_{\tau=0}^{t-1} e^{x_\tau}\right)}{u'(c_0)}.$$

(4.13)

To keep things simple at this stage, consider the case of a power utility function with relative aversion γ. Using independence, equation (4.13) can then be rewritten as:

$$r_t = \delta - \frac{1}{t} \sum_{\tau=0}^{t-1} \ln\left(Ee^{-\gamma x_\tau}\right).$$

(4.14)

Because the process is iid, this can be rewritten as:

$$r_t = \delta - \ln\left(Ee^{-\gamma x_1}\right).$$

(4.15)

Thus, in the case of power utility functions and an iid process for the growth rate of the economy, the term structure of the efficient discount rate is completely flat. In the special case of a normal distribution for x, the extended Ramsey rule (3.23) gives us the level of this constant discount rate. This result can be found for example in Hansen and Singleton (1983).

This case, which is the discrete version of a Brownian motion for the growth of the economy, serves as a benchmark for the analysis of the term structure of discount rates. It is therefore important to understand its nature. When the growth rate of the economy follows a random walk with a constant positive trend, the wealth effect goes up exponentially with the time horizon. If $g = 2\%$, one expects to be 2% wealthier next year, and 5000% wealthier in 200 years. This exponentially increasing wealth effect justifies taking an exponentially decreasing discount factor. This requires a constant discount rate. Similarly, the random walk in the growth rate entails an exponentially increasing level of uncertainty about future consumption. This is equivalent to a linearly increasing variance for $\ln c_t$. Indeed, it follows that:

$$Var(\ln c_t - \ln c_0) = Var\left(\sum_{\tau=0}^{t-1} x_\tau\right) = t\sigma^2. \tag{4.16}$$

The exponentially increasing precautionary effect that this implies should impact the discount factor exponentially. In other words, it should affect the discount rate uniformly with respect to the time horizon. Combining these two elements implies that the term structure of discount rates is flat.

A SIMPLE EXTENSION: MEAN-REVERTING GROWTH PROCESS

Following Bansal and Yaron (2004), for example, the two growth processes that have been considered in this chapter can be combined in the following simple model:

$$\begin{cases} c_{t+1} = c_t e^{x_t} \\ x_t = \mu + y_t + \varepsilon_{xt}, \\ y_t = \phi y_{t-1} + \varepsilon_{yt} \end{cases} \tag{4.17}$$

For some initial state characterized by y_{-1}, where ε_{xt} and ε_{yt} are independent and serially independent with mean zero and variance σ_x^2 and σ_y^2, respectively. The state variable y_t exhibits some persistence. As earlier, parameter ϕ, which is between 0 and 1, represents the degree of persistence in the expected growth rate process. When ε_x and ε_y are uniformly zero, this model is equivalent to the story of deterministic "diminishing expectations." When ϕ is zero, the model returns to a pure random walk.

This autoregressive model of order 1—an AR(1)—illustrates the notion of mean-reversion. Suppose that the expected growth rate equals its historical level $\mu(y_{-1}=0)$, and that a positive shock ε_{y0} affects the expected growth rate between dates 0 and 1, so that y_0 is larger than 0. Contrary to a random walk, this shock will have some persistence. For example, the expected growth rate between dates t and $t+1$ will be $Ex_t | \varepsilon_{y0} = \mu + \phi^t \varepsilon_{y0}$. However, in the long run, the expected growth rate will revert to the mean. But at each date, a new persistent shock may affect the growth rate of the economy, in addition to the pure noise ε_{xt}.

The efficient term structure is determined in this case by characterizing the distribution of c_t. By forward induction of (4.17), it follows that:

$$\ln c_t - \ln c_0 = \mu t + y_{-1}\phi \frac{1-\phi^t}{1-\phi} + \sum_{\tau=0}^{t-1} \frac{1-\phi^{t-\tau}}{1-\phi}\varepsilon_{y\tau} + \sum_{\tau=0}^{t-1}\varepsilon_{x\tau}. \qquad (4.18)$$

The ε terms are assumed to be normally distributed; therefore so too is $\ln c_t - \ln c_0$. Its mean is the sum of the first two terms in the right-hand side of equality (4.18). Its annualized variance equals:

$$t^{-1} Var(\ln c_t) = \frac{\sigma_y^2}{(1-\phi)^2}\left[1 - 2\phi\frac{\phi^t-1}{t(\phi-1)} + \phi^2\frac{\phi^{2t}-1}{t(\phi^2-1)}\right] + \sigma_x^2. \qquad (4.19)$$

Observe that the annualized variance of log consumption tends to $(\sigma_y^2/(1-\phi)^2)+\sigma_x^2$, which is larger than the short-run uncertainty measured by $Var\, x_0 = \sigma_y^2 + \sigma_x^2$. The long-run risk is increasing in the degree of persistence of shocks on the expected growth rate of consumption. This is because of the positive serial correlation in growth rates. More generally, the analysis of the right-hand side of (4.19) shows that the annualized variance of future log consumption goes up smoothly from $\sigma_y^2 + \sigma_x^2$ to $(\sigma_y^2/(1-\phi)^2)+\sigma_x^2$ when t goes from 1 to infinity.

Suppose that u is a power function with relative aversion γ. The pricing formula (4.1) can therefore be rewritten as:

$$r_t = \delta - \frac{1}{t}\ln E[e^{-\gamma(\ln c_t - \ln c_0)}]. \tag{4.20}$$

The normality of $\ln c_t - \ln c_0$ means that lemma 1 can be used to obtain that:

$$r_t = \delta + \gamma t^{-1}E[\ln c_t - \ln c_0] - 0.5\gamma^2 t^{-1} Var(\ln c_t). \tag{4.21}$$

Finally, using the properties of the mean and variance of log consumption, the term structure of the discount rate can be characterized as follows:

$$
\begin{aligned}
r_t = \delta + \gamma\left[\mu + y_{-1}\phi\frac{1-\phi^t}{t(1-\phi)}\right] \\
- 0.5\gamma^2\left[\frac{\sigma_y^2}{(1-\phi)^2}\left[1 - 2\phi\frac{\phi^t-1}{t(\phi-1)} + \phi^2\frac{\phi^{2t}-1}{t(\phi^2-1)}\right] + \sigma_x^2\right].
\end{aligned} \tag{4.22}
$$

This equation can be rewritten as:

$$
\begin{aligned}
r_t = \delta + \gamma\mu - 0.5\gamma^2\left[\sigma_x^2 + \frac{\sigma_y^2}{(1-\phi)^2}\right] \\
+ \left[\gamma y_{-1}\phi\frac{1-\phi^t}{t(1-\phi)} - 0.5\gamma^2\frac{\sigma_y^2}{(1-\phi)^2}\left[\phi^2\frac{\phi^{2t}-1}{t(\phi^2-1)} - 2\phi\frac{\phi^t-1}{t(\phi-1)}\right]\right].
\end{aligned} \tag{4.23}
$$

Observe that the last bracketed term of this equation is the only one that depends upon t and that it vanishes when t tends to infinity. It is this transitory term which shapes the term structure. The first three terms in (4.23) determine the long-term discount rate. Indeed, it yields:

$$r_\infty = \delta + \gamma\mu - 0.5\gamma^2\left[\sigma_x^2 + \frac{\sigma_y^2}{(1-\phi)^2}\right]. \tag{4.24}$$

The long-term wealth effect is still measured by $\gamma\mu$. The long-term precautionary effect is increasing in ϕ, therefore this effect is magnified by persistence. It can be concluded that if shocks on the growth rate of the economy are persistent, the rate at which very distant cash flows should be discounted is reduced. This is because of the increased long-term risk that the positive correlation of growth rates generates. To make this more precise, consider experts who believe that the growth rate of our economy follows a random walk. In order to estimate the efficient discount rate, they would use observations of past growth rates to estimate μ and σ. In particular, they would use the observed volatility of the growth rate to estimate σ. With a large data set, they would obtain $\sigma_y^2 + \sigma_x^2$ for the variance of changes in log consumption. Therefore, using the extended Ramsey rule, the recommendation would be a flat discount rate given by:

$$r_1 = \delta + \gamma\mu - 0.5\gamma^2(\sigma_y^2 + \sigma_x^2), \tag{4.25}$$

which is obviously larger than r_∞. In fact, by proceeding in this way, experts would provide the correct answer, but only for the short-term discount rate, and only when the past growth rate of the economy was equal to its historical mean ($y_{-1} = 0$).

The term structure is given by the last term in equation (4.23). The part of that term including y_{-1} corresponds to the "diminishing expectations" story that was explained earlier in the chapter. It yields a decreasing shape for the term structure if the economy is currently experiencing a growth rate above its historical mean. This effect is switched off by assuming that $y_{-1} = 0$. In that case, the second term inside the brackets in (4.23) tells us how the discount rate goes down from the short-term rate r_1 given by (4.25) to $r_\infty < r_1$. The annualized variance of log consumption is increasing with the time horizon when there is persistence. Contrary to the pure Brownian case, this gives a decreasing term structure.

Let $r_{t \to t+1}$ denote the rate that should be used at date t to discount cash flows occurring at date $t+1$. This is the short-term interest rate. Notice that the short-term interest rate in this model also follows an AR(1) process since using the pricing formula (4.21) for $t = 1$ yields

$$\begin{cases} r_{t \to t+1} = \delta + \gamma\mu - 0.5\gamma^2(\sigma_y^2 + \sigma_x^2) + \gamma\phi y_{t-1} \\ y_t = \phi y_{t-1} + \varepsilon_{yt}. \end{cases} \tag{4.26}$$

Vasicek (1977) was interested in determining the shape of the yield curve by using the standard arbitrage method in finance under the assumption of an AR(1) for the short-term interest rate. He got equilibrium interest rates for different maturities that are equivalent to formula (4.22). The degree of persistence ϕ is the same for economic growth and for the short-term interest rate. This is interesting because the degree of persistence of the latter has been well documented in the literature on the term structure of the interest rate. One important critique that has been made regarding Vasicek's model is that the short-term interest rate expressed by (4.26) can become negative. This is a problem if a predictive model for the equilibrium interest rate is wanted, since the interest rate must be nonnegative (otherwise consumers will prefer to hold cash). This critique does not hold for our normative analysis. It may indeed be efficient to use a negative discount rate, in particular when a significant economic depression is predicted for the future.

Bansal and Yaron (2004) consider the following calibration of the model, using annual growth data for the United States for the period 1929–1998. Taking a month as the unit period, they obtained $\mu = 0.0015$, $\sigma_x = 0.0078$, $\sigma_y = 0.00034$, and $\phi = 0.979$. Using this ϕ yields a half-life for shocks of 32 months. This implies that the model is useful to justify differences in discount rates for maturities expressed in years, but not really for maturities expressed in decades or centuries. In other words, Vasicek's model and mean-reversion in the growth rate are useful to explain the term structure of interest rates for maturities that are treated by financial markets, up to two or three decades.

Figure 4.1 describes how the term structure of interest/discount rates evolves along the business cycle. In addition to the Bansal-Yaron's parameter values given earlier, it is assumed that the rate of impatience is $\delta = 0$ and relative aversion is $\gamma = 2$. Three term structures are represented in this figure. When the recent growth rate is exactly at its historical mean ($y_0 = 0$, which corresponds to an annual growth rate of 1.8%), the yield curve is decreasing. This slope describes the increasing precautionary effect coming from the increasing annualized variance of future log consumption due to the persistence of shocks. During a downturn (illustrated by a low growth rate $y_0 = -0.1\%$/month, which corresponds to an annual growth rate of 0.6%), the yield curve is upward sloping. This shape is mostly expressing an accelerating wealth effect generated by rising growth expectations, which are rising because of mean reversion. On the contrary, when the economy is booming with $y_0 = 0.1\%$/month (corresponding to an annual growth rate of 3%), the yield curve is decreasing because of diminishing expectations. The long-term interest rate is not affected by the business

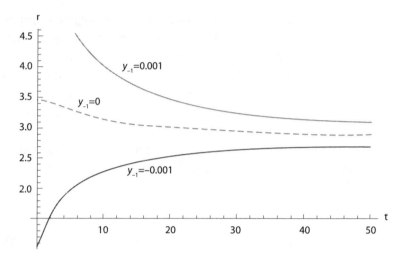

Figure 4.1. The efficient discount rate (in %) as a function of the maturity t (in years). Using the month as the unit period, the parameter values are $\delta = 0$, $\mu = 0.0015$, $\sigma_x = 0.0078$, $\sigma_y = 0.00034$, $\phi = 0.979$, and $\gamma = 2$.

cycle because the long-term growth rate in this model is deterministic and long-term uncertainty remains constant.

SUMMARY OF MAIN RESULTS

1. The shape of the term structure of discount rates is determined by the way the wealth effect and the precautionary effects evolve with the time horizon.

2. When the growth rate of consumption is constant, then consumption increases exponentially, and the intertemporal rate of substitution, which is the discount factor, decreases exponentially. This requires that the discount rate is constant.

3. The simplest extension of this to uncertainty is to assume that the growth rate of the economy follows a random walk. In that case, the variance of *log* consumption increases linearly, which yields an exponentially increasing precautionary effect for the discount

factor. This justifies a constant precautionary effect on the discount rate, yielding a crucial result for the theory of efficient discount rates: *When the growth rate of the economy follows a random walk and when relative aversion is constant, the discount rate should be independent of the maturity of the project to be evaluated.*

4. A simple extension of the random walk for the growth rate of the economy is when the growth rate follows an autoregressive process of order 1. Mean-reversion has two consequences for the previous result. First, the term structure becomes sensitive to the business cycle. When the economy is booming, the short-term interest rate is large because of the wealth effect. However, the wealth effect becomes relatively less powerful in the longer term because the economy is expected to revert to a smaller growth rate. The result is a downward sloping term structure. The opposite effect arises in a downturn. The second effect of mean-reversion is to introduce some positive serial correlation in the growth rate. Compared to the case of a random walk, with correlation the long-term risk of the economy is magnified. This reinforces the precautionary effect over time, which acts to make the term structure downward sloping. This would be the case when the current growth rate of the economy is at its historical mean.

REFERENCES

Bansal, R., and A. Yaron (2004), Risks for the long run: a potential resolution of asset pricing puzzles, *Journal of Finance*, 59, 1481–1509.

Hansen, L., and K. Singleton (1983), Stochastic consumption, risk aversion and the temporal behavior of assets returns, *Journal of Political Economy*, 91, 249–268.

Vasicek, O. (1977), An equilibrium characterization of the term structure, *Journal of Financial Economics*, 5, 177–188.

5

Markov Switches and Extreme Events

The economic history of the world has one obvious feature: for thousands of years, per capita consumption remained close to subsistence level. Society followed Malthus' Law, whereby any technical progress led to an increase in population rather than an improvement in welfare. For example, Clark (2007) estimates that the daily wage in Babylon (1880–1600 BC) was around 15 pounds of wheat. In the golden age of Pericles in Athens, it was approximately 26 pounds. In England in about 1780, it was only 13 pounds.

Thanks to the industrial revolution, the western world escaped this miserable economic trap toward the end of the eighteenth century. The trend rate of growth of per capita consumption rose from 0% to 2%. The origin of this radical transformation lies beyond the scope of this book. However, the possibility of such a dramatic switch in the dynamics of economic growth has important implications for the term structure of the discount rate over the longer term. For issues such as climate change or nuclear waste, or more generally sustainable development, the time horizon under consideration is of the order of several centuries. To form our attitude toward generations who will live in the distant future, we need to form beliefs about their level of prosperity. It is rather myopic to use historical data from only the most recent century to form our beliefs about the growth of the economy over the next *several* centuries.

Economies undergo radical transformations. One such radical transformation was called the "industrial revolution" which has had a long-lasting effect on economic growth. Who knows whether there will be a reversion to the pre-industrial age, at least in terms of an absence of growth, in the distant future? Other less persistent—but more frequent—transformations observed in the past were wars or great economic depressions. It is important to include the possibility of such changes in the dynamics of growth in the analysis of the term structure of the discount rate.

THE ROLE OF EXTREME EVENTS ON THE LEVEL OF DISCOUNT RATES

The easiest way to examine the effect of extreme events on the discount rate is to assume a random walk, which implies that the term structure is flat. Observe that this result does not depend on the distribution of the annual growth rate. Normality was assumed in the previous two chapters just to get an analytical expression for expectations. Suppose instead that the increase in log consumption follows an iid process characterized by a non-normal random variable x. More precisely, suppose that with a small probability p, there is a catastrophe that causes a percentage reduction in consumption of λ, which is large. This is an extreme event. Otherwise, there is business as usual growth, with an increase in log consumption that is drawn from random variable x_{bau}. In short we assume that

$$\ln c_{t+1} - \ln c_t \sim (p, \ln(1-\lambda); 1-p, x_{bau}). \tag{5.1}$$

Under the assumption of constant relative aversion, the efficient discount rate equals

$$r_1 = \delta - \ln[p(1-\lambda)^{-\gamma} + (1-p)Ee^{-\gamma x_{bau}}]. \tag{5.2}$$

Assuming that x_{bau} is normally distributed with mean μ_{bau} and variance σ^2_{bau} allows us to rewrite this equation as follows:

$$r_1 = \delta - \ln[p(1-\lambda)^{-\gamma} + (1-p)e^{-\gamma\mu_{bau} + 0.5\gamma^2\sigma^2_{bau}}]. \tag{5.3}$$

If λ is large enough, the possibility of a catastrophe reduces the intensity of the wealth effect, and raises the intensity of the precautionary effect, thereby reducing the efficient discount rate.

Barro (2006) collected data on extreme macroeconomic events across different countries during the last century. His analysis of these events *"suggests a disaster probability of 1.5–2% per year with a distribution of*

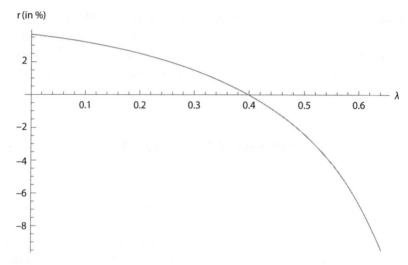

Figure 5.1. The efficient discount rate for different size λ of the catastrophe. Parameter values: $\delta = 0$, $\mu_{bau} = 2\%$, $\sigma_{bau} = 3.6\%$, $\gamma = 2$, $p = 2\%$.

declines in per capita GDP ranging between 15% and 64%." Figure 5.1 was generated with a disaster probability of 2%, and examines the level of the (flat) discount rate for different magnitudes λ of decline in GDP following a disaster. The standard values are retained for the trend and volatility in BAU growth and for the preference parameters.

For small disaster losses, a discount rate of 3.6% is obtained as before. However, when the size of the potential loss exceeds 40%, the efficient discount rate becomes negative. Further increases in the size of the loss, beyond 40%, cause the discount rate to rapidly become deeply negative. When λ tends to 100%, the efficient discount rate tends to −100%, independent of the probability of the catastrophe. In spite of the small probability of a catastrophe, society should sacrifice virtually all of current wealth to avoid the risk of experiencing zero consumption in the future. This is because marginal utility of consumption tends to infinity when consumption tends to zero—a specific property of power utility functions. Weitzman (2007) commented that people *"dread the thickened-left-tail heightened probability of a negative-growth disaster that they find scary, disruptive, and without precedent."*

TWO-STATE MARKOV PROCESS

In the previous section, we assumed that the economic growth rate follows a random walk. Catastrophes have a permanent effect on the level of consumption, but not on its growth rate. In this section, we consider an alternative stochastic process in which the growth rate of consumption is subject to persistent shocks. In the long run, if persistent, even small shocks on the growth rate will have dramatic consequences on the level of consumption in the long run. China, which was by far the wealthiest nation at the end of the fifteenth century, experienced a persistent reduction in its growth rate until the early 1990s. As a result, it became one of the poorest nations in the world by the late 1950s, facing a dramatic famine during the Great Leap Forward, which killed more than 30 million people. However, over the last twenty years or so, China's growth rate has switched to a much higher rate of around 10% per year.

To model this type of dynamic process, a two-state Markov chain for the trend of the economic growth is considered. There are two states of the world, $s = g$ and $s = b$, yielding different expected changes in log consumption μ^g and μ^b, with $\mu^g > \mu^b$. In each period, there is a constant state-dependent probability, π^s, that the state will switch to the other one. This probability is less than ½. We can thus describe this stochastic process as follows:

$$\begin{cases} c_{t+1} = c_t e^{x_t} \\ x_t = \mu^{s_t} + \varepsilon_t \\ P[s_{t+1} = b \mid s_t = g] = \pi^g; \quad P[s_{t+1} = g \mid s_t = b] = \pi^b \end{cases} \tag{5.4}$$

where ε_t is iid normal with mean zero and variance σ^2. We suppose that the state of nature s is observable. Because the wealth effect and the precautionary effect will obviously depend upon this state of nature, so will the discount rates. Let r_t^s denote the term structure of discount rates that prevails in state s.

Suppose that relative risk aversion is a constant, γ, and let us denote $-g = b$ and $-b = g$. We have that

$$
\begin{aligned}
\frac{E[u'(c_1)|\,s]}{u'(c_0)} &= (1-\pi^s)Ee^{-\gamma(\mu^s+\varepsilon_0)} + \pi^s Ee^{-\gamma(\mu^{-s}+\varepsilon_0)} \\
&= e^{0.5\gamma^2\sigma^2}[(1-\pi^s)e^{-\gamma\mu^s} + \pi^s e^{-\gamma\mu^{-s}}].
\end{aligned}
\tag{5.5}
$$

Equation (4.1) can then be rewritten as

$$
r_1^s = \delta + \gamma m_1^s - 0.5\gamma^2\sigma^2,
\tag{5.6}
$$

where the exponential of m_1^s is the precautionary equivalent of lottery (exp μ^s, $1-\pi^s$; exp μ^{-s}, π^s):

$$
e^{-\gamma m_1^s} = (1-\pi^s)e^{-\gamma\mu^s} + \pi^s e^{-\gamma\mu^{-s}}.
\tag{5.7}
$$

r_1^s is the discount rate for a one-period horizon when the current state is s. Notice that term γm_1^s in (5.6) contains a wealth effect and a precautionary effect, since m is the volatility-free component of the precautionary equivalent growth rate of consumption. It takes into account the risk of a Markov switch during the period. Because μ^g is larger than μ^b and π^s is smaller than $\frac{1}{2}$, we have that m_1^g is larger than m_1^b. This implies that the short-term discount rate is larger in the good state than in the bad state.

When we explore the possible dynamic evolution of the economy two periods ahead, things become more complex since the economic regime can switch twice. However, we can proceed as above by using a recursive method. Without going into details, we obtain that

$$
r_t^s = \delta + \gamma\frac{m_t^s}{t} - 0.5\gamma^2\sigma^2,
\tag{5.8}
$$

where m_t^s is defined recursively from m_1^s as follows:

$$
e^{-\gamma m_{t+1}^s} = (1-\pi^s)e^{-\gamma(\mu^s+m_t^s)} + \pi^s e^{-\gamma(\mu^{-s}+m_t^{-s})}.
\tag{5.9}
$$

We thus obtain two state-dependent term structures, r_t^g and r_t^b, for the efficient discount rate. If the current economic state is the good one, the short-term discount rate is high because the probability to stay in that high-growth state is larger than $\frac{1}{2}$. However, in the longer run, the probability of a switch to the low-growth state increases, which implies a reduction of the wealth effect in a way similar to the "diminishing expectation" presented in the previous chapter. The term structure of the efficient discount rates is thus downward sloping in the good regime. In contrast, the term structure is upward sloping in the bad state. In the distant future, the probability distribution of the two states becomes independent of the initial state. When t tends to infinity, the probability to be in the good regime at date t tends to its unconditional value $\pi^b/(\pi^b + \pi^g)$.

NUMERICAL ILLUSTRATIONS

We hereafter examine two numerical illustrations of this model. The first one is based on an estimation of a two-state regime-switching process for the U.S. economy using the annual per capita consumption data covering the period 1890–1994. Table 5.1 reproduces the estimates from Cecchetti, Lam, and Mark (2000).

The estimates in the table reveal that the low-growth state is moderately persistent but very bad, with consumption growth of $\mu^b = -6.78\%$. On the contrary, the high-growth state, with consumption growth of 2.25%, is highly persistent. The unconditional probability of being in the good state is 96%. The unconditional expected growth rate is 1.89%.

Figure 5.2 illustrates the two state-dependent term structures using the estimates in table 5.1 for the values of the parameters of the Markov process, together with $\delta = 0$ and $\gamma = 2$. The two curves have an asymptote at $r_\infty = 3.26\%$. The short-term rate in the good regime equals $r_1^g = 4.3\%$, whereas in the bad regime it equals $r_1^b = -13.8\%$. The main driver of this result is the difference between the wealth effects in the two states. In the bad state, the recession is expected to be deep in the short term. Much

TABLE **5.1.**
Estimates of the regime-switching consumption process

μ^g	μ^b	π^g	π^b	σ
2.25%	-6.78%	2.2%	48.4%	3.13%

Source: Cecchetti et al. (2000, table 2)

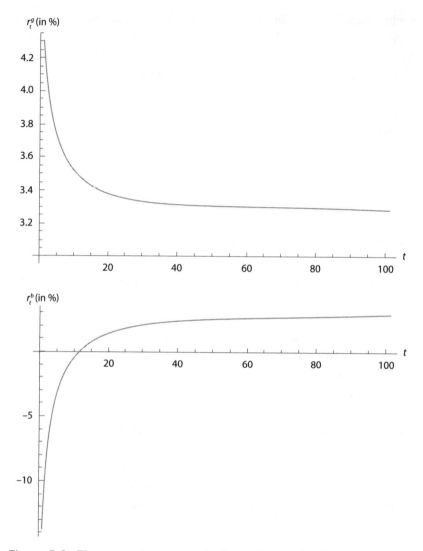

Figure 5.2. The term structures of discount rates in the two regimes under the two-state regime-switching regime model of table 5.1. *Source:* Cecchetti et al. (2000), and own computation.

should be done to transfer consumption forward to the next few years, when consumption is expected to be lower. Also, the uncertainty about the time at which the economy will switch back to the good state implies a large precautionary effect. This is a situation in which the wealth effect and the precautionary effect reinforce each other. The discount rate is negative for time horizons up to eleven years.

As pointed out in the introduction of this chapter, this calibration, based on data covering the period 1890–1994, fails to recognize a crucial feature of economic history. Over at least 6 millennia, the trend of economic growth has been around 0%, until the end of the seventeenth century, when the western world switched to a trend of around 2%. To model this switching of economic regime, the two-state Markov process presented in this chapter is used, with two possible growth trends described in table 5.2. It is assumed that there is a uniform probability of 1% per year to switch from the current state to the other state. In figure 5.3, the two state-dependent term structures are represented, taking standard values for the other parameters ($\delta = 0\%$, $\gamma = 2$, and $\sigma = 3.6\%$). In the good state, the discount rate goes down from 3.74% to 0.77% from 1 to 500 years. In the bad state, it goes from -0.26% to 0.48% over the same range of time horizons. They both converge to 0.6% in the very long run.

This alternative example illustrates the long-lasting effects of uncertainty on the term structure of the discount rate. In the short run, the risk of switching state adds little to uncertainty over future consumption. However, because the shock on the growth rate is persistent, the risk accumulates over time at a faster pace than when there is no serial correlation. The precautionary effect is magnified by the state switching dynamics. In the high-growth regime, this first explanation of the long downward-sloping term

TABLE 5.2.
An alternative hypothetical two-state Markov process
freely adapted from the history of humanity

μ^g	μ^b	π^g	π^b	σ
2%	0%	1%	1%	3.6%

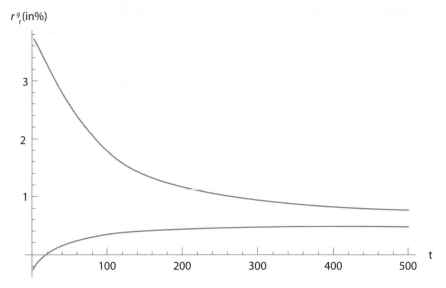

Figure 5.3. The term structures of discount rates in the two regimes under the alternative two-state Markov process of table 5.2.

structure reinforces a declining wealth effect arising because of diminishing expectations. In the short run, the expected growth rate is close to 2%, thereby yielding a wealth effect on the discount rate equaling $\gamma \times 2\% = 4\%$. In the longer run, the probability of being in the good state is 50%, so that the expected trend is only 1%. So the wealth effect in the distant future amounts to $\gamma \times 1\% = 2\%$. In the low-growth regime, the improving outlook acts to produce an upward sloping term structure, although this is partially countered by the precautionary effect.

In the literature, all calibration exercises of the term structure of interest rates rely on macroeconomic data covering a fraction of the last two centuries, during which time the western world experienced a growth trend around 2%. This approach makes sense when one wants to discount cash flows maturing in the next few years. However, it is flawed if cash flows occurring in the more distant future are being discounted. A smaller rate should be used for these cash flows because of the possibility of switching abruptly and persistently to a lower growth regime. The change in magnitude over time of both the wealth effect and the precautionary effect support this result.

Of course, a more realistic model would entail more than two regimes. In particular, one should recognize the possibility of a regime with a growth rate of consumption larger than the one that we experienced over the two centuries in the western world. Let us imagine a world with dematerialized consumptions, free sources of renewable energy, or efficient markets for the allocation of capital or employment.

SUMMARY OF MAIN RESULTS

1. The history of humanity contains many examples of abrupt and persistent shocks to the trend of regional economic growth. In this chapter, we model this by a two-regime Markov process.
2. Because of the persistence of shocks, the precautionary effect is increasing with the time horizon. In the good regime, this goes together with the diminishing expectation effect to generate a decreasing term structure of discount rates. In the bad regime, the wealth effect is increasing with the maturity, and this effect usually dominates the increasing precautionary effect to yield an increasing term structure.

REFERENCES

Barro, R. J. (2006), Rare disasters and asset markets in the twentieth century, *Quarterly Journal of Economics*, 121, 823–866.

Cecchetti, S. G., P.-S. Lam, and N. C. Mark (2000), Asset pricing with distorted beliefs: are equity returns too good to be true, *American Economic Review*, 90, 787–805.

Clark, G. (2007), *Farewell to Alms. A Brief Economic History of the World*, Princeton: Princeton University Press.

Weitzman, M. L. (2007), Subjective expectations and asset-return puzzles, *American Economic Review*, 97(4), 1102–1130.

6

———◁○▷———

Parametric Uncertainty and Fat Tails

This book started the analysis of discount rates by considering a sure rate of growth of consumption. The analysis was extended by recognizing that economic growth is uncertain. In the previous chapter, it was noted that the parameters governing this uncertainty may be unstable. In this chapter, we go one step further by recognizing that the probability distribution for economic growth is itself subject to some parametric uncertainty.

Estimation of the parameters governing a stochastic process, such as the mean or the volatility, can be performed using a data set of past realizations of this process. However, this sample may not contain all possible scenarios that could occur in the future. For example, until the early 1970s, the Mexican currency was pegged to the dollar, so that the estimation of trend and volatility of the exchange rate of the peso were close to zero. Thus, the econometric analysis suggested a very small exchange risk. Based on this data it was therefore quite hard to explain the large premium which was observed between Mexican and U.S. interest rates. This was called the "peso problem." The sharp devaluation of the peso in 1976 provided the solution to the puzzle: the data did not contain this small probability event, although most investors had it in mind.

In a similar way to the peso problem, there is a limited data set for the dynamics of economic growth. The absence of a sufficiently large data set to estimate the long-term growth process of the economy implies that its parameters are uncertain and subject to learning in the future. This problem is particularly crucial when its parameters are unstable, or when the dynamic process entails low-probability extreme events. The rarer the event, the less precise is our estimate of its likelihood. This builds a bridge between the problem of parametric uncertainty, and the one of extreme events.

UNCERTAIN GROWTH

Suppose that the dynamic process $c_0, c_1, c_2, \ldots$ is a function of a parameter θ. The true value of θ is unknown. For the sake of simplicity, suppose that θ can take n possible values $\theta = 1, \ldots, n$. Our prior beliefs about θ at date 0 are characterized by a probability distribution $(q_1, \ldots, q_n)$, $q_\theta > 0$, $\sum q_\theta = 1$, where q_θ is the probability that the true value of the parameter be θ. By the law of iterated expectations, we have that

$$Eu'(c_t) = \sum_{\theta=1}^{n} q_\theta E[u'(c_t)|\theta]. \tag{6.1}$$

It implies that the pricing formula (4.1) can be rewritten as

$$r_t = \delta - \frac{1}{t} \ln \sum_{\theta=1}^{n} q_\theta \frac{E[u'(c_t)|\theta]}{u'(c_0)}. \tag{6.2}$$

Let $r_{t\theta}$ denote the discount rate that would be efficient for horizon t if we knew for sure that the true value of the parameter was θ. This means that $r_{t\theta}$ is defined as

$$r_{t\theta} = \delta - \frac{1}{t} \ln \frac{E[u'(c_t)|\theta]}{u'(c_0)}. \tag{6.3}$$

Combining equations (6.2) and (6.3) yields that

$$e^{-r_t t} = \sum_{\theta=1}^{n} q_\theta e^{-r_{t\theta} t}. \tag{6.4}$$

In other words, the socially efficient discount factor under parametric uncertainty equals the expectation of the conditionally efficient discount factors (the discount factors that would be efficient for each value of the parameter if it was known with certainty).

Notice that the expectation concerns the discount factors, not the discount rates. In fact, the socially efficient discount rate defined by (6.4) can be interpreted as the certainty equivalent rate of the uncertain rates $r_{t\theta}$,

$\theta = 1,\dots,n$, under the implicit utility function $h(r) = -\exp(-rt)$. This function is increasing and concave, with an index of concavity measured by t. It implies that the certainty equivalent r_t is smaller than the mean of the uncertain $r_{t\theta}$. However, at the limit, we obtain

$$\lim_{t \to 0} r_t = \lim_{t \to 0} \frac{\sum_{\theta=1}^{n} q_\theta r_{t\theta} e^{-r_{t\theta}t}}{\sum_{\theta=1}^{n} q_\theta e^{-r_{t\theta}t}} = Er_{0\theta}. \tag{6.5}$$

Moreover, as long as the support of $r_{t\theta}$ remains bounded, r_t tends to the lower bound of this support when t tends to infinity. Indeed, using L'Hopital's rule, we have that

$$\lim_{t \to \infty} r_t = -\lim_{t \to \infty} \frac{1}{t} \ln \sum_{\theta=1}^{n} q_\theta e^{-r_{t\theta}t} = \lim_{t \to \infty} \frac{\sum_{\theta=1}^{n} q_\theta r_{t\theta} e^{-r_{t\theta}t}}{\sum_{\theta=1}^{n} q_\theta e^{-r_{t\theta}t}}. \tag{6.6}$$

Let $r_\infty^{\min}$ denote the smallest possible discount rate when t tends to infinity: $r_\infty^{\min} = \lim_{t \to \infty} \min_\theta r_{t\theta}$. Then, the previous equation implies that

$$\lim_{t \to \infty} r_t = \lim_{t \to \infty} \frac{\sum_{\theta=1}^{n} q_\theta r_{t\theta} e^{(r_\infty^{\min} - r_{t\theta})t}}{\sum_{\theta=1}^{n} q_\theta e^{(r_\infty^{\min} - r_{t\theta})t}} = r_\infty^{\min}. \tag{6.7}$$

The rate at which cash flows occurring in the short term should be discounted is equal to the expectation of the conditionally efficient discount rate. Moreover, as long as the support of $r_{t\theta}$ remains bounded, r_t tends to the lower bound of this support when t tends to infinity. In order to get an intuition for these results, let us examine the simplest case when the stochastic process governing $\ln c_t$ is a random walk conditional on θ.

CONDITIONAL ON θ, THE GROWTH PROCESS IS A RANDOM WALK

A special case of the model we mentioned is as follows:

$$\begin{cases} c_{t+1} = c_t e^{x_t} \\ x_0, x_1, \dots | \theta \ i.i.d. \sim N(\mu_\theta, \sigma_\theta) \, \forall \theta. \end{cases} \tag{6.8}$$

This is a discrete version of an arithmetic Brownian motion with an unknown trend and/or volatility. Although this process is a random walk conditional on θ, x_t exhibits some serial correlation. Suppose for example that only the trend μ_θ is subject to parametric uncertainty. Then, using Bayes' rule, the observation of a large x_0 yields an upward revision to beliefs about the trend of economic growth.

Conditional on θ, the dynamic process of x_t is a normal random walk. As seen before, equation (6.3) has an analytical solution in that case:

$$r_{t\theta} = \delta + \gamma\mu_\theta - 0.5\gamma^2\sigma_\theta^2. \tag{6.9}$$

In particular, $r_{t\theta}$ is independent of t. Under the hidden structure characterized by $(\mu_\theta, \sigma_\theta)$, $\theta = 1,\ldots,n$, the term structure of the socially efficient discount rate is obtained by rewriting equation (6.4) as follows:

$$r_t = \delta - \frac{1}{t}\ln\sum_{\theta=1}^{n} q_\theta e^{(-\gamma\mu_\theta + 0.5\gamma^2\sigma_\theta^2)t}. \tag{6.10}$$

The socially efficient discount rate under this parametric uncertainty is equal to the expected value of $r_\theta = \delta + \gamma\mu_\theta - 0.5\gamma^2\sigma_\theta^2$ for short maturities, is decreasing with t, and tends to the smallest possible value of r_θ when t tends to infinity.

Following Gollier (2008), the intuition for these results is based on the observation that the parametric uncertainty plays a crucial role in shaping the uncertainty surrounding consumption in the distant future. To illustrate this, let us assume that the volatility of the growth of log consumption is known and equal to $\sigma = 3.6\%$, but the trend μ is unknown. It can be either 1% or 3% with equal probability. In figure 6.1, we draw the distribution of $\ln c_t/c_0$ for $t = 1$, 10, and 100. Ex ante, the distribution of $\ln c_1/c_0$ is a mixture of two normal densities. However, the uncertainty affecting the trend is a second-order source of uncertainty compared to the volatility of the growth rate. So, in the short run, assuming a trend of $(1\% + 3\%)/2$ to determine the efficient discount rate is a good approximation. In contrast, the uncertainty affecting consumption in one century's time is mostly a result of the uncertainty over the growth trend. Conditional on the growth trend, $\mu = 1\%$ or $\mu = 3\%$, the expectation of c_{100}/c_0 is $\exp(100(\mu + 0.5 \times 0.036^2))$, which equals 3.5 or 26. The magnitude of the uncertainty from this source can be compared to that from the intrinsic volatility of growth.

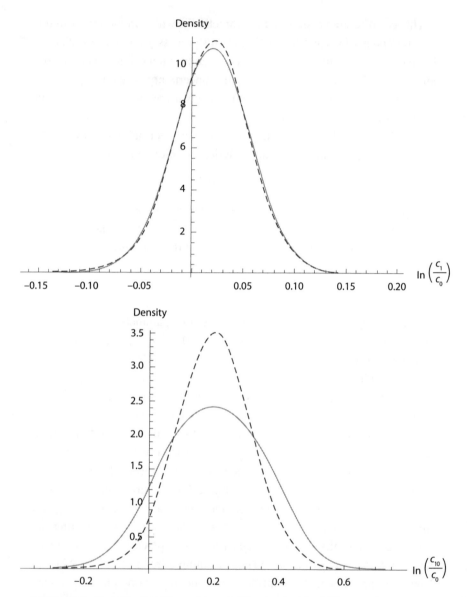

Figure 6.1. Density function of $\ln c_t/c_0$ for $t = 1$, 10, 100, and 200, under the assumption that $\mu \sim (1\%, 1/2; 3\%, 1/2)$ and $\sigma = 3.6\%$. The dashed curve is the density function without parametric uncertainty and $\mu = 2\%$.

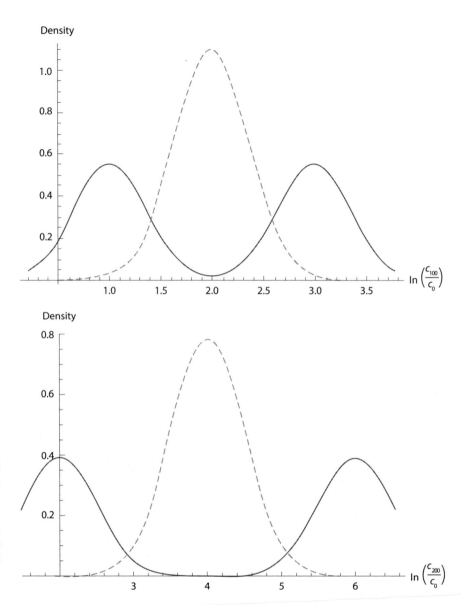

Figure 6.1. (*continued*)

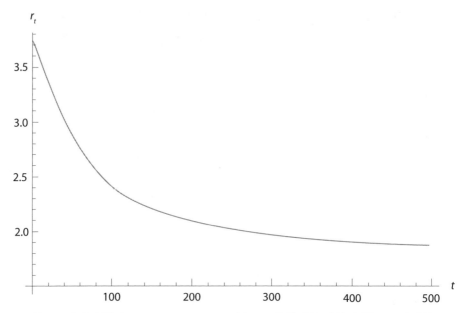

Figure 6.2. Efficient term structure with $\mu \sim (1\%, 1/2; 3\%, 1/2)$, $\sigma = 3.6\%$, $\delta = 0\%$, and $\gamma = 2$.

Assuming $\mu = 2\%$ and $\sigma = 3.6\%$, the 95% confidence interval for $\ln c_{100}/c_0$ is [1.29, 2.71].

The bottom line is that parametric uncertainty entails fatter tails for the distribution of future consumption. The thickness of the tails increases with the time horizon. Integrating out parameter uncertainty by Bayes' rule spreads apart probabilities and thickens the tails of the posterior distribution for predicting the future growth rate of consumption. This explains why the term structure of discount rates is decreasing. Indeed, the growing gap of uncertainty, compared to the random walk hypothesis with the mean trend, magnifies the precautionary effect in the distant future. We get a decreasing term structure because the precautionary effect tends to reduce the discount rate. In the long run, the fear of a low economic growth rate of 1% dominates all other considerations about how to value the future. Under the assumption that $\delta = 0\%$ and $\gamma = 2$, the discount rate converges to $r_\infty = 2 \times 1\% - 0.5 \times 2^2 \times 0.036^2 = 1.7\%$, as shown in figure 6.2.

THE CASE OF AN UNKNOWN TREND OF ECONOMIC GROWTH

When the growth of log consumption conditional on θ is normally distributed, the term structure of efficient discount rates is characterized by equation (6.10), which is rewritten as follows:

$$r_t = \delta - \frac{1}{t} \ln E e^{(-\gamma \mu_\theta + 0.5\gamma^2 \sigma_\theta^2)t}. \tag{6.11}$$

Hereafter θ is allowed to have a continuous distribution. In this section, it is supposed that the volatility of the growth rate of consumption is known, so that $\sigma_\theta = \sigma$ for all θ. However, more sophisticated prior distributions for μ_θ are considered than the two-state case from the previous section. Suppose that μ_θ is normally distributed with mean μ_0 and variance σ_0^2. σ_0 can be interpreted as a measure of the degree of uncertainty about the true growth of log consumption. Observe from (6.11) that once again this is a situation requiring the expectation of the exponential of a normally distributed random variable to be computed. Using lemma 1, it is obtained that:

$$r_t = \delta - \frac{1}{t} \ln e^{(-\gamma\mu_0 + 0.5\gamma^2 t \sigma_0^2 + 0.5\gamma^2 \sigma^2)t} = \delta + \gamma\mu_0 - 0.5\gamma^2(\sigma^2 + \sigma_0^2 t). \tag{6.12}$$

This expression can alternatively be derived from the well-known property that if the conditional distribution $\ln c_t/c_0$ given (μ, σ) is normal with mean μt and variance $\sigma^2 t$, and if μt is itself normally distributed with mean $\mu_0 t$ and variance $\sigma_0^2 t^2$, then the unconditional distribution of $\ln c_t/c_0$ is also normal with mean $\mu_0 t$ and variance $\sigma^2 t + \sigma_0^2 t^2$. Define $g_t = \mu_0 + 0.5(\sigma^2 + \sigma_0^2 t)$ as the expected growth rate of consumption in the time interval $[0,t]$. This allows equation (6.12) to be rewritten as

$$r_t = \delta + \gamma g_t - 0.5\gamma(\gamma + 1)(\sigma^2 + \sigma_0^2 t). \tag{6.13}$$

The term structure of efficient discount rates (6.13) is linearly decreasing in maturity, t. It tends to min $r_\theta = -\infty$ when t tends to infinity. The support of r_θ is unbounded below because the expected growth of log consumption is normally distributed. The possibility that the true growth trend for the economy is a large negative number is central to the valuation of distant cash flows. Although the probability of such an event may be very small, the scenario of a vanishing GDP per capita is greatly feared by the representative agent. When combined with the property that $\lim_{c \to 0} u'(c)$ is infinite for power utility functions, it implies that there is a very high social value for transfers of wealth to distant dates where there is the possibility of close to zero per capita consumption.

One can question the normality of the prior beliefs on the trend of log consumption, or more generally the nature and origin of these prior beliefs. It is possible to approach these questions by using Bayesian inference. Suppose that our current beliefs about the future growth of the economy combines primitive beliefs about it—which may be uninformative—and the observation of a sample of T past realizations of growth of log consumption $(x_{-T}, \ldots, x_{-1})$. Suppose that the primitive beliefs take the form of three assumptions. First, changes in log consumption are independent and normally distributed. Second, the variance of the change in log consumption is a known constant σ^2. Third, the mean μ of the change in log consumption is normally distributed with mean μ^* and variance σ^{*2}. The observation of the recent changes $(x_{-T}, \ldots, x_{-1})$ affects these beliefs. Using Bayes' rule, it follows that

$$P[\mu | \mu^*, \sigma^*, \sigma, x_{-T}, \ldots, x_{-1}] = \frac{P[x_{-T}, \ldots, x_{-1} | \mu, \sigma] P[\mu | \mu^*, \sigma^*]}{P[x_{-T}, \ldots, x_{-1}]}. \quad (6.14)$$

It is well-known that this process of revising beliefs yields a posterior distribution for the change in $\ln c$ which is normally distributed with mean:

$$E[\mu | \mu^*, \sigma^*, \sigma, x_{-T}, \ldots, x_{-1}] = \mu_0 = \frac{\mu^* (\sigma^*)^{-2} + m (\sigma^2/T)^{-1}}{(\sigma^*)^{-2} + (\sigma^2/T)^{-1}}, \quad (6.15)$$

where $m = T^{-1} \sum_{\tau = -T}^{-1} x_\tau$ is the sample mean for changes in $\ln c$. See for example Leamer (1978, theorem 2.3). The new expected growth, μ_0, is a weighted average of the prior expectation and of the sample mean. A large sample mean pushes beliefs upward. The sensitiveness of posterior beliefs is an increasing function of the relative precision $(\sigma^2/T)^{-1}$ of the sample information relative to the precision σ^{-2*} of prior beliefs. The posterior variance of μ is equal to

$$Var[\mu | \mu^*, \sigma^*, \sigma, x_{-T}, \ldots, x_{-1}] = \sigma_0^2 = ((\sigma^*)^{-2} + (\sigma^2/T)^{-1})^{-1}. \quad (6.16)$$

The posterior (μ_0, σ_0) can then be considered as the updated mean and standard deviation for the change in log consumption. It can be plugged into equation (6.12) to determine the socially efficient discount rates. A special case arises when the prior beliefs are uninformative. This can be approximated by assuming that σ^* is very large. Equations (6.15) and (6.16) then become

$$\mu_0 = m \quad \text{and} \quad \sigma_0^2 = \frac{\sigma^2}{T}. \tag{6.17}$$

In this case, the beliefs at date 0 are entirely determined by the observation of economic growth. They are normal, with mean and variance given by (6.17). This is the standard way of justifying a normal distribution for the prior beliefs. Notice that this yields a linearly decreasing term structure.

THE CASE OF AN UNKNOWN VOLATILITY OF ECONOMIC GROWTH

In a sequence of two recent papers, Weitzman (2007, 2009) considers an alternative model in which the unknown parameter for the distribution of $\ln c_{t+1}/c_t$ is its volatility rather than its mean. Suppose that $\mu_\theta = \mu$ for all θ. The plausible distribution for the volatility must of course have its support in $\mathbb{R}_+$, which excludes the normal distribution. As has already been observed, it is often more convenient to work with the precision, $p_\theta = \sigma_\theta^{-2}$, rather than the variance. When the precision is unknown, it is standard in the literature to assume that it has a gamma distribution: $p_\theta \sim \Gamma(a,b)$. The gamma distribution has two parameters, a shape parameter $a > 0$, and a scale parameter $b > 0$. Its density function is

$$f(p;a,b) = p^{a-1} \frac{e^{-p/b}}{b^a \Gamma(a)} \quad \text{for all } p > 0. \tag{6.18}$$

The gamma function extends the factorial one to non-integer numbers, with $\Gamma(a) = (a-1)!$ when a is a natural integer.

The mean and variance of p_θ are respectively equal to ab and ab^2. Remember that the observed volatility of yearly changes in log consumption is around 3.6%, which gives a precision of approximately $(0.036)^{-2} \approx 800$. In figure 6.3, four different gamma densities are drawn, all with the same mean $ab = 800$.

The remaining challenge is to determine the shape of the term structure of discount rates under this specification. It is characterized by equation (6.11) which is rewritten as follows:

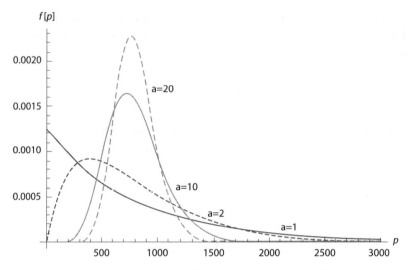

Figure 6.3. Gamma densities for different parameters (a, b) with the same $Ep = ab = 800$.

$$r_t = \delta + \gamma\mu - \frac{1}{t}\ln Ee^{0.5\gamma^2 t/p_\theta} = \delta + \gamma\mu - \frac{1}{t}\ln \int_0^\infty e^{0.5\gamma^2 t/p} f(p;a,b)dp. \quad (6.19)$$

The integral in this equation is unbounded. It is the moment-generating function evaluated at $0.5\gamma^2 t$ for the random variable $1/p$, which has an inverted-gamma distribution. The precautionary effect is infinite, independent of the degree of parametric uncertainty!

An alternative way to view this problem is achieved by characterizing the unconditional distribution of x_t. Conditional on σ_θ, it is normal. Combining a normal distribution of mean μ with a gamma distribution $\Gamma(a, b)$ for its uncertain precision yields an unconditional distribution that is a Student's t-distribution. This distribution has $v = 2a$ degrees of freedom, with mean μ and variance $1/(a - 1)b$:

$$\left. \begin{array}{c} x|p \sim N(\mu, \sigma = 1/\sqrt{p}) \\ p \sim \Gamma(a, b) \end{array} \right\} \Rightarrow \frac{x - \mu}{1/\sqrt{ab}} \sim Student(2a). \quad (6.20)$$

The Student's t-distribution has fatter tails than the corresponding normal distribution with the same mean and variance. In figure 6.4, we draw different unconditional distributions for the annual change in log

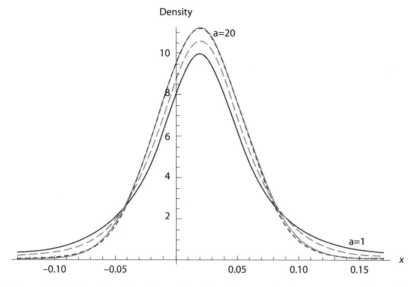

Figure 6.4. Density functions for the change in log consumption. We assume that $(x - 0.02)\sqrt{800}$ is a Student's t-distribution with $2a$ degrees of freedom, $a = 1, 2, 10$ and 20. The dashed curve is the density of $N(0.02, 1/\sqrt{800})$.

consumption by using the same parameters of the gamma distribution as in the previous figure: $(a,b) = (1{,}800), (2{,}400), (10{,}80)$, and $(20{,}40)$. We assume that x has a mean of $\mu = 2\%$, so that $(x - 0.02)\sqrt{800}$ is a Student's t-distribution with $2a$ degrees of freedom. When a tends to infinity, the Student's t-distribution tends to normal. However, a finite parameter a has the effect of thickening the tails of the distribution compared to the normal one. Just as for other sources of parametric uncertainty, the parametric uncertainty about the volatility of the growth process makes the distribution of the growth rate riskier.

The differences between the normal distribution and the Student's t-distribution may look quite marginal in figure 6.4. However, the tails of the distributions are significantly different. There is relatively much more probability mass in the Student's t-distribution than in the normal one. Let us define function $g(t;v)$ as the ratio of probabilities that $x_s(v)$ and x_N are smaller than t, where $x_s(v)$ and x_N are respectively the Student's t-distribution with v degrees of freedom, and the standardized normal distribution:

TABLE 6.1.
Ratio $g(t;v)$ of probabilities in the left tail

	$t = -2$	$t = -4$	$t = -6$	$t = -8$
$v = 1$	6.49	2462.14	5.33×10^7	6.48×10^{13}
$v = 10$	1.61	39.76	66952.4	9.64×10^9

$$g(t;v) = \frac{P[x_S(v) \leq t]}{P[x_N \leq t]}. \tag{6.21}$$

Table 6.1 shows how big g can be in the left tail.

What is special with this specific parametric uncertainty is that the tails of the unconditional distribution of x are particularly thick. They are so thick that the precautionary effect becomes infinite. This can be checked in the following way. We have that

$$r_1 = \delta - \ln E e^{-\gamma x_0} = \delta - \ln M_x(-\gamma), \tag{6.22}$$

where $M_x(k) = E e^{xk}$ is the moment-generating function of random variable x. For $x \sim N(\mu,\sigma)$, we know that $M_x(k) = \exp(\mu k + 0.5\sigma^2 k^2)$. However, the Student's t-distribution has an unbounded moment-generating function. Therefore, $r_1 = -\infty$.

It can be argued that this result is driven by the fact that "too much" parametric uncertainty is contained in the gamma distribution for the precision p. This point again raises the question of the status of our beliefs about the distribution of the uncertain parameter. Suppose that the only source of information is the observation of the past volatility of economic growth. Suppose that the true distribution of x_t is normal. Using Bayes' rule, it can be proved that updating the normal-gamma prior beliefs using the observation of $(x_{-T}, \ldots, x_{-1})$ yields a normal-gamma posterior belief (see Leamer 1978, theorem 2.4). In particular, if μ is known and if the prior on σ is uninformative, the posterior distribution of $p = 1/\sigma^2$ must be a gamma distribution. Thus, the use of an inverse-gamma distribution for the precision is a natural way to model the uncertainty affecting the variance of a Brownian process.

The unboundedness of the efficient discount rate in this case is a consequence of the Inada property $u'(0) = +\infty$ of the utility function, and from the standard marginalist approach to economic valuation. The representative agent places enormous value on any investment that yields a sure consumption, $\varepsilon > 0$, in the future. Once these investments are implemented, the probability that future consumption will fall below $\varepsilon > 0$ will be zero, and the discount rate will be bounded.

SUMMARY OF MAIN RESULTS

1. A simple way to generate a decreasing structure of discount rates is to recognize that some parameters of the consumption growth process are uncertain. Parametric uncertainty about the trend is of limited importance in the short run, but in the long run is of huge significance. In particular, it tends to magnify the long term risk (fatter tails) and the associated precautionary effect for long horizons.
2. For each time horizon, the efficient discount factor is the expected value of the efficient discount factors conditional to each plausible value of the parameters. As a consequence, for distant futures, the efficient unconditional discount rate tends to the smallest plausible conditional discount rate.
3. Suppose that consumption follows a geometric Brownian motion with an uncertain trend. If this trend is normally distributed, then the term structure of discount rates is linearly decreasing.
4. Suppose alternatively that consumption follows a geometric Brownian motion with an uncertain variance. If the variance follows an inverse gamma distribution, the efficient discount rate is unbounded below for all time horizons.

REFERENCES

Gollier, C. (2008), Discounting with fat-tailed economic growth, *Journal of Risk and Uncertainty*, 37, 171–186.

Leamer, E. E. (1978), *Specification Searches: Ad Hoc Inference with Nonexperimental Data*, New York: John Wiley.

Weitzman, M. L. (2007), Subjective expectations and asset-return puzzle, *American Economic Review*, 97, 1102–1130.

Weitzman, M. L. (2009), On modeling and interpreting the economics of catastrophic climate change, *Review of Economics and Statistics*, 91 (1), 1–19.

7

The Weitzman Argument

In the first chapter, it was shown that there are essentially two methods to determine the socially efficient discount rate. The first method is based on the marginal rate of intertemporal substitution. It leads to the Ramsey rule and to a variety of extensions that have been analyzed in detail in the previous chapters. The other method is based on the rate of return of capital. At equilibrium, the two methods should lead to the same result, which is the equilibrium interest rate.

Let us re-examine the reason why the discount rate should be equalized to the rate of return of risk-free capital in the economy. It is a simple arbitrage argument. Let r denote the rate of return of capital, which is also the equilibrium interest rate if financial markets are efficient. Consider an investment project that yields, after t years, a single sure cash flow F per dollar invested today. This dollar can alternatively be safely invested in the capital market to yield $\exp(rt)$ dollars in t years. The investment project therefore should only be implemented if its future payoff, F, exceeds $\exp(rt)$. An alternative way to express this decision rule is to implement the project if the net future value $NFV = F - \exp(rt)$ is positive.

The NFV is the net future benefit of the investment when compared to an alternative investment in the productive capital of the economy. Behind this positive NFV rule, there is the important notion of the opportunity cost of capital, which tells us that what is invested in one project cannot be invested in other projects. For example, our efforts in favor of fighting global warming will reduce the resources available to fight malaria or poverty in developing countries.

The net future value of the project is what the stakeholders get at date t from their investment when financing its initial unit cost by a loan at the interest rate r. An alternative strategy for impatient investors would be to anticipate the future benefit of their investment by borrowing today $F\exp(-rt)$ at rate r, in such a way that the reimbursement F of the loan at date t perfectly offsets the cash flow of the project. When doing so, stakeholders get only one immediate benefit from the investment project equal to its net present value $NPV = -1 + F\exp(-rt)$. It is thus optimal to invest in the project if its NPV is positive. Obviously, because for any particular project the NPV and the $NFV = NPV \times \exp(rt)$ are proportional to each other, they must have the same sign, so that the two decision rules always yield the same decision.

An important practical limitation of this approach is that there is no market for risk-free assets with very long maturities. Typically, government bonds have maturities that do not exceed thirty years. Market interest rates do not reveal the rate of return on capital for longer time horizons. Therefore, to apply the arbitrage argument presented earlier, it is necessary to compare the sure investment project with a "roll-over" strategy in which the transfer of cash flows is made via a sequence of credit contracts scattered through time. For the latter, there is a "reinvestment risk"; it cannot be known what the credit market conditions will be in the future. To avoid this difficulty, an alternative approach to using market interest rates would be to try to guess what the rate of return on capital will be in the future. However, there are difficulties with this too. Although economists have tried for decades to build realistic models of economic growth, it must be recognized that the predictive power of these models is not impressive.

Neither neoclassical growth models nor endogenous growth models provide reliable predictions for the expected return on capital over long time horizons. The driver of growth identified in neoclassical growth theory is capital accumulation. However, the buildup of capital stock provides only a partial explanation for economic growth. The predominant driver of growth in the long run is exogenous. It is contained in the famous "Solow residual" which has been interpreted as representing technological and scientific progress. The model provides no insight into what can be expected for the future rate of progress in these fields, or the level of innovation. Longer term growth rates are therefore largely determined by exogenous assumptions.

The more recent endogenous growth theory tries to model the production of new knowledge, but at this stage, it is not able to help very much with characterizing the rate of return of capital over the next two hundred years. In summary, more sophistication is required to apply the arbitrage arguments mentioned previously in the context of sustainable development.

Following Weitzman (1998, 2001) and Gollier and Weitzman (2010), let us accept that there is unavoidable uncertainty over the rate of return of capital r when the investment decision must be made. It is assumed that r will be constant in the future, is uncertain this morning but will be known with certainty at the end of the day. To keep it simple, let us consider a numerical example in which r will be either 5% or 1% with equal probabilities. Thus, the opportunity cost of capital cannot be evaluated without error today. One dollar invested today in the productive capital of the economy will yield either $\exp(0.05t)$ or $\exp(0.01t)$ dollars at date t. So, it is hard to compare this benefit to the sure benefit F of the investment project. The NFV of this project is uncertain. One possible decision rule under uncertainty is to require that the sure cash flow of the project is larger than the expected cash flow of the investment in the productive capital of the economy, or alternatively that the expected NFV is positive. This is referred to as the expected NFV rule. It is equivalent to a rule which requires that the investment has an internal rate of return larger than a critical rate R_t^F which is defined as follows:

$$e^{R_t^F t} = E e^{rt} \tag{7.1}$$

Weitzman (1998) provides an alternative decision rule under uncertainty which yields opposite results: A sure investment project should be implemented if its expected NPV is positive. In spite of the fact that this rule is equivalent to the expected NFV rule when there is no uncertainty (as was already explained), the decision rules are not equivalent when there is uncertainty. If the future benefit is offset by borrowing $F\exp(-rt)$ once the rate r will be known, the net present benefit of the investment is equal to $-1 + E[F\exp(-rt)]$, which is equivalent to discounting F at a rate R_t^P defined as

$$e^{-R_t^P t} = E e^{-rt}. \tag{7.2}$$

As observed by Gollier (2004), using the positive expected NFV rule or the positive expected NPV rule leads to opposite results concerning the choice of the discount rate. In particular, it is obtained that

$$\forall t: \quad \min r \leq R_t^P \leq Er \leq R_t^F \leq \max r. \tag{7.3}$$

Moreover, the minimum and maximum bounds correspond to the asymptotic values of R_t^P and R_t^F respectively, when t tends to infinity. The NPV approach is more favorable to the evaluation of sure investment projects than the NFV approach, and this difference increases with the time horizon.

The analysis has also shown that the two rules differ by the date at which the risk associated with the alternative investment in the economy is allocated. Under the NFV approach, cash flows and risk are all transferred to the terminal date of the project, whereas they are all transferred to today under the NPV approach. This is a paradox, because of the huge difference in the practical consequences of the two approaches. In the spirit of the Modigliani–Miller's Theorem, the evaluation of an investment project should not depend on the way that it is financed. In the absence of a clear description of the stakeholders' preferences toward risk and time, it is not possible to determine which rule should be preferred, and which discount rate should be selected.

THE CASE OF THE LOGARITHMIC UTILITY FUNCTION

A surprising result of the expected NFV approach is that uncertainty affecting an investment project in the productive capital of the economy biases us to prefer this risky project against the sure one. This suggests that introducing risk aversion into the picture should make us favor the expected NPV rule which acts in the opposite direction.

Consistently, throughout this book, what matters for stakeholders is not the payoff of the project itself, but rather the utility that it generates. Before extending the analysis to a more general case, this section supposes that the utility function is logarithmic, $u(c) = \ln c$. An important property of this function is that a change in the interest rate does not affect saving. The wealth effect perfectly compensates the substitution effect. This implies that at the end of the day, when r is observed, the level of consumption c_0 is insensitive to this information (this will be shown later in the chapter). However, consumption in the distant future will be highly sensitive to r. It can be shown that the optimal consumption at date t is proportional to

$\exp(rt)$. Thus, at the beginning of the day, there is absolutely no uncertainty about the optimal consumption at the end of the day, but there is a huge uncertainty about consumption in the distant future.

Let us consider the expected NPV approach in this context. Remember that the NPV rule is based on the assumption that all cash flows from the sure marginal investment project are transformed into additional consumption at the end of the day, and only at that time. This additional consumption is uncertain (it depends upon the unknown r), but it is marginal. Because consumption c_0 at date 0 is risk-free, adding this marginal risk to initial wealth increases welfare if and only if the expected NPV is positive. Risk aversion is irrelevant. This is because (independent) risk is a second-order effect in the expected utility model (Segal and Spivak 1990). When introducing a small lottery into an initially risk-free situation, the first-order expectation effect always dominates. This can be seen from observing that, by the Arrow–Pratt approximation (3.3), the risk premium for small risk is proportional to the variance of the payoff, that is, to the square of the size of the risk. This means that the NPV formula (7.2) is perfectly valid when the representative agent has a logarithmic utility function.

What of the alternative expected NFV approach? This approach relies on the assumption that all the costs and benefits of the sure investment project are transferred to the terminal date t. Observe that the NFV is negatively related to the interest rate r, since the loan used to finance the initial cost of the project will yield a larger repayment at the terminal date when the interest rate is large. This means that the NFV of the sure project is negatively correlated with c_t. In other words, implementing the sure project by this financing strategy provides some hedging against the macroeconomic risk at date t. This is positively valued by consumers, something that equation (7.1) of the expected NFV approach fails to take into account. Therefore, this equation misprices the future.

To sum up, given a logarithmic utility function, when the sure investment project is implemented and cash flows are transferred to the present (the NPV approach), one can assume that the representative agent is risk neutral. This is because current consumption is risk-free. In contrast, taking the NFV approach, when the sure project is implemented and cash flows are transferred to the terminal date, this strategy serves as an insurance against wider macroeconomic risk. The risk neutrality assumption, implicit in equation

(7.1), therefore cannot be sustained. Thus, when the representative agent has a logarithmic utility function, Weitzman's formula (7.2) is right.

When the utility function of the representative agent is not logarithmic, the problem is more complex, because the optimal level of today's consumption c_0 will react to changes in the rate of return of capital. Therefore, neither of the two rules (7.1) and (7.2) is valid. The next section is devoted to the analysis of this more general case.

TAKING ACCOUNT OF PREFERENCES TOWARD RISK AND TIME

When considering the expected NFV rule with risk aversion, the marginal additional consumption $F - \exp(rt)$ occurring at date t has a different marginal effect on utility in different future states of the world. This is because of the differing levels of consumption, c_t, that will be realized in these different states. The underlying strategy of financing the initial cost by a loan at rate r increases the expected utility at date t if

$$E[u'(c_t)(F - e^{rt})] \geq 0. \tag{7.4}$$

This is equivalent to using a discount rate R_t^F implicitly defined as follows:

$$R_t^F = \frac{1}{t} \ln \frac{E[u'(c_t)e^{rt}]}{Eu'(c_t)}. \tag{7.5}$$

This formula generalizes equation (7.1) to the case of risk aversion. Because c_t and r are likely to be correlated, the two equations are not equivalent. In fact, because GDP per capita is expected to be larger when the return on capital is larger, a negative correlation between $u'(c_t)$ and r is expected. This implies that the numerator in equation (7.5) should be smaller than the product of $Eu'(c_t)$ and $E\exp(rt)$. In turn, this implies that the right-hand side of this equation should be smaller than the one in equation (7.1). Risk aversion should have a negative impact on the discount rate recommended under the expected NFV approach, and this effect is increasing with maturity. The intuition for this result is that investing in the productive capital of the economy yields a risk that has a positive correlation with wider macroeconomic risk which cannot be diversified. The associated risk premium of this strategy is increasing with the time horizon, favoring investment in the risk-free project.

The same method should also be used under the expected NPV approach. Remember that this approach is based on the assumption that the future cash flow of the risk-free project is offset by a loan of $F\exp(-rt)$ at the end of the day. This strategy raises the expected utility of current consumption if

$$E[u'(c_0)(Fe^{-rt} - 1)] \geq 0. \tag{7.6}$$

This is equivalent to using a discount rate R_t^P defined as

$$R_t^P = -\frac{1}{t}\ln\frac{E[u'(c_0)e^{-rt}]}{Eu'(c_0)}. \tag{7.7}$$

Under risk neutrality (u' constant), this equation is equivalent to (7.2). The choice of consumption c_0 will in general depend upon the observation of the rate of return of capital at the end of the day. If the substitution effect dominates the wealth effect, c_0 and r are negatively correlated. This means that investing in the productive capital of the economy rather than in the safe investment project plays the role of insurance against low consumption in the short run. This reduces the relative attractiveness of the sure project under the expected NPV approach. This tends to raise the discount rate R_t^P.

TAKING ACCOUNT OF THE OPTIMALITY OF CONSUMPTION GROWTH

The introduction of risk aversion acts to reduce the gap between the two discount rates described by the inequalities in equation (7.3), by raising the lower rate and reducing the higher one. It is possible to go one step further by showing that the two approaches are in fact equivalent if it is assumed that consumers optimize their consumption plan contingent on their information about the future rate of return of capital. At the end of the day, r is realized, and consumers can decide how much to save or to borrow at that interest rate. Consider a marginal increase in saving at date 0 by 1 to finance an increase in consumption at date t by $\exp(rt)$. This marginal change in the consumption plan has no effect on welfare if

$$u'(c_0) = e^{-\delta t}e^{rt}u'(c_t). \tag{7.8}$$

This is an optimality condition, which must hold for all possible realizations of r. This means that c_0 and c_t depend upon random variable r. If this condition is plugged into equation (7.7), it follows that:

$$R_t^P = -\frac{1}{t}\ln\frac{E[u'(c_0)e^{-rt}]}{Eu'(c_0)} = \frac{1}{t}\ln\frac{E[u'(c_t)e^{rt}]}{Eu'(c_t)} = R_t^F. \qquad (7.9)$$

Observe thus that $R_t^P = R_t^F$ for all t! It can be concluded that once risk and risk aversion are properly combined with intertemporal optimization, the NPV and NFV approaches are equivalent. Moreover, these approaches are equivalent to the one on which the Ramsey rule and the previous chapters are based. Indeed, it also follows that:

$$R_t^P = -\frac{1}{t}\ln\frac{E[u'(c_0)e^{-rt}]}{Eu'(c_0)} = \delta - \frac{1}{t}\ln\frac{Eu'(c_t)}{Eu'(c_0)} \qquad (7.10)$$

The only difference with respect to what has been presented earlier in this book comes from the possibility that c_0 is random.

THE TERM STRUCTURE OF DISCOUNT RATES

In this model, in which shocks on capital productivity are permanent, risks affecting consumption growth are also permanent, as seen from equation (7.8). This implies that risk increases with maturity. This yields a decreasing term structure of discount rates. The property that the term structure must be decreasing can be proved by rewriting equation (7.9) as

$$r_t = R_t^F = R_t^P = -\frac{1}{t}\ln\frac{E[u'(c_0)e^{-rt}]}{Eu'(c_0)} = -\frac{1}{t}\ln E^*[e^{-rt}], \qquad (7.11)$$

where E^* is the standard risk-neutral expectation operator in which for any function F of r, we have $E^*[F(r)] = E[u'(c_0(r))F(r)]/E[u'(c_0(r))]$. Observe that the efficient term structure under this specification is equivalent to the Weitzman's NPV formula (7.2) up to the risk-neutral transformation of the probability distribution. This implies that we get the same qualitative properties for the term structure as those generated by equation (7.2): it is decreasing and tends to the smallest possible rate of return of capital.

Let us examine this point in greater detail by characterizing the optimal allocation of risk and consumption through time. Suppose, as before, that relative risk aversion is a positive constant γ, so that $u'(c) = c^{-\gamma}$. One can solve equation (7.8) together with the intertemporal budget constraint

$$\int_0^\infty e^{-rt} c_t \, dt = k_0,$$ (7.12)

where k_0 is the initial level of capital per capita in the economy. A solution to this maximization program exists if $r(1-\gamma) < \delta$, which is true in particular when γ is greater than unity. The solution is written as

$$c_t = k_0 \left(\frac{\delta - r(1-\gamma)}{\gamma} \right) e^{\frac{r-\delta}{\gamma} t}.$$ (7.13)

Observe first that the initial consumption c_0 is independent of the random variable r when γ equals unity. This confirms the property that initial consumption is not sensitive to the interest rate when the utility function is logarithmic ($\gamma = 1$). Observe also that, conditional on r, c_t has a constant growth rate $g(r) = (r - \delta)/\gamma$. It is notable that this implies that the ex post equilibrium interest rate is $r = \delta + \gamma g$, which is the Ramsey rule. The problem is to determine the socially efficient discount rate before r is revealed. The fact is that ex post consumption will grow at a constant rate that is unknown ex ante. This simple model is thus equivalent to the following stochastic process for the growth of log consumption:

$$\begin{cases} c_{t+1} = c_t e^{g(\theta)} \\ c_0 = k_0 (\theta - g(\theta)) \end{cases}$$ (7.14)

This is a special case of the general problem of parametric uncertainty that we examined in the previous chapter, but with an uncertain discrete jump in initial consumption. The arithmetic Brownian motion for log consumption is degenerate, with zero volatility, so that uncertainty is fully resolved at date 0. The riskiness of consumption increases exponentially through time, rather than linearly as in the case of log consumption following a Brownian motion.

Following Weitzman (2010), let us calibrate this model by assuming that the uncertainty about the future rate of return of capital is governed by a gamma distribution:

$$f(r; a, b) = r^{a-1} \frac{e^{-r/b}}{b^a \Gamma(a)} \quad \text{for all } r > 0,$$ (7.15)

where a and b are two positive constants. This implies that the mean rate of return is $Er = \mu = ab$ and its variance is $Var(r) = \sigma^2 = ab^2$. Suppose that $\delta = 0$ and $\gamma > 1$,[1] which implies from equation (7.13) that $c_0 = k_0(\gamma - 1)r/\gamma$. The Ramsey pricing formula (7.10) can then be written as follows:

$$r_t = -\frac{1}{t}\ln\frac{Er^{-\gamma}e^{-rt}}{Er^{-\gamma}} = -\frac{1}{t}\ln\frac{\int_0^\infty r^{-\gamma+a-1}e^{-r(t+b^{-1})}\,dr}{\int_0^\infty r^{-\gamma+a-1}e^{-rb^{-1}}\,dr}. \qquad (7.16)$$

The two integrals in this expression have an analytical solution. Indeed, because the integral of the density $f(r;k,h)$ must be equal to 1, we must have that

$$\int_0^\infty r^{h-1}e^{-r/k}\,dr = k^h\Gamma(h). \qquad (7.17)$$

Suppose that $\gamma < a$. We can then apply this property twice in (7.16) for $h = a - \gamma > 0$ and respectively $k = (t + b^{-1})^{-1}$ and $k = b$. It yields

$$r_t = -\frac{1}{t}\ln\frac{(t+b^{-1})^{\gamma-a}\Gamma(a-\gamma)}{b^{a-\gamma}\Gamma(a-\gamma)} = \frac{a-\gamma}{t}\ln(1+tb). \qquad (7.18)$$

It is easier to rewrite this equation with parameters (μ, σ) rather than (a, b). This substitution yields the risk-adjusted Weitzman's formula

$$r_t = \frac{(\mu/\sigma)^2 - \gamma}{t}\ln\left(1 + \frac{t\sigma^2}{\mu}\right). \qquad (7.19)$$

As long as γ is smaller than $a = (\mu/\sigma)^2$, this term structure is decreasing, and tends to zero when t tends to infinity. Observe also that $r_0 = \mu - (\gamma\sigma^2/\mu)$. Interestingly enough, an increase in risk aversion shifts the term structure downward in this model. This is because consumption c_0 is increasing in r, whereas the NPV is decreasing in r. This implies that investing in a safe project in this context provides a hedge for the immediate consumption risk. An increase in risk aversion makes safe projects more attractive. This is expressed by a smaller discount rate.

---

[1] There is a discountinuity of the term structure with respect to γ at $\gamma = 1$. A similar analysis to the one presented in the text yields $r_t = (\mu^2/t\sigma^2)\ln(1 + (t\sigma^2/\mu))$.

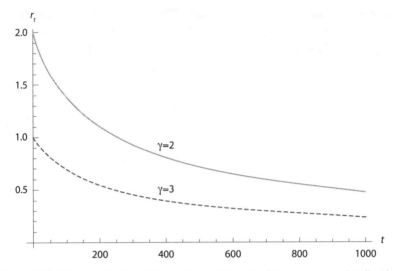

Figure 7.1. Discount rate with $\gamma = 2$ and 3 and with a gamma distribution for the permanent shock on the future return of capital. The mean future rate has a mean of 4% and a standard deviation of 2%.

Notice that equation (7.19) is equivalent to a hyperbolic discounting rule, since we have that

$$e^{-r_t t} = \frac{a_1}{1 + a_2 t}. \tag{7.20}$$

This is the functional form suggested by Loewenstein and Prelec (1991), to describe observed discounting behaviors. In figure 7.1, the discount rates are computed for a gamma distribution of the rate of return of capital with mean $\mu = 4\%$ and standard deviation $\sigma = 2\%$, together with $\gamma = 2$ and 3. Examine in particular the term structure for our benchmark calibration with $\gamma = 2$. Compared to the expected rate of return of capital of 4%, we see that the ex ante short-term efficient discount rate is only 2%. This illustrates the effect of risk aversion. The further reduction in the discount rate for longer maturities illustrates the growing precautionary effect.

The model proposed in this chapter is highly unrealistic because it makes the assumption that the uncertainty on the future return of productive capital will be completely revealed to us at the end of the day. This assumption on the permanency of the initial shock on interest rates is the driving force of the decreasing nature of discount rates. In reality, interest rates are subject to partially persistent shocks scattered through time. Newell and Pizer (2003), and Groom, Koundouri, Panopoulou, and Pantelidis (2007), have estimated the degree of permanency of shocks on interest rates, and have shown that it has a crucial role in the shape of the term structure of efficient discount rates.

SUMMARY OF MAIN RESULTS

1. Weitzman (1998, 2001, 2010) examines a model in which the exogeneous rate of return of capital is constant but random. Safe investment projects must be evaluated and implemented before this uncertainty can be fully revealed, i.e., before knowing the opportunity cost of capital.

2. A simple rule of thumb in this context would be to compute the net present value for each possible discount rate, and to implement the project if the expected NPV is positive. If the evaluator uses this approach, this is as if one would discount cash flows at a rate that is decreasing with maturity. This approach is implicitly based on the assumptions that the stakeholders are risk-neutral and transfer the net benefits of the project to an increase in immediate consumption. Opposite results prevail if one assumes that the net benefit is consumed at the maturity of the project.

3. Fisher equivalence property: We have shown in this chapter that the evaluation of a sure (marginal) investment project is independent of how cash flows are allocated through time, as soon as it is recognized that economic agents are risk-averse and that they optimize their consumption plans.

4. Finally, once risk aversion and optimal consumption planning are introduced into the model, it has been shown that the term structure of discount rates should be decreasing in the context proposed by Weitzman. This is due to the increasing precautionary effect generated by the persistency of shocks in this economy.

REFERENCES

Gollier, C. (2004), Maximizing the expected net future value as an alternative strategy to gamma discounting, *Finance Research Letters*, 1, 85–89.

Gollier, C., and M. L. Weitzman (2010), How should the distant future be discounted when discount rates are uncertain? *Economic Letters*, 107 (3), 350–353.

Groom, B., P. Koundouri, E. Panopoulou, and T. Pantelidis (2007), An econometric approach to estimating long-run discount rates, *Journal of Applied Econometrics*, 22, 641–656.

Loewenstein, G., and D. Prelec (1991), Negative time preference, *American Economic Review*, 81, 347–352.

Newell, R., and W. Pizer (2003), Discounting the benefits of climate change mitigation: how much do uncertain rates increase valuations? *Journal of Environmental Economics and Management*, 46 (1), 52–71.

Segal, U., and A. Spivak (1990), First order versus second order risk aversion, *Journal of Economic Theory*, 51, 111–125.

Weitzman, M. L. (1998), Why the far-distant future should be discounted at its lowest possible rate? *Journal of Environmental Economics and Management*, 36, 201–208.

Weitzman, M. L. (2001), Gamma discounting, *American Economic Review*, 91, 260–271.

Weitzman, M. L. (2010), Risk-adjusted gamma discounting, *Journal of Environmental Economics and Management*, 60, 1–13.

8

A Theory of the Decreasing
Term Structure of Discount Rates

This chapter completes part II of the book. It aims to provide a unified theoretical foundation to the term structure of discount rates. To do this it develops a benchmark model based on two assumptions: individual preferences toward risk, and the nature of the uncertainty over economic growth. We have shown that constant relative risk aversion, combined with a random walk for the growth of log consumption, yields a flat term structure for efficient discount rates. In this chapter, these two assumptions are relaxed by using a stochastic dominance approach.

The first step is to explore the link between the current long-term discount rate and expectations about what the future short-term discount rate will be.

THE CURRENT LONG DISCOUNT RATE AND
FUTURE SHORT DISCOUNT RATES

We limit the analysis to three equally distant dates, $t = 0$, 1, and 2. We assume that c_0 is known. At date $t = 0$, the short and long discount rates are, respectively

$$r_1 = \delta - \ln \frac{Eu'(c_1)}{u'(c_0)} \tag{8.1}$$

and

$$r_2 = \delta - \frac{1}{2}\ln\frac{Eu'(c_2)}{u'(c_0)}. \tag{8.2}$$

Suppose now that we are at date $t = 1$, with a realized level of consumption c_1. At that date under that state of nature, one should use a short rate denoted $r_{1 \to 2}(c_1)$ to discount a sure cash flow occurring one period later at date $t = 2$. To keep the notation simple, we write $r_{1 \to 2} = r_{12}$. This future short rate is as usual characterized by the following equation:

$$r_{12}(c_1) = \delta - \ln\frac{E[u'(c_2)|c_1]}{u'(c_1)}. \tag{8.3}$$

We want to link these three rates r_1, r_2, and r_{12}. This can be done by rewriting equation (8.2) as follows:

$$
\begin{aligned}
r_2 &= \delta - \frac{1}{2}\ln\frac{Eu'(c_2)}{u'(c_0)} \\
&= \delta - \frac{1}{2}\ln E\left[\frac{E[u'(c_2)|c_1]}{u'(c_1)}\frac{u'(c_1)}{Eu'(c_1)}\frac{Eu'(c_1)}{u'(c_0)}\right] \\
&= -\frac{1}{2}\ln\left(e^{-r_1}E\left[e^{-r_{12}(c_1)}\frac{u'(c_1)}{Eu'(c_1)}\right]\right).
\end{aligned}
\tag{8.4}
$$

This implies that

$$r_2 = 0.5(r_1 + R_{12}) \tag{8.5}$$

where R_{12} is defined as follows:

$$e^{-R_{12}} = \frac{Eu'(c_1)e^{-r_{12}(c_1)}}{Eu'(c_1)}. \tag{8.6}$$

Equation (8.5) tells us that the long rate today is the average of the short rate r_1 today and R_{12}. Observe that the discount factor $\exp(-R_{12})$ is the risk-neutral expectation of the future discount factor $\exp(-r_{12}(c_1))$, using the risk-neutral probabilities for the distribution of the states of nature at date $t = 1$. Rate R_{12}, measured at date $t = 0$, depends upon the uncertainty about the immediate growth rate and upon the correlation of this growth rate with the interest rate that will prevail in the future. R_{12} can also be interpreted as the certainty equivalent of the future short rate r_{12}. To keep terminology simple, let us refer to R_{12} as the forward interest rate. It lies somewhere between the smallest and the largest possible future short rates. Using equations (8.3) and (8.6), R_{12} can be rewritten as

$$R_{12} = \delta - \ln\frac{Eu'(c_2)}{Eu'(c_1)}. \tag{8.7}$$

It should not be a surprise that the discount factor to be used at date 0, to evaluate a transfer of consumption from date 1 to date 2, is equal to $\exp(-\delta)Eu'(c_2)/Eu'(c_1)$. Evaluated today, this is indeed the marginal rate of substitution between c_1 and c_2. Remember that, by the first theorem of welfare economics, the efficient discount rate is also the equilibrium interest rate in a frictionless economy. In the same spirit, R_{12} is the equilibrium forward interest rate, that is, the rate of return for a credit contract at date 0 offering a loan at date 1 with maturity at date 2.

Equations (8.5) and (8.6) also describe the links between current long rates and expectations about future shorter rates. It states that the following two investment strategies have the same effect on the expected utility at date 1. Under both strategies, consumption is reduced by ε at date 2 to fund an investment to increase consumption at date 1.

The first investment strategy is safe. It consists of borrowing long to invest short. More specifically, $\varepsilon\exp(-2r_2)$ is borrowed at date 0, which requires a reimbursement of ε at date 2. This loan is used at date zero to invest in a short bond that yields a sure payoff $\varepsilon\exp(-2r_2)\exp(r_1)$ at date 1. The increase in utility at date 1 is thus equal to that marginal sure increase in consumption multiplied by $Eu'(c_1)$. The second investment strategy is risky. It consists of borrowing $\varepsilon\exp(-r_{12})$ at date 1 that requires the same reimbursement ε at date 2. Seen from date 0, this is a risky strategy because the increased consumption at date 1 will depend upon the prevailing short-term rate $r_{12}(c_1)$ at date 1. The increase in expected utility at date 1 is given by $\varepsilon E\exp(-r_{12})u'(c_1)$. At equilibrium, the two strategies must have the same effect on welfare. The following condition must therefore be satisfied:

$$\varepsilon e^{-2r_2}e^{r_1}Eu'(c_1) = \varepsilon Ee^{-r_{12}}u'(c_1), \tag{8.8}$$

which is equivalent to equation (8.4), which in turn yields property (8.5). This simple arbitrage argument explains why the long rate today must increase when investors expect the future interest rate to go up. It also explains the role of risk aversion in this relationship.

A vast literature on the term structure of interest rates has examined these interactions. Until seminal works by Vasicek (1977) and Cox, Ingersoll, and Ross (1985), economists based their analysis on the "Pure Expectations Hypothesis," which states that the long rate today is the mean of the sequence of current and future short rates. Cochrane (2005, section 19.2) provides a useful analysis of this approach. It is similar to equations (8.5) and (8.6), but with a linear utility function u in (8.6). In spite of its inappropriate assumption of risk neutrality, this theory is compatible with the crucial idea that the current long rate tells us something about the investors' expectation about the future rates.

DECREASING TERM STRUCTURE

There are two ways to write the condition that the long rate is smaller than the short one: $r_2 \leq r_1$. First, from property (8.5), it is the case if the current short interest rate, r_1, is larger than the forward rate R_{12}:

$$r_1 \geq R_{12}. \tag{8.9}$$

Second, conditions (8.1) and (8.2) can be used more directly to get that r_2 is smaller than r_1 if:

$$\delta - \frac{1}{2}\ln\frac{Eu'(c_2)}{u'(c_0)} \leq \delta - \ln\frac{Eu'(c_1)}{u'(c_0)}, \tag{8.10}$$

which requires that:

$$u'(c_0)Eu'(c_2) \geq (Eu'(c_1))^2. \tag{8.11}$$

Of course, given equations (8.1) and (8.7), these two approaches yield exactly the same condition for a decreasing term structure.

THE CASE OF AN IID DYNAMIC GROWTH PROCESS

In this section, the case in which the log of consumption exhibits no serial correlation is examined. What is sought is the condition on u that yields a decreasing term structure. Let $x_t = \log c_{t+1} - \log c_t$ denote the change in log consumption between dates t and $t+1$. We assume that (x_0, x_1) are iid. It is easier to use variable $y_t = \exp(x_t) = c_{t+1}/c_t$, which is the relative change in consumption between dates t and $t+1$. Condition (8.11) for a decreasing term structure can therefore be rewritten as follows:

$$u'(c_0) Eu'(c_0 y_0 y_1) \geq (Eu'(c_0 y_0))^2. \tag{8.12}$$

Let us first consider the special case of power utility functions with $u'(c) = c^{-\gamma}$. That condition is then equivalent to

$$Ey_0^{-\gamma} y_1^{-\gamma} \geq (Ey_0^{-\gamma})^2. \tag{8.13}$$

Because y_0 and y_1 are independent, the left-hand side of this inequality equals $Ey_0^{-\gamma} Ey_1^{-\gamma}$, which in turn is equal to the right-hand side of (8.13) since y_0 and y_1 are identically distributed. We conclude that condition (8.13) holds as an equality, which implies that the term structure of discount rates is flat.

Under constant relative risk aversion, the short-term rate r_{12} is independent of c_1. Indeed, from (8.3), we have that

$$r_{12}(c_1) = \delta - \ln \frac{E[u'(c_2)|c_1]}{u'(c_1)} = \delta - \ln \frac{E(c_1 y_1)^{-\gamma}}{c_1^{-\gamma}} = \delta - \ln Ey_1^{-\gamma}. \tag{8.14}$$

It is a crucial property of the power utility function that the equilibrium interest rate is independent of the level of economic development. There is empirical support for this independence. During the twentieth century, GDP per capita was multiplied by a factor around 7 in the developed world, but no clear trend for the short-term interest rate has been observed. This is illustrated in figure 8.1, in which the series of short-term real interest rates between 1900 and 2006 in the United States is drawn. This argues in favor of constant relative risk aversion. If, in addition, expectations remain stable over time, implying that y_0 and y_1 are identically distributed, then comparing (8.14) and (8.1) implies that $r_1 = R_{12} = r_{12}$. In turn, this implies that the term structure is flat.

Let us relax the assumption that relative risk aversion is constant. Instead, the case where r_{12} is decreasing with c_1 is examined. From (8.3), this is the case if $f(c_1)$ is increasing in c_1 where:

$$f(c_1) = \frac{Eu'(c_1 y_1)}{u'(c_1)}. \tag{8.15}$$

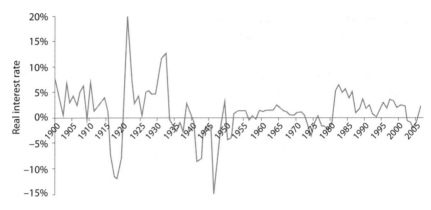

Figure 8.1. Real Bill rates in the United States in the twentieth century. *Source*: Morningstar France.

Derivating with respect to consumption:

$$f'(c) = \frac{u'(c)Ey_1 u''(cy_1) - u''(c)Eu'(cy_1)}{u'(c)^2} \tag{8.16}$$

which is positive if:

$$-\frac{Ey_1 u''(cy_1)}{Eu'(cy_1)} \leq -\frac{u''(c)}{u'(c)}. \tag{8.17}$$

This is equivalent to:

$$E\left[\frac{u'(cy_1)}{Eu'(cy_1)}R(cy_1)\right] \leq R(c), \tag{8.18}$$

where $R(c) = -cu''(c)/u'(c)$ is relative risk aversion. Suppose that consumption never falls (y_1 is almost surely larger than unity). If relative risk aversion is decreasing, this implies that $R(cy_1)$ is smaller than $R(c)$ almost surely. This implies that condition (8.18) always holds. Therefore, under the assumption that consumption never falls, decreasing relative risk aversion implies that the future short-term rate r_{12} is decreasing in c_1. This implies that $r_{12}(c_1)$ is almost surely less than $r_{12}(c_0)$. Under the assumption that y_0 and y_1 are iid, this also means that $r_{12}(c_1)$ is almost surely less than r_1. So is its certainty equivalent R_{12}. By equation (8.5), this implies that r_2 is less than r_1. Thus, when consumption never falls and growth exhibits no serial correlation, decreasing relative risk aversion is sufficient for a decreasing term structure. This condition is also necessary if we do not specify the distribution of y_1 with support in $[1,+\infty[$. This result is in Gollier (2002a, 2002b).

In figure 8.2, we draw the term structure of discount rates in the special case of a modified power function with a minimum level of subsistence k:

$$u(c) = \frac{(c-k)^{1-\gamma}}{1-\gamma}, \tag{8.19}$$

This function is increasing and concave in its domain $]k,+\infty[$. Parameter k is interpreted as a minimum level of subsistence since when consumption goes to the level k, utility goes to $-\infty$. It is easily checked that $R(c)=\gamma c/(c-k)$ under this specification. The function is decreasing in its relevant domain. It tends to infinity when consumption approaches the minimum level of subsistence, and it converges to γ for large consumption levels.

Let us normalize k to unity and consider $c_0 = 2$ as a benchmark. It is also assumed that the growth rate of the economy is a sure 2% per year, and that $\gamma = 1$, so that, as assumed elsewhere in this book, the relative risk aversion today is $R(2) = 2$. Using the Ramsey rule, which states that the interest rate net of the rate of impatience—which is assumed to be 0%—must be equal to the product of relative risk aversion and the growth rate of consumption. A short discount rate of $2\times2\% = 4\%$ is obtained. For very long maturities, the relevant R to be used in the Ramsey rule is $R(+\infty) = 1$, which yields a long discount rate equaling $1\times2\% = 2\%$.

In figure 8.2, current consumption c_0 is taken to be 20%, 50%, or 100% larger than the minimum level of subsistence. Figure 8.2 therefore also depicts the situation for less developed countries whose GDP per capita is closer to the minimum level of subsistence. For the case where $c_0 = 1.2$, the marginal utility of consumption is considerably larger today than in the benchmark case, which implies that reducing today's consumption to invest for the future is a lower priority. This takes the form of a large discount rate $r = R(1.2)\times2\% = 12\%$ in the short run. This may explain why poorer countries are observed to be more short-termist in relation to various public investments such as education or infrastructure.

Under the assumption of never decreasing consumption, the term structure is decreasing with maturity if and only if relative risk aversion is

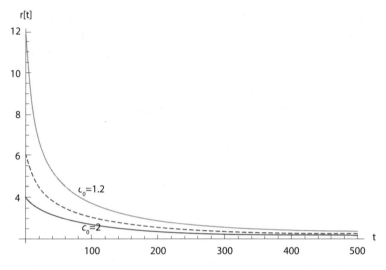

Figure 8.2. The term structure of discount rates with $\delta = 0\%$, $x_t = 2\%$, $u'(c) = (c = 1^{-1})$, $c_0 = 1.2$, 1.5, and 2.

decreasing with wealth. The intuition for this result is simple. The intensity of the wealth effect is proportional to R, which measures the aversion to intertemporal inequality. In a growing economy, this effect decreases over time when R is decreasing with wealth. This implies that interest rates will tend to go down in the future. This generates in turn a decreasing term structure of interest rates today. However, this approach is at odds with the empirical observations that the short-term interest rate is independent of the degree of economic development. In the next section, an alternative approach is considered to justify the type of downward sloping term structure which would be consistent with the analysis presented in the second part of the book.

A CONCEPT OF CONCORDANCE: "LARGE VALUES OF x_1 GO WITH LARGE VALUES OF x_2"

This section is devoted to the analysis of the impact on the forward interest rate of serial correlation in the growth rate of the economy. Up to now in this chapter, we examined the case of random walk for the change in log consumption, and we relaxed the assumption that relative risk aversion is constant. In the remainder of this chapter, we examine the role of serial correlation in the change of log consumption.

The forward rate is characterized by the following equality:

$$R_{12} = \delta - \ln \frac{Eu'(c_0 e^{x_0 + x_1})}{Eu'(c_0 e^{x_0})}. \tag{8.20}$$

This equation makes explicit that serial correlation in the growth of log consumption matters, as illustrated in the previous chapters. In the special case without serial correlation and constant relative risk aversion, we know that $R_{12} = r_{12} = r_1$, so that, according to condition (8.5), the term structure is flat. From now on in this chapter, the assumption of serial independence is relaxed in a framework in which there is no a priori specification of the utility function u.

In the general expected utility model, the coefficient of correlation between two random variables as x_1 and x_2 is usually insufficient to characterize the role of the statistical relationship on an expectation as $Eu'(c_0 e^{x_0 + x_1})$, that is, on the term structure of discount rates. The full joint distribution function is generally required to determine the forward discount rate. Following Tchen (1980) and Epstein and Tanny (1980), the idea that "greater values of x_1 go with greater values of x_2" is now formalized. To do this, consider an initial distribution function F for the pair of random variables (x_1, x_2), with $F(t_1, t_2) = P[x_1 \leq t_1 \cap x_2 \leq t_2]$. Consider another pair of random variables $(\hat{x}_1, \hat{x}_2)$ with cumulative distribution function (cdf) $\hat{F}$. A "marginal-preserving increase in concordance" (MPIC) is defined as any transformation of distribution F into distribution $\hat{F}$ that takes the following form: Consider two pairs (t_1, t_2) and (t'_1, t'_2) such that $t'_1 > t_1$ and $t'_2 > t_2$. $\hat{F}$ is obtained from F by adding probability mass ε in a small neighborhood of (t_1, t_2) and (t'_1, t'_2), while subtracting probability mass ε in a small neighborhood of (t_1, t'_2) and (t_1, t'_2). This is depicted in figure 8.3.

This MPIC clearly increases the correlation between the two random variables, without affecting the marginal distributions of the two random variables. Observe also that the new cdf, $\hat{F}$, obtained through a MPIC uniformly raises the cdf: for all (t_1, t_2), $\hat{F}(t_1, t_2) \geq F(t_1, t_2)$. Following Tchen (1980), this inequality defines the notion of "more concordance" for any

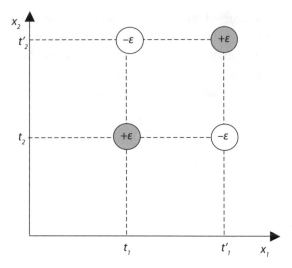

Figure 8.3. Transfer of probability mass in a marginal-preserving increase in concordance.

two cdfs F and $\hat{F}$ with the same marginals $\hat{F}(t_1,+\infty)=F(t_1,+\infty)$ $\forall t_1 \in \mathbb{R}$, and $\hat{F}(+\infty,t_2)=F(+\infty,t_2)$ $\forall t_2 \in \mathbb{R}$:

$$\hat{F} \succ_c F \Leftrightarrow \forall (t_1,t_2) \in \mathbb{R}^2, \hat{F}(t_1,t_2) \geq F(t_1,t_2). \qquad (8.21)$$

A more concordant cdf concentrates more probability mass in any South-West and North-East quadrangles of $\mathbb{R}^2$. Tchen (1980, theorem 1) and Epstein and Tanny (1980) show that two cdfs with the same marginals can be ranked by this notion of increasing concordance if and only if the more concordant cdf can be obtained from the less concordant one through a sequence of MPICs. It is interesting to observe that, by dividing both sides of the inequality in (8.21) by $\hat{F}(t_1,+\infty)=F(t_1,+\infty)$, this definition is equivalent to

$$\hat{F} \succ_c F \Leftrightarrow \forall(t_1,t_2) \in \mathbb{R}^2, P[\hat{x}_2 \leq t_2 | \hat{x}_1 \leq t_1] \geq P[x_2 \leq t_2 | x_1 \leq t_1]. \quad (8.22)$$

This is in turn equivalent to the following definition of an increase in concordance, which relies on the notion of First-order Stochastic Dominance (FSD):

$$\hat{F} \succ_c F \iff \forall t_1 \in \mathbb{R}, \hat{x}_2 | \hat{x}_1 \leq t_1 \text{ is FSD−dominated by } x_2 | x_1 \leq t_1. \quad (8.23)$$

This can be seen clearly in figure 8.3. Suppose that the MPIC represented in this figure is undertaken, and that the information is received that x_1 is smaller than some $t \in]t_1, t_1'[$. What remains visible to the left of t is the downward transfer of probability mass that happens in the neighborhood of t_1, which is a FSD deterioration in the conditional distribution of x_2. Conditional on the fact that x_1 is smaller than any threshold t_1, the probability distribution of $\hat{x}_2$ is a deterioration of x_2 in the sense of FSD. This means that some probability mass of this conditional distribution is transferred from the high values of x_2 to the lower ones. Under the new distribution, there is always more probability mass in the left tail of the distribution of $x_2 | x_1 \leq t_1$.

In words, this means that the present and the future changes in consumption are more strongly correlated after a sequence of MPICs. Bad news in the first period is bad news for the second period's distribution of consumption. In the statistical literature, this notion is referred to as the "stochastic increasing positive dependence," because x_2 is more likely to take on a larger value when x_1 increases (see for example Joe 1997). It is closely related to the notion of "positive quadrant dependence" proposed by Lehmann (1966). Gollier (2007) was too restrictive in identifying the notion of more concordance with respect to a pair of independent random variables with the stronger condition of "positive FSD dependence" that requires that $x_2 | x_1 = t_1$ be ordered by first-degree stochastic dominance.

CONCORDANCE AND SUPERMODULARITY

Suppose that we are interested in the effect of an increase in concordance on the expectation of some function $h : \mathbb{R}^2 \to \mathbb{R}$. Let us first consider the effect of an elementary MPIC defined by pairs (t_1, t_2) and (t_1', t_2') such that $t_1' > t_1$ and $t_2' > t_2$, as in figure 8.3. Obviously, this MPIC increases the expectation of h if and only if

$$h(t_1, t_2) + h(t_1', t_2') \geq h(t_1', t_2) + h(t_1, t_2'). \quad (8.24)$$

Because the two pairs (t_1, t_2) and (t_1', t_2') are arbitrary, this condition must hold for all such pairs such that $t_1' > t_1$ and $t_2' > t_2$. This condition is necessary and sufficient for an increase in concordance to raise the expectation of h because any increase in concordance can be expressed as a sequence of MPICs. It happens that this condition is well-known in mathematical economics. It is referred to as the "supermodularity of h."

If h represents a von Neumann-Morgenstern utility function in $\mathbb{R}^2$, taking condition (8.24) and dividing both sides of the inequality by 2, implies that one would prefer a lottery yielding payoff (t_1, t_2) or (t'_1, t'_2) with equal probabilities to another lottery yielding payoff (t'_1, t_2) and (t_1, t'_2) with equal probabilities. This would be the case, for example, for complement goods where x_1 and x_2 are respectively the number of left and right shoes in the consumption bundle. Condition (8.24) thus defines a notion of complementarity between x_1 and x_2. Two goods are complements if the marginal utility of the first is increasing in the consumption of the second, that is, if the cross derivative of the utility function is positive.

Observe that if h is twice differentiable, replacing (t'_1, t'_2) by $(t_1 + dx, t_2 + dy)$, inequality (8.24) is equivalent to

$$h_{12}(t_1, t_2)\, dx\, dy \geq 0 \qquad (8.25)$$

for all $dx > 0$ and $dy > 0$. A simple integration argument implies that when h is twice differentiable, the supermodularity of h is equivalent to its having a positive cross derivative.

The following lemma summarizes the findings so far. The formal proof of the lemma is in Tchen (1980), Epstein and Tanny (1980), or Meyer and Strulovici (2011).

Lemma 2: *Consider a bivariate function h. The following conditions are equivalent:*

- *For any two pairs of random variables (x_1, x_2) and $(\hat{x}_1, \hat{x}_2)$ such that $(\hat{x}_1, \hat{x}_2)$ is more concordant than (x_1, x_2), $Eh(\hat{x}_1, \hat{x}_2) \geq Eh(x_1, x_2)$.*
- *h is supermodular.*

Moreover, assuming that h is twice differentiable, Tchen (1980, theorem 2) shows that

$$Eh(\hat{x}_1, \hat{x}_2) - Eh(x_1, x_2) = \iint h_{12}(t_1, t_2)[\hat{F}(t_1, t_2) - F(t_1, t_2)]\, dt_1\, dt_2. \qquad (8.26)$$

This can be obtained by a double integration by parts. By the definition (8.21) of an increase in concordance, we see that equation (8.26) provides a simple proof for this lemma.

An immediate application of the lemma is to apply it to function $h(x_1, x_2) = x_1 x_2$, which is supermodular. Lemma 2 tells us that an increase in concordance raises the expectation of h. Since the marginal distributions are preserved because $E\hat{x}_i = Ex_i$, this shows that an increase in concordance necessarily raises the covariance between the two random variables.

THE EFFECT OF AN INCREASE IN CONCORDANCE OF ECONOMIC GROWTH ON THE FORWARD DISCOUNT RATE

There is a clear link between the notions of supermodularity and of an increase in concordance. Consider two dynamic processes for the growth of consumption (shown in figure 8.4).

The perfect positive concordant pair of random variables in (a) is obtained from the perfect negative concordant pair in (b) through a MPIC transferring all the probability mass from the upward diagonal of the rectangle to the downward one. In the two cases, the marginal distributions of x_1 and x_2 are the same: $x_t \sim (1\%, 1/2; 3\%, 1/2)$, but they are perfectly positively correlated in case (a), whereas they are perfectly negatively correlated in case (b).

Define

$$h(x_1, x_2) = u'(c_0 e^{x_0 + x_1}). \tag{8.27}$$

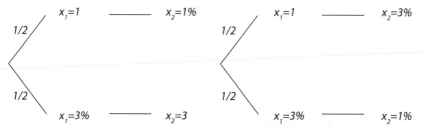

Figure 8.4. Illustrations of perfect positive and negative concordance.

Equation (8.20) tells us that the forward discount rate R_{12} is negatively affected by an increase in concordance if Eh is positively affected by it. Using lemma 2, this requires that h is supermodular. It follows that

$$h_{12}(x_1, x_2) = c_2 u''(c_2)[1 - P(c_2)], \qquad (8.28)$$

where $c_2 = c_0 \exp(x_1 + x_2)$ is consumption at date $t = 2$ and $P(c) = -cu''(c)/u'(c)$ is the index of relative prudence. This proves the following proposition:

Proposition: *Any increase in concordance in the growth of log consumption reduces the forward discount rate if and only if relative prudence is uniformly larger than unity.*

By equation (8.5), $P \geq 1$ is also necessary and sufficient to reduce the long discount rate. Now, remember that combining the assumption of iid (x_1, x_2) with constant relative risk aversion implies a flat term structure. Remember also that constant relative risk aversion implies that relative prudence is also constant and is equal to relative risk aversion plus one. Thus, when relative risk aversion is constant, it must be that relative prudence is larger than unity. Thus, under this assumption, the term structure of discount rates is decreasing if, for the same marginal cdf, the growth process exhibits more concordance than in the case of serial independence.

The intuition for this result is based on the observation that the second moment of c_2 is the expectation of a supermodular function of (x_1, x_2). Indeed, function

$$h(x_1, x_2) = (c_0 e^{x_1 + x_2})^2 \qquad (8.29)$$

is supermodular. It implies that an increase in concordance for the change in log consumption tends to raise the variance of c_2. This reduces the forward discount rate under prudence. However, observe also that the expectation of c_2 is increased by the concordance in (x_1, x_2), since $h(x_1, x_2) = c_0 \exp(x_1 + x_2)$ is supermodular. This wealth effect goes against the precautionary effect. This explains why positive prudence is not sufficient to determine the sign of the effect of an increase in concordance of *log consumption*. Using lemma 2, it is easy to check that positive prudence is necessary and sufficient when the dynamic process of *consumption* exhibits more concordance than in the case of independence. Heinzel (2011) shows how to generalize this analysis to higher orders of stochastic dependence and to higher derivatives of the utility function.

UNIFIED EXPLANATION FOR A DECREASING TERM STRUCTURE OF DISCOUNT RATES

The stochastic processes that we examined in chapters 4 (mean-reversion), 5 (Markov switches), and 6 (parametric uncertainty) exhibited some forms of stochastic dependence in serial changes of log consumption. Their common feature is the increased concordance of successive changes in log consumption compared to the case of a random walk. This provides a common underlying explanation for the decreasing term structure derived for each of these models. The simplest illustration of this is obtained in the case of Markov switches. Suppose that there are two regimes, one with a sure growth rate of 2%, and one with no growth. There is a 1% probability to switch from one regime to the other every year. Figure 8.5 (left) describes the probability distribution for the growth rate in the first two years, assuming that one experienced a good state in the previous year. Figure 8.5

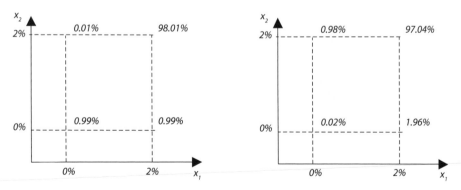

Figure 8.5. A two-state Markov process (left) that is more concordant than in the case of independence (right). The switching probability in each period is 1%.

(right) describes the probability distribution with no serial correlation, but with the same marginal probabilities as in the original distribution on the left. We see that the Markov-switch process is more concordant than in the case of independence, since it is obtained from the latter through a MPIC of a probability mass of 0.97%.

Alternatively, consider the mean-reverting process $x_{t+1} = \phi x_t + (1 - \phi) \mu + \varepsilon_t$, with $\phi \in [0, 1]$ and where ε_t is normally distributed with mean 0 and volatility σ. We have seen in chapter 4 that this yields a decreasing term structure under CRRA when $x_0 = \mu$, which guarantees that $Ex_1 = Ex_2$. In figure 8.6, the iso-density curves of (x_1, x_2) are depicted, together with the curves for the pair of independent random variables with the same marginal distributions $(x_1 \sim N(\mu, \sigma^2)$ and $x_2 \sim N(\mu, (1 + \phi^2)\sigma^2))$. We clearly see that the pair exhibiting mean-reversion exhibits more concordance than the corresponding independent pair. A similar observation can be made for the case of parametric uncertainty.

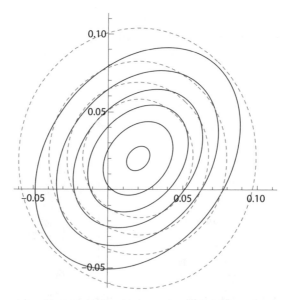

Figure 8.6. Iso-density curves in the case of mean-reversion with $\mu = 2\%$, $\sigma = 3.6\%$, and $\phi = 0.3$. The dashed curves correspond to the iso-density curves of the pair of random variables with the same marginal distributions.

SUMMARY OF MAIN RESULTS

1. By a simple arbitrage argument, the term structure of interest rates is decreasing if the short-term interest rate is larger than the forward rate. The forward discount factor is the risk-neutral expectation of the future short-term discount factor. It contains a risk premium.

2. If the growth rate of consumption follows a random walk but is always non-negative, the forward interest rate is smaller than the short rate if and only if relative risk aversion is decreasing. In this context, this is also necessary and sufficient for a decreasing term structure. This may explain a greater degree of short-termism in public investments observed in developing countries whose citizens are close to their subsistence level of consumption.

3. Stochastic models of economic growth with mean-reversion, Markov switches, and parametric uncertainty all exhibit some forms of positive statistical dependence of successive growth rates. Because this tends to magnify the long-term risk, it is the driving force of the decreasing nature of the term structure. We formalize this idea by the notion of concordance, in which probability masses are transferred in favor of more concordant growth rates without changing the marginal distributions. This family of changes in the joint distribution of growth rates reduces the forward rate and makes the term structure more downward sloping if and only if relative prudence is larger than unity.

REFERENCES

Cochrane, J. H. (2005), *Asset Pricing. Revised Edition*, Princeton: Princeton University Press.

Cox, J., J. Ingersoll, and S. Ross (1985), A theory of the term structure of interest rates, *Econometrica*, 53, 385–403.

Epstein, L. G., and S. M. Tanny (1980), Increasing generalized correlation: a definition and some economic consequences, *Canadian Journal of Economics*, 13, 16–34.

Gollier, C. (2002a), Discounting an uncertain future, *Journal of Public Economics*, 85, 149–166.

Gollier, C. (2002b), Time horizon and the discount rate, *Journal of Economic Theory*, 107, 463–473.

Gollier, C. (2007), The consumption-based determinants of the term structure of discount rates, *Mathematics and Financial Economics*, 1 (2), 81–102.

Heinzel, C. (2011), Term structure of interest rates under multivariate $\vec{s}$-ordered consumption growth, mimeo, Toulouse School of Economics.

Joe, H. (1997), *Multivariate Models and Dependence Concepts*, London: Chapman and Hall/CRC.

Lehmann, E. L. (1966), Some concepts of dependence, *Annals of Mathematical Statistics*, 37, 1153–1173.

Meyer, M., and B. Strulovici (2011), *The supermodular stochastic ordering*, Nuffield College, Oxford University.

Tchen, A. H. (1980), Inequalities for distributions with given marginals, *Annals of Probability*, 8, 814–827.

Vasicek, O. (1977), An equilibrium characterization of the term structure, *Journal of Financial Economics*, 5, 177–188.

PART III

—◄o►—

EXTENSIONS

9

Inequalities

In the canonical models of the term structure presented earlier in this book, a single agent was assumed to benefit from the cash flow that the investment project under scrutiny generates. Another way to interpret this model is that there is more than one person, perhaps many people, who all have the same (perfectly concordant) consumption levels and the same share of the project's cash flows. Of course, the real world is quite different. In particular, our societies are unequal, and people are unequally affected by macroeconomic shocks. Moreover, the costs and benefits of most public policies are not spread equally across citizens. This can be illustrated by considering global efforts to curb emissions of greenhouse gases. It is plausible that most of the cost of these efforts will be borne by the western world, whereas the biggest beneficiaries will be the populations of the countries which are most vulnerable to climate change, many of them in the developing world. Climate change mitigation therefore has some additional value by virtue of helping to reduce global wealth inequality. Even abstracting from the heterogeneous allocation of costs and benefits, the existence of huge wealth inequalities between and within countries necessitates an adaptation of the canonical model.

The aim of this chapter is to make adaptations to the model developed so far, to recognize inequalities as crucial features of our world. Two models are considered. In the first model, inequalities in society are introduced in the model examined in part I of this book. However, it is assumed that individuals in this unequal society are able to share risk efficiently, and that they can implement mutually beneficial long-term credit contracts. In the second model, these assumptions are relaxed.

DESCRIPTION OF THE ECONOMY

Suppose that the economy is composed of N agents, all with infinite life expectancy. These agents can be interpreted as family dynasties, or countries. They are indexed by $i = 1, 2, \ldots, N$. To keep the model simple, it is assumed that all the agents have identical preferences, which are classically represented by the rate of pure time preference, δ,[1] and an increasing and concave utility function u. The analysis focuses first on the discount rate to be used at date 0 for a sure cash flow at date t.

At date 0, there is some inequality in the endowment for each agent, $(z_{10}, \ldots, z_{N0})$, where z_{i0} is agent i's endowment of the single consumption good at that date. At date 0, the distribution of the endowment occurring at date t is not known. This uncertainty is characterized by S possible states of nature, $s = 1, 2, \ldots, S$, and by the associated state probabilities $(p_1, \ldots, p_S)$, with $\Sigma_s p_s = 1$. Let z_{is} denote the endowment of agent i at date t in state s. Observe that $s = 0$ designates date 0 rather than a possible state to occur at date t. The income per capita in state s (or at date 0) is defined as:

$$z_s = \frac{1}{N} \sum_{i=1}^{N} z_{is}. \tag{9.1}$$

It is assumed that there exists at date 0 a complete market of insurance and credit contracts. In other words, from now on it is assumed that for each $s = 1, \ldots, S$, there exists a contract for the delivery of one unit of the consumption good at date t if and only if state s is realized. Moreover, there exists a competitive market for each of these "Arrow–Debreu securities." An Arrow–Debreu security can be interpreted as an insurance contract, in which an indemnity is paid by the counterpart of the contract if a specific event occurs. Any risky asset can be interpreted as a bundle of Arrow–Debreu securities. A special case is the risk-free asset, which is

---

[1] Gollier and Zeckhauser (2005) examine the effect of heterogeneous rates of impatience.

characterized as a bundle containing exactly one unit of each of the Arrow–Debreu securities. Let Π_s denote the equilibrium price of the Arrow–Debreu security associated with state s. It is useful at this stage to also define the state price per unit of probability $\pi_s = \Pi_s/p_s$, $s = 1, \ldots, S$, and $\pi_0 = \Pi_0$.

A competitive equilibrium is characterized by the vector $(\Pi_0, \ldots, \Pi_S)$ of Arrow–Debreu securities at date 0, and by a matrix $(c_{is})^{i=1,\ldots,N}_{s=0,1,\ldots,S}$ of actual consumption levels in the economy. Observe that $c_{is} - z_{is}$ is the demand for the Arrow–Debreu security s by agent i. The equilibrium must satisfy two sets of conditions:

Each agent maximizes his welfare under the intertemporal budget constraint, $\forall i = 1, \ldots, N$:

$$\max_{c_{is}} u(c_{i0}) + e^{-\delta t} \sum_{s=1}^{S} p_s u(c_{is}) \quad s.t. \quad \Pi_0(c_{i0} - z_{i0}) + \sum_{s=1}^{S} \Pi_s(c_{is} - z_{is}) = 0. \quad (9.2)$$

Markets clear: $\forall s = 0, 1, \ldots, S$:

$$\sum_{i=1}^{N}(c_{is} - z_{is}) = 0. \quad (9.3)$$

Observe that condition (9.3) can be rewritten as a feasibility condition:

$$\frac{1}{N}\sum_{i=1}^{N} c_{is} = z_s, \quad (9.4)$$

Of course, if agents have all the same preferences and the same endowments ($z_{is} = z_s$ for all $s = 0, 1, \ldots, S$), there is no trade at equilibrium. The canonical model described earlier in this book applies. However, if the endowment is unequally allocated at date 0 or in some states at date t, some additional work is required to define a "representative agent" in this economy.

EXISTENCE OF A REPRESENTATIVE AGENT

The first-order condition associated to program (9.2) can be written as:

$$\begin{cases} u'(c_{i0}) = \lambda_i \pi_0 \\ u'(c_{is}) = \lambda_i e^{-\delta t} \pi_s, \quad s = 1, \ldots, S, \end{cases} \quad (9.5)$$

where λ_i is the lagrangian multiplier associated to agent i's budget constraint. The competitive equilibrium is the solution of this set of $N(S + 1)$ first-order conditions (9.5) combined with the $S + 1$ market-clearing conditions (9.4). Standard theorems from General Equilibrium Theory can be used to prove the existence and the unicity (up to a normalization of the vector of prices) of the competitive equilibrium, and to prove that it is Pareto-efficient.

An important property of the competitive equilibrium is the mutuality principle. This principle requires that if there are two states at date t, say $s = a$ and $s = b$, such that the wealth per capita are the same, i.e., $z_a = z_b$, then all agents will enjoy the same consumption level in the two states, i.e., $c_{ia} = c_{ib}$ for all $i = 1,\ldots,N$. It also implies that the two states' price per unit of probability must be the same, i.e., $\pi_a = \pi_b$. The simplest way to prove this is to check that the sets of equations corresponding to the two states are equivalent. More intuitively, the mutuality principle implies that all diversifiable risks are diversified at equilibrium. Suppose for example that there are only two states, and that the wealth levels per capita are the same in the two states. This means that there is no aggregate risk in the economy. Applied in this context, the mutuality principle states that all agents are fully insured at equilibrium. Departing from this rule would force people to face zero-mean risks, which because of risk aversion is a Pareto-inferior allocation.

The mutuality principle means that state-dependent variables c_{is} and π_s depend upon state s only through the level of wealth per capita z_s. In other words, there exist functions C_i and v' such that $c_{is} = C_i(z_s)$ and $\pi_s = v'(z_s)$ for all $s = 1,\ldots,S$. Equation (9.5) can thus be rewritten as:

$$\forall (s, s') \in \{1,\ldots,S\}^2,\ \forall i \in \{1,\ldots,N\}: \quad \frac{u'(c_{is})}{u'(c_{is'})} = \frac{v'(z_s)}{v'(z_{s'})}, \qquad (9.6)$$

As is well known, the equilibrium is characterized by the equalization across all agents of their marginal rate of substitution of consumption for any pair of states. Equation (9.6) tells us that the equilibrium marginal rate of substitution is the same as in an economy in which all agents consume the income per capita, z_s, but where the utility function u is replaced by function v when computing the ratio of marginal utility.

Suppose without loss of generality that there exists a state s' such that $z_0 = z_{s'}$. Equation (9.5) implies that $c_{i0} = c_{is'} = C_i(z_0)$ for all i, and $\pi_0 = e^{-\delta t}\pi_{s'} = e^{-\delta t}v'(z_0)$. Therefore it also follows that:

$$\forall s \in \{1,\ldots,S\}, \ \forall i \in \{1,\ldots,N\}: \quad \frac{u'(c_{is})}{u'(c_{i0})} = \frac{v'(z_s)}{v'(z_0)}, \tag{9.7}$$

At equilibrium, the marginal rates of substitution between consumption at date 0 and in any specific state at date t are equalized across agents. They are equal to the marginal rate of substitution of an agent whose consumption is equal to the income per capita at date 0 and in any state at date t, but where the original utility function u is replaced by function v. From now on, this function is referred to as "the utility function of the representative agent." This agent consumes the income per capita in all states and at all dates. An egalitarian economy composed by N identical agents with this utility function v would price all assets in this economy in exactly the same way as in the unequal economy described in the previous section. This section has shown that the existence of a complete set of competitive markets for Arrow–Debreu securities implies the existence of such a representative agent, as initially shown by Wilson (1968). In the next section, the utility function v of the representative agent is characterized.

CHARACTERIZATION OF THE REPRESENTATIVE AGENT

We have seen in the previous section that the utility function v of the representative agent can be derived from the original utility function by solving the following set of equalities: for all z:

$$u'(C_i(z)) = \lambda_i v'(z) \quad i = 1,\ldots,N,$$
$$\frac{1}{N}\sum_{i=1}^{N} C_i(z) = z \tag{9.8}$$

Notice that this set of equations characterizes the solution of the following "cake-sharing" problem:

$$v(z) = \max_{(C_1,\ldots,C_N)} \frac{1}{N}\sum_{i=1}^{N} \lambda_i^{-1} u(C_i) \quad s.t. \quad \frac{1}{N}\sum_{i=1}^{N} C_i = z. \tag{9.9}$$

The competitive allocation of risk maximizes the social welfare in each state of nature, where the social welfare function is the sum of individual utilities weighted by λ_i^{-1}.

The unequal distribution of wealth in the economy is entirely concentrated in the vector of lagrange multipliers $(\lambda_1, \ldots, \lambda_N)$. If, for all agents, their endowment has the same market value, the λ_i would all be the same, thereby trivially yielding the solution: $v \equiv u$ and $C_i(z) = z$ for all z. Suppose alternatively that the market values of the individual endowment are unequal, so that the lagrange multipliers are heterogeneous. Fully differentiating the previous equations with respect to z yields:

$$u''(C_i(z))\frac{dC_i}{dz} = \lambda_i v''(z) \quad i = 1, \ldots, N,$$

$$\frac{1}{N}\sum_{i=1}^{N} \frac{dC_i}{dz} = 1$$

(9.10)

Let $T(c) = -u'(c)/u''(c)$ and $T_v(z) = -v'(z)/v''(z)$ denote the degree of absolute risk tolerance for the utility function of the original agent and of the representative agent respectively. Observe that absolute risk tolerance is just the inverse of absolute risk aversion. Using (9.8), the first equality in (9.10) can be rewritten as:

$$\frac{dC_i}{dz} = \frac{T(C_i(z))}{T_v(z)} \quad i = 1, \ldots, N.$$

(9.11)

This formula is intuitive. It states that the share of the aggregate risk borne by agent i—which is measured by the sensitiveness of agent i's consumption to collective income per capita—is proportional to agent i's degree of absolute risk tolerance. More risk-tolerant agents bear a larger share of the aggregate risk. Using the second equality in (9.10) implies that it must be the case that:

$$T_v(z) = \frac{1}{N}\sum_{i=1}^{N} T(C_i(z)).$$

(9.12)

This equation, which was first derived by Wilson (1968), tells us that the degree of risk tolerance of the representative agent is the mean of the absolute risk tolerance of the original agents evaluated at their actual level of consumption. This equation fully characterizes the utility function v of the representative agent in this unequal economy. Once v is obtained, it is possible to determine the socially efficient discount rate by using the standard pricing formula in the canonical model:

$$r_t = \delta - \frac{1}{t} \ln \frac{Ev'(z_t)}{v'(z_0)}, \tag{9.13}$$

where z_t is the random variable which is distributed as $(z_1, p_1; \ldots; z_S, p_S)$. It is obtained, as usual, by considering a marginal investment project in which the income per capita at date 0 is reduced by ε to increase the income per capita in all states at date t by $\varepsilon \exp(r_t t)$. The r_t defined in (9.13) is the one for which, at the margin, this investment project has no effect on the intertemporal social welfare $(v(z_0) + e^{-\delta t} Ev(z_t))$. It is assumed that benefits and costs are added and subtracted to aggregate wealth, and are then reallocated in the population according to the cake-sharing rule derived from program (9.9) and described by rule (9.11). In other words, this means that markets for Arrow–Debreu securities remain active after the investment decision is made.

THE IMPACT OF WEALTH INEQUALITY ON THE EFFICIENT DISCOUNT RATE

In order to explore the effect of wealth inequality on the efficient discount rate, let us first examine the special case of an economy in which agents have the same classical power utility function with $u'(c) = c^{-\gamma}$. This implies that $T(c) = c/\gamma$, which in turn implies that:

$$\forall z: \quad T_v(z) = \frac{1}{N} \sum_{i=1}^{N} T(C_i(z)) = \frac{1}{N} \sum_{i=1}^{N} \frac{C_i(z)}{\gamma} = \frac{z}{\gamma}. \tag{9.14}$$

The implication is that the utility function of the representative agent is also a power function, with the same constant relative risk aversion as u. This proves that, under this specification, wealth inequality has absolutely no effect on the shape of the utility function of the representative agent, and therefore on the efficient discount rate. The power utility function is widely used by economists; therefore it can be concluded that the presence of (large) wealth inequalities around the world is not enough, in itself, to justify a departure from the extended Ramsey rule which also relies on a power utility function.

More generally, if the utility function u exhibits linear risk tolerance, the representative agent will have the same utility function u, whatever the

degree of wealth inequality in the economy. By contrast, if the utility function u exhibits a convex risk tolerance T, Jensen's inequality implies that:

$$\forall z: \; T_v(z) = \frac{1}{N} \sum_{i=1}^{N} T(C_i(z)) \geq T\left(\frac{1}{N} \sum_{i=1}^{N} C_i(z)\right) = T(z). \qquad (9.15)$$

The opposite result holds if risk tolerance is concave. A simple result is
obtained in the special case of a certain growth rate between dates 0 and
t. Suppose that T is convex, so that $T_v(z)$ is larger than $T(z)$ for all z. This
means that v is less concave than u in the Arrow–Pratt sense, or that there
exists an increasing and convex function ξ such that $v(z) = \xi(u(z))$ for all
z. This implies in turn that if $z_t \geq z_0$, i.e., if $\xi'(u(z_t)) \geq \xi'(u(z_0))$, we obtain:

$$r_t = \delta - \frac{1}{t} \ln \frac{v'(z_t)}{v'(z_0)} = \delta - \frac{1}{t} \ln \frac{\xi'(u(z_t))u'(z_t)}{\xi'(u(z_0))u'(z_0)} \leq \delta - \frac{1}{t} \ln \frac{u'(z_t)}{u'(z_0)}, \qquad (9.16)$$

This means that if the sure growth of the economy is positive, and if
risk tolerance is convex, then wealth inequality reduces the efficient discount rate. Assuming that economic growth is uncertain makes the problem
considerably more complex, because it requires the degree of prudence of
the representative agent to be described in addition to their risk tolerance
(Gollier 2001).

EPITAPH FOR LONG-TERM RISK-SHARING ALLOCATIONS

Up to now this chapter has assumed that agents can credibly commit to
share risk efficiently over long time horizons. This assumption fits quite
well with the reality of the western world over time horizons corresponding
to life expectancies, in which people can write legally enforceable insurance and credit contracts. The assumption is far from perfect, however,
because of the existence of transaction costs and asymmetric information
that result in credit constraints for households. Further, if time horizon t
exceeds the lifetime of the current generation, risk-sharing arrangements
can only be implicit, which raises a commitment problem. An alternative
view is that the agents described earlier are governments that commit their
citizens to intergenerational risk-sharing contracts. However, this is quite
unrealistic. Even within the European Union, countries have only limited

commitments to assist other countries in economic distress, as illustrated by the absence of solidarity within the EU during the financial crisis observed since 2008.

The potential social value of international risk-sharing is enormous, in particular when a long-term perspective is taken. Imagine, for a moment, Marco Polo as a plenipotential ambassador for the western world going to China to sign a treaty of risk-sharing with the eastern world, each party committing to financially compensate the other in case of a persistent divergence in their respective growth rates. Imagine for another moment that today we were able to create a global "Commonwealth" for a progressive mutual assistance scheme where unlucky countries would get positive transfers from the lucky ones over the next two centuries. In both these examples, there exists a large set of mutually beneficial risk-sharing contracts, which are not currently implemented—even at the margin—because of the huge commitment and moral hazard problems that they would generate.

This means that the model presented earlier in this chapter is unrealistic, in particular for the time horizons that correspond to global investment projects and sustainable development generally. It is a useful benchmark, however, since it is the classical model used in the modern theory of finance, which relies heavily on the existence of a representative agent.

THE CASE OF INEFFICIENT RISK SHARING

We hereafter take dynastic or country-specific consumption growth as completely exogenous. An extreme interpretation of this model is that there are no transfers at all between parties in this community, and that each agent consumes at each date its exogenous endowment of the consumption good. Let c_{it} denote the consumption of agent i at date t. The dynamic stochastic process of $(c_1, \ldots, c_N)$ is not specified at this stage, but it may exhibit temporal and geographical correlations. Intertemporal marginal rates of substitution are not equalized between agents because this allocation is not Pareto efficient. This implies that agents will in general use different discount rates to evaluate any reallocation of consumption through time. It also means that, contrary to the case of efficient risk-sharing examined earlier in this chapter, the law of a single discount rate (for a specific time horizon) is lost. The discount rate to be used to evaluate a collective investment project depends upon how costs and benefits are allocated within the economy.

Let us consider an "egalitarian" investment project that allocates costs and benefits in a non-discriminatory way. More specifically, consider a safe investment project that reduces consumption of all agents by ε at date 0, and that raises consumption of all agents by $\varepsilon \exp(r_t t)$ at date t. We are looking for the critical internal rate of return for the project that has no effect at the margin on intertemporal social welfare. Intertemporal social welfare is defined, as before, as the discounted sum of the flow of temporal welfare. The welfare at date t is arbitrarily defined as the sum of the individual felicities weighted by Pareto weights $(q_1, \ldots, q_N)$, with $\Sigma_i q_i = 1$. Thus, the objective function is defined as:

$$W_0 = \sum_{t=0}^{N} e^{-\delta t} \sum_{i=1}^{N} q_i E u(c_{it}). \tag{9.17}$$

Following the same path as in chapter 2, the critical internal rate of return of the safe project is characterized by the following rule:

$$r_t = \delta - \frac{1}{t} \ln \frac{\displaystyle\sum_{i=1}^{N} q_i E u'(c_{it})}{\displaystyle\sum_{i=1}^{N} q_i u'(c_{i0})}. \tag{9.18}$$

Consider the efficient discount rate that should be used by agent i if they alone bear the full costs and benefits of the project:

$$r_{it} = \delta - \frac{1}{t} \ln \frac{E u'(c_{it})}{u'(c_{i0})}. \tag{9.19}$$

Following Emmerling (2010), let us also define the inequality-neutral Pareto weights $(\hat{q}_1, \ldots, \hat{q}_N)$ such that:

$$\hat{q}_i = q_i \frac{u'(c_{i0})}{\displaystyle\sum_{j=1}^{N} q_j u'(c_{j0})}. \tag{9.20}$$

Using equation (9.18), it is then easy to check that the efficient discount rate r_t for an egalitarian cash flow at date t is linked to the individual discount rates $(r_{1t}, \ldots, r_{Nt})$ in the following way:

$$e^{-r_t t} = \sum_{i=1}^{N} \hat{q}_i e^{-r_{it} t}. \tag{9.21}$$

The efficient discount factor is a weighted mean of the individual discount factors. This is reminiscent of equation (6.4) that describes the term structure of efficient discount rates when there is a single representative agent with utility function u, but in which there is some uncertainty about the true stochastic process for the growth of per capita consumption. Equation (9.21) describes the efficient discount rate in an economy with a representative agent who faces a stochastic process c_{it} with probability $\hat{q}_i$, $i = 1, \ldots, N$. In this model, there is therefore a formal equivalence between the fact that different agents may face different destinies, and the fact that all agents face the same uncertain destiny. This equivalence is an illustration of John Rawls' concept of the veil of ignorance. It follows that the analysis in this section can be limited by referring to the results presented in chapter 6. For example, for distant time horizons, the efficient discount rate tends to the smallest individual long-term discount rate. The equivalence with the model of parametric uncertainty is perfect only when there is no inequality of consumption at date 0; otherwise the Pareto weights need to be biased.

To illustrate, consider a specification similar to that which was examined in chapter 6:

$$\begin{cases} c_{it+1} = c_{it} e^{x_{it}} \\ x_{i0}, x_{i1}, \ldots \text{ i.i.d.} \sim N(\mu_i, \sigma_i) \quad \forall i = 1, \ldots, N. \end{cases} \tag{9.22}$$

Under constant relative risk aversion γ, it implies that:

$$r_{it} = r_i = \delta + \gamma \mu_i - 0.5 \gamma^2 \sigma_i^2. \tag{9.23}$$

Combined with equation (9.21), this implies that the efficient discount rate r_t is decreasing and tends to the smallest r_i when t tends to infinity. Moreover, r_t satisfies the following property:

$$\lim_{t \to 0} r_t = \sum_{i=1}^{N} \hat{q}_i r_i. \tag{9.24}$$

The short-term discount rate is the weighted mean of the individual discount rates. The intuition is the same as in the framework of parametric uncertainty. For the very distant future, what really matters when evaluating a project is whether it can improve the welfare of the poorest agent. The true shape of the term structure depends upon the distorted Pareto weights $\hat{q}_i$, which depends upon our ethical values $(q_1, \ldots, q_N)$, the initial degree of inequality $(c_{10}, \ldots, c_{N0})$, and its correlation with the distribution of economic growth.

ECONOMIC CONVERGENCE AND THE DISCOUNT RATE

In order to have a more precise description of the term structure, it is necessary to specify the degree of convergence of economic development. Let us first consider an economy without any convergence, in which the current level of development of a country is uninformative about its future economic growth. More precisely, suppose that $\log c_{i0}$ is independent of the distribution of the growth rate x_{it}. Let X_{it} be the cumulative growth of log consumption between 0 and t. Under constant relative risk aversion γ, this implies that:

$$\frac{\sum_{i=1}^{N} q_i E u'(c_{it})}{\sum_{i=1}^{N} q_i u'(c_{i0})} = \frac{\sum_{i=1}^{N} q_i E \exp(-\gamma \ln c_{i0} - \gamma X_{it})}{\sum_{i=1}^{N} q_i \exp(-\gamma \ln c_{i0})}$$

$$= \frac{\left(\sum_{i=1}^{N} q_i \exp(-\gamma \ln c_{i0})\right)\left(\sum_{i=1}^{N} q_i E \exp(-\gamma X_{it})\right)}{\sum_{i=1}^{N} q_i \exp(-\gamma \ln c_{i0})}. \tag{9.25}$$

The second equality is a direct consequence of the no-convergence hypothesis. This implies in turn that:

$$r_t = \delta - \frac{1}{t} \ln \sum_{i=1}^{N} q_i E \exp(-\gamma X_{it}). \tag{9.26}$$

This means that the term structure of discount rates is independent of the initial distribution of wealth in this framework. Only the unequal expectation about future growth matters.

Let us now consider the case of economic convergence. An economy is characterized by its initial allocation of consumption $c_0 \sim (c_{10}, q_0; \ldots; c_{N0}, q_N)$

and by its individual expectations $X_t \sim (X_{1t}, q_1; \ldots; X_{Nt}, q_t)$. Following Gollier (2010), it can be said that economic convergence increases in this economy if the pair of random variables $(\ln c_0, X_t)$ becomes *less* concordant, as defined in chapter 8. Remember that this means that the new distribution of $(\ln c_0, X_t)$ is obtained from the initial one by a sequence of marginal-preserving *reductions* in concordance. In other words, for initially poor agents, growth prospects are FSD-improved, whereas they are FSD-deteriorated for the initially wealthy agents. Those transfers in probability are made in such a way that the unconditional distribution of growth is unchanged.

Lemma 2 in chapter 8 is useful for evaluating the impact of economic convergence on the efficient discount rate. Observe that the numerator in the right-hand side of equation (9.18) can be expressed as:

$$\sum_{i=1}^{N} q_i Eu'(c_{it}) = Eu'(c_0 e^{X_t}) = Eu'(\exp(\ln c_0 + X_t)). \qquad (9.27)$$

Lemma 2 in chapter 8 tells us that a reduction of concordance of $\ln c_0$ and X_t, that is an increase in economic convergence, reduces this numerator if and only if $h(x_1, x_2) = u'(\exp(x_1 + x_2))$ is supermodular. This is true if and only if relative prudence is uniformly larger than unity. Therefore, it can be concluded that economic convergence raises the efficient discount rate if relative prudence is larger than unity. This is the case, for example, with constant relative risk aversion, for which equation (9.26) underestimates the true discount rate for all time horizons. Symmetrically, economic divergence tends to reduce the discount rate. This is reminiscent of the idea that saving and investing are a substitute to the reduction of future risks.

To illustrate, consider a global economy with two equally populated countries. Country $i = 1$ has a GDP per capita at date 0 that is normalized to one. Country $i = 2$ has a GDP per capita at date 0 that is fifty times larger. Our ethical values impose $q_1 = q_2 = 1/2$. Suppose that, in economy A, the two countries converge, with country 1 enjoying a constant growth rate of 3%, whereas the growth rate of the wealthier country 2 is only 1%. These growth rates imply that the two countries will have the same per capita consumption level in just a bit less than two hundred years. Consider alternatively an economy B with the same initial distribution of consumption levels, $(c_{10}, c_{20}) = (1, 50)$, but the same uncertain growth rate for the two countries, which will be either 1% or 3% with equal probabilities. Clearly,

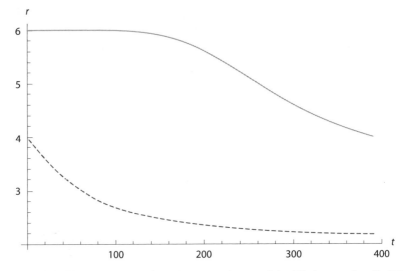

Figure 9.1. Term structure in a two-country model with $(c_{10}, c_{20}) = (1, 50)$ and $(x_{1t}, x_{2t}) = (3\%, 1\%)$. It is assumed that $\gamma = 2$ and $\delta = 0\%$. The dashed curve corresponds to the case where the two countries face an uncertain constant growth rate of either 1% or 3% with equal probabilities.

economy A exhibits more economic convergence than economy B, as defined. In figure 9.1, we have drawn the term structure of efficient discount rates in these two economies. As expected, the two curves are decreasing, and the discount rates are larger when there is convergence.

A SIMPLE CALIBRATION EXERCISE

What is known about economic convergence? The classical economic theory of economic growth provides an argument for it, since decreasing marginal productivity of capital implies that wealthier countries should grow at a smaller rate. Furthermore, poorer countries can replicate successful production methods, technologies, and institutions which were implemented earlier by more developed countries. However, in spite of the existence of some successful newly developed countries such as India, Singapore, South Korea, China, or Brazil, many poor countries seem to be permanently underdeveloped, whereas some others are becoming ever poorer (for example, Haïti and Zimbabwe). According to Clark (2007), the industrial revolution has reduced inequalities within societies, but it has increased them between societies. This process has been labeled "the Great Divergence" (Pomeranz 2000).

Accepting that history is full of periods of global divergence, in contrast the last forty years have been characterized by a global convergence between countries. In the following calibration exercise, the focus is on estimating the level of convergence during the period 1969 to 2009. The calibration examined in Gollier (2010) is based on the ERS International Macroeconomic data set that gives us estimation of the GDP per capita for 190 countries during this period. A set of thirteen regions that are relatively homogenous in size and in socioeconomic structure were defined because of the extremely large heterogeneity of the 190 country sizes. This data set is summarized in table 9.1 and figure 9.2.

Let us first assume that there is no economic convergence. Under the assumption of constant absolute risk aversion, we know that the initial

TABLE 9.1.
Global economic convergence during the period 1969–2009

Region	Population 2009	GDP/cap 1969	GDP/cap 2009	Annualized growth rate
North America	340 699 331	20 745	41 213	1,72%
Latin America	585 675 448	2 841	5 242	1,53%
EU15	387 805 629	15 834	33 410	1,87%
EU27- EU15	103 777 223	3 452	9 053	2,41%
Former Soviet Union	276 203 629	2 773	4 302	1,10%
China	1 338 612 968	128	2 494	7,43%
Japan	127 078 679	13 466	32 818	2,23%
Southeast Asia	593 051 249	454	1 829	3,48%
South Asia	1 566 502 232	247	814	2,98%
Oceania	36 460 398	14 075	24 662	1,40%
Middle East	279 897 739	3 319	5 415	1,22%
North Africa	161 140 693	1 013	2 359	2,11%
Sub-Saharan Africa	828 412 224	1 030	997	−0,08%

Source: ERS International Macroeconomic data set

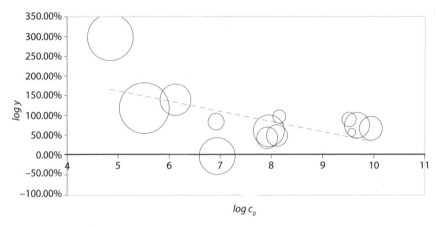

Figure 9.2. Global economic convergence over the period 1969–2009. c_0 is the GDP/cap in 1969 (expressed in USD of 2005), and $X = \ln y$ is the total growth rate over the period. The surface of the circle is proportional to the population size in 2009. Source: ERS International Macroeconomic data set.

inequalities do not matter for the determination of the discount rate. Equation (9.26) can therefore be used, which is rewritten as:

$$r_t = \delta - \frac{1}{t}\ln E\exp(-\gamma X_t). \qquad (9.28)$$

The regional data set previouslydescribed yields $\mu = E\ln X_t = 0.9047$ and $\sigma^2 = Var\ln X_t = 0.5128$. Assuming that $\ln X_t$ is normally distributed, $\gamma = 2$ and $\delta = 0$, lemma 1 implies that:

$$r_{40} = \delta + \gamma\frac{\mu}{40} - 0.5\gamma^2\frac{\sigma^2}{40} = 2\times 2.26\% - 2\times 1.28\% = 1.96\%. \quad (9.29)$$

It is notable that this calibration, based on a comparison of the growth rates of thirteen regions during the same period, generates a much smaller discount rate than the 3.6% obtained in chapter 3 using the growth rate of the U.S. economy throughout the twentieth century. This is because the annualized standard deviation of growth rates is much larger in the cross-section data (11.3%) than in the time-series data of the U.S. economy (3.6%). The precautionary effect is therefore much larger.

Let us now recognize that economic growth rates across regions are not independent. The degree of economic convergence is estimated through the following simple regression:

$$X_t = 2.89 - 0.26 \ln c_0 + \varepsilon. \tag{9.30}$$

The t-statistic of the slope coefficient β equals -2.41, so that it is significantly different from 0. The R^2 of the regression is 0.35. Therefore, economies are converging. Notice that this is mostly due to the extraordinary growth rates observed in China and India in the last two decades.

These numbers can be plugged into equation (9.18), weighting countries by their population in 2009. It follows that:

$$r_{40} = \delta - \frac{1}{40} \ln \frac{(E \exp(-\gamma(2.89 + \varepsilon))) \sum_{i=1}^{13} q_i c_i^{-\gamma(1+\beta)}}{\sum_{i=1}^{13} q_i c_i^{-\gamma}}, \tag{9.31}$$

where c_i is the GDP per capita of region i in 2009, and $\beta = -0.26$. Using lemma 1 with the fact that the variance of the residuals in (9.30) is $Var\varepsilon = 0.31$ gives $r_{40} = 4.06\%$. The effect of economic convergence, which is positive as expected, is surprisingly large.

SUMMARY OF MAIN RESULTS

1. The (extended) Ramsey rule is based on the assumption of the existence of a representative agent. This is a meaningful assumption if the heterogeneity of preferences and of incomes is limited. Alternatively, we have shown that there exists a representative agent if risks and credit are efficiently allocated in the economy.
2. Under the assumption of an efficient risk and credit allocation, inequilities are irrelevant for the discount rate if relative risk aversion is constant. In the absence of risk on growth, the impact of inequalities on the discount rate depends upon whether absolute prudence is concave or convex in consumption.
3. Because of agency problem, global long-term risks are not efficiently shared. Behind the veil of ignorance, inequalities in the

growth of individual consumption play a role equivalent to parametric uncertainty, as examined in chapter 6.

4. Behind the veil of ignorance, economic convergence reduces the long-term risk on consumption, thereby raising the long discount rate under prudence.

REFERENCES

Clark, G. (2007), *A Farewell to Alms: A Brief History of the World*, Princeton: Princeton University Press.

Emmerling, J. (2010), Discounting and intergenerational equity, mimeo, Toulouse School of Economics.

Gollier, C. (2001), Wealth inequality and asset pricing, *Review of Economic Studies*, 68, 181–203.

Gollier, C. (2010), Discounting, inequalities and economic convergence, mimeo, Toulouse School of Economics.

Gollier, C., and R. J. Zeckhauser (2005), Aggregation of heterogeneous time preferences, *Journal of Political Economy*, 113, 878–898.

Pomeranz, K. (2000), *The Great Divergence: China, Europe, and the Making of the Modern World Economy*, Princeton: Princeton University Press.

Wilson, R. (1968), The theory of syndicates, *Econometrica*, 36, 113–132.

10

———◀◯▶———

Discounting Non-monetary Benefits

Environmentalists are often quite skeptical about using standard cost-benefit analysis to shape environmental policies because environmental damages incurred in the distant future are claimed to receive insufficient weight in the economic evaluation. From their viewpoint this may be caused either because future environmental assets are undervalued, or because the economic discount rate is too large. In this chapter, we address these two questions together by defining an ecological discount rate compatible with social welfare when the representative agent cares about both the economic and ecological environments faced by future generations. This ecological rate at which future environmental damages are discounted may be much smaller than the economic rate at which economic damages are discounted, because of the integration of a potentially increasing willingness to pay for the environment into the ecological discount rate. This increased interest in environmental assets is modeled in this chapter by the potential for increased scarcity of these assets, which drives their value upward through time. We show that the uncertainties surrounding the future evolution of environmental quality and the economy tend to reduce the discount rates, in particular if they are positively correlated.

The determinants of human happiness, or utility, are many and varied. They include the consumption of goods and services, the quality of the environment, health, life expectancy, and social status. Up to this point in the book, the analysis has been simplified by assuming that utility is derived from a univariate variable that was referred to as consumption, or income. This approach relies on the notion of an *indirect* utility function, which characterizes the maximum utility that can be extracted from a given income. The function assumes that individuals select the optimal bundle of the determinants of their utility level given their budget constraint.

It must be recognized, however, that the indirect utility function approach is often unsatisfactory for at least two reasons. First, many of the determinants of utility are not tradable market goods. This category includes, for example, various environmental assets and health. Second, the indirect utility function depends upon the vector of prices of the tradable goods and services whose prices fluctuate over time because of changes in their relative scarcity. Therefore, the indirect utility function also changes over time. Think for example of the relative price of oil, of land, of masterpieces of art, or more prosaically of the services of a plumber. When valuing a project that generates multidimensional impacts scattered over a long time span, it is crucial to take into account these transformations of the indirect utility function, and the changing relative value of the project's impacts.

The main economic justification for discounting is based on the wealth effect. If one believes that future generations will be wealthier than we are, one more unit of consumption is more valuable to us than to them. This is because of decreasing marginal utility of consumption. However, a large proportion of the impacts of our actions, for example the emission of greenhouse gases, affect the quality of the environment for future generations rather than their level of consumption. The environmental impacts may take the form of increased temperatures, reduced biodiversity, or the destruction of environmental assets such as forests. In this chapter, the question of how to discount future changes in the quality of the environment is addressed. If it is believed that the environment is deteriorating over time, and if it is assumed that the marginal utility of environmental quality is decreasing, then improvements to environmental quality is more valuable to future generations than to us. This argument, which is symmetric to the Ramsey wealth effect, supports the use of a smaller discount rate for changes in the environment than for changes in consumption. The full characterization of this "ecological" discount rate should also take into account the potential substitutability between environmental assets and consumption, and the uncertainty that affects the dynamics of consumption and environmental quality. This chapter is based on Gollier (2010).

This analysis can be applied to other attributes of social welfare. For example, the evaluation of health and safety policies must take account of the impacts on lives saved and improved quality of life. Should we value them differently as a function of the time at which they occur? Cropper, Aydede, and Portney (1994) used a survey of 3,000 respondents to show that people attach less importance to saving life in the future than to saving life today. Discounting human lives is an important issue, discussed, for example, by Cropper and Portney (1990) and Cropper, Hammitt, and Robinson (2011).

TWO METHODS TO EVALUATE FUTURE NON-FINANCIAL BENEFITS

There are two possible methods to evaluate the present monetary value of a certain environmental impact which will occur in the future. The classical method consists of first measuring the future monetary value of the impact, and second discounting this monetary value back to the present. This involves a pricing formula to value future changes in environmental quality, and an economic discount rate to discount these monetarized impacts. The problem of discounting monetary flows is the core of the first three parts of this book.

The second approach, first suggested by Malinvaud (1953), consists in first discounting the future environmental impact to transform it into an equivalent environmental impact happening in the present, and then measuring the monetary value of this immediate impact. This involves an ecological discount rate, to discount environmental impacts. Of course, these two methods are strictly equivalent. However, in the case of certainty, the two discount rates (economic and ecological) differ if the monetary value of environmental assets evolves over time. This has been shown by Guesnerie (2004), Weikard and Zhu (2005), and Hoel and Sterner (2007).

The classical method, using a monetary discount factor, is not well adapted to dealing with uncertainty. Indeed, the value of environmental assets in the future depends upon the evolution of their relative scarcity, which is unknown. As a result, for any particular project, there is uncertainty over the monetary value of its environmental impacts. This is a problem because the economic discount rate is used to discount *sure* future monetary benefits. It is therefore necessary to compute a certainty equivalent value.

This requires the use of a stochastic discount factor, which determines at the same time the risk premium and the economic discount rate. Standard pricing formulas exist that can be borrowed from the theory of finance, but they are seldom used in cost-benefit analyses of environmental projects because of their complexity. In this chapter, we describe in detail the alternative method based on the ecological discount rate. The ecological discount factor associated with date t is the number of units of immediate sure environmental impact that has the same effect on intergenerational welfare as a unit of environmental impact at date t. The (shadow) price of an immediate environmental impact can then be used to value environmental projects. This alternative method is simpler because it is not necessary to compute certainty equivalent future values.

A SIMPLE MODEL OF THE ECOLOGICAL DISCOUNT RATE

To keep the notation simple, it is assumed that the representative agent's felicity is affected by two determinants or "goods," available in quantities (c_{1t}, c_{2t}) at date t. It is conceptually straightforward, though it makes heavy demands on notation, to extend this model to more than two dimensions. Determinant 1 is hereafter assumed to be an aggregated consumption good, whereas c_{2t} is an index of the quality of the environment, which includes, for example, how hospitable the climate is, the "use" and "non-use" values of biodiversity, the impact on human morbidity of various pollutants, and life expectancy. The felicity at any date t is a function, U, of the available quantities (c_{1t}, c_{2t}) of the two goods. U is assumed to be increasing and concave. The intertemporal social welfare is measured by the discounted value of the flow of temporal expected felicity:

$$W = \sum_{t=0}^{\infty} e^{-\delta t} EU(c_{1t}, c_{2t}). \qquad (10.1)$$

The expectation is linked to the fact that, seen from date 0, the future evolution of the availability of the consumption good and of the quality of the environment is uncertain.

The economic discount rate is examined first. Let us consider a simple marginal project that would reduce consumption by $\varepsilon \exp(-r_t t)$ today, and that would raise consumption by a sure amount ε at date t, leaving the environment unaffected by the action. The internal rate of return r_t that is such that implementing the project has no effect on W at the margin is called the "*economic* discount rate," and is denoted r_{1t}:

$$r_{1t} = \delta - \frac{1}{t} \ln \frac{EU_1(c_{1t}, c_{2t})}{U_1(c_{10}, c_{20})},\qquad(10.2)$$

where $U_i(c_1, c_2)$ is the partial derivative of U with respect to c_i. This economic discount rate allows the value of different consumption increments at different dates to be compared.

Consider alternatively an investment project that increases the environmental quality by ε at date t. The standard way to include this environmental impact in the cost-benefit analysis would be to first express this impact in future monetary terms. The instantaneous value v_t of the environment at date t is measured by the marginal rate of substitution between consumption and the environment:

$$v_t = -\frac{dc_{1t}}{dc_{2t}}\bigg|_U = \frac{U_2(c_{1t}, c_{2t})}{U_1(c_{1t}, c_{2t})}.\qquad(10.3)$$

If the quality of the environment was tradable, v_t would be its equilibrium price, taking the aggregate consumption good as the numeraire. More generally, v_t is the instantaneous willingness to pay for a one-unit improvement in environmental quality. Its evolution over time is uncertain, so that seen from $t=0$, v_t is a random variable, as is the future monetary benefit εv_t of the sure improvement in environmental quality. This implies that in spite of the fact that an investment project with a sure ecological benefit is being considered, its monetary benefit is uncertain. Up to now, this book has focused on the valuation of sure cash flows; extending the analysis to the valuation of uncertain projects will be carried out later in this book.

A much simpler approach is to define an ecological discount rate. Consider a marginal project that would increase environmental quality by a sure amount ε at date t, but would reduce the environmental quality by $\varepsilon \exp(-rt)$ today. Implementing this project would be socially efficient if

$$r \geq r_{2t} = \delta - \frac{1}{t} \ln \frac{EU_2(c_{1t}, c_{2t})}{U_2(c_{10}, c_{20})}.\qquad(10.4)$$

This equation defines the *ecological* discount rate r_{2t} for the time horizon t. It allows the comparison of sure changes in environmental quality at different dates. In particular, an increase in environmental quality by ε at date t has an effect on intertemporal welfare that is equivalent to an increase in current environmental quality by $\varepsilon \exp(-r_{2t}t)$. In monetary terms, this is equal to $v_0 \varepsilon \exp(-r_{2t}t)$, where v_0 is the current value of one unit of environmental quality.

To sum up, the benefit of a unit increment in environmental quality at date t should be accounted for in the evaluation of a project as equivalent to an immediate increase in consumption by $v_0 \varepsilon \exp(-r_{2t}t)$. This really means that environmental costs and benefits should be discounted at the ecological rate r_{2t}, which does not have to be the same as the economic discount rate r_{1t}. The potential discrepancy between the economic discount rate and the ecological discount rate takes into account the stochastic changes in the relative social valuation of the environment.

DETERMINANTS OF THE ECOLOGICAL DISCOUNT RATE

In this section, we examine the determinants of the rate r_{2t} with which a sure increase in environmental quality at date t should be discounted. It is characterized by equation (10.4). Let us first focus on the role of the level of c_{2t} and the uncertainty surrounding it. A better environmental quality in the future raises the ecological discount rate, ceteris paribus, because U is concave in c_2. This effect is symmetric to the wealth effect presented in chapter 2. One is ready to sacrifice less today if the future quality of the environment is larger because of the decreasing marginal utility of environmental quality. This is referred to as "the ecological growth effect."

If it is assumed that U_2 is convex in c_2, then the uncertainty surrounding c_{2t} reduces the ecological discount rate. This effect, referred to as the "ecological prudence effect," is analogous to the precautionary effect for monetary cash flows described in chapter 3. The basic idea is that one should do more to improve future environmental quality if it is more uncertain.

It is also necessary to take into account changes in GDP per capita, c_{1t}, on the level of the ecological discount rate. Suppose for example that the two goods are substitutes, which requires that the marginal utility of c_2 is decreasing in c_1. In other words, suppose that U_{12} is negative. Then, an increase in the GDP per capita at date t reduces the marginal utility of environmental quality at that date. Therefore, it raises the ecological discount rate. This is referred to as "the substitution effect."

One difficulty is to determine whether consumption and the environment are substitutes ($U_{12} \leq 0$) or complements ($U_{12} \geq 0$). Fortunately, there is a simple way to answer this question. Consider an arbitrary situation characterized by (c_1, c_2), an arbitrary reduction in consumption $l_1 > 0$, and an arbitrary reduction in environmental quality $l_2 > 0$. Consider two lotteries. Lottery A is a fifty-fifty chance of facing the monetary loss or the environmental loss. Lottery B is a fifty-fifty chance of facing the two losses simultaneously, or to lose nothing. If one prefers A to B, it must be that U_{12} is negative. Indeed, it means that:

$$\frac{1}{2} U(c_1 - l_1, c_2) + \frac{1}{2} U(c_1, c_2 - l_2) \geq \frac{1}{2} U(c_1 - l_1, c_2 - l_2) + \frac{1}{2} U(c_1, c_2), \quad (10.5)$$

which is equivalent to:

$$\int_{c_2 - l_2}^{c_2} U_2(c_1 - l_1, y) \, dy \geq \int_{c_2 - l_2}^{c_2} U_2(c_1, y) \, dy. \quad (10.6)$$

This requires that U_{12} is negative, or U is supermodular. Richard (1975), Epstein and Tanny (1980), Bommier (2007), and Eeckhoudt, Rey, and Schlesinger (2007) analyze this idea of "correlation aversion," which is another way to say that the two goods are substitutes.

A more complex problem is to evaluate the effect of uncertainty about economic growth on the ecological discount rate. Obviously, a zero-mean risk on c_{1t} raises $EU_2(c_{1t}, c_{2t})$ if U_2 is convex in its first argument. This effect is referred to as the "cross-prudence in consumption" effect. In order to evaluate whether condition $U_{211} \geq 0$ is reasonable, the approach of Eeckhoudt et al. (2007) can be followed. They use a multidimensional version of equation (3.12), and again consider an arbitrary initial situation (c_1, c_2), an arbitrary zero-mean risk in consumption ε_1, and an arbitrary reduction in environmental quality $l_2 > 0$. Consider two lotteries. Lottery A is a fifty-fifty chance to face the monetary risk or the environmental loss. Lottery B is a fifty-fifty chance to face the monetary risk and the environmental loss simultaneously, or to lose nothing. If one prefers A to B, it must be that U_{211} is positive. Indeed, this preference implies that:

$$\frac{1}{2}EU(c_1 + \varepsilon_1, c_2) + \frac{1}{2}U(c_1, c_2 - l_2) \geq \frac{1}{2}EU(c_1 + \varepsilon_1, c_2 - l_2)$$
$$+ \frac{1}{2}U(c_1, c_2),$$

(10.7)

which is equivalent to:

$$\int_{c_2 - l_2}^{c_2} EU_2(c_1 + \varepsilon_1, y)\,dy \geq \int_{c_2 - l_2}^{c_2} U_2(c_1, y)\,dy.$$

(10.8)

This requires that U_2 is convex in c_1. The preference of lottery A over lottery B provides an economic justification to reduce the ecological discount rate when the economic growth rate becomes more uncertain.

Finally, the existence of a positive correlation between economic growth and improvement in environmental quality provides a last determinant of the ecological discount rate. As many readers may now anticipate, this is formalized by a positive statistical dependence of (c_1, c_2) through the notion of an increase in concordance. Using lemma 2 of chapter 8, an increase in concordance raises $EU_2(c_1, c_2)$ if and only if U_2 is supermodular, that is, if U_{221} is positive. By symmetry to the notion of cross-prudence in consumption, this means that the representative agent is cross-prudent toward the environment. They prefer a lottery with a fifty-fifty chance to face either a sure monetary loss or a zero-mean environmental risk in isolation rather than a lottery with a fifty-fifty chance of facing both together or facing no risk at all. Under this assumption, the existence of a positive correlation in the economic and ecological growth rates raises $EU_2(c_1, c_2)$, thereby reducing the efficient ecological discount rate. Intuitively, one wants to do more for the future when the economic and ecological risks are positively correlated than when they are independent. This is the "correlation effect."

In this section, we assumed the sign of the cross-derivatives of the utility function to guarantee that the representative agent always prefers to incur one of the two harms for certain, with the only uncertainty being about which one will be received, as opposed to a 50-50 gamble of receiving the two harms simultaneously, or receiving neither. Following a terminology introduced by Eeckhoudt and Schlesinger (2006), pairs of harms are "mutually aggravating."

Under this set of assumptions on U, the following factors raise the ecological discount rate:

- An increase in future environmental quality;
- An increase in future GDP per capita.

On the contrary, the following factors reduce it:

- An increase in the uncertainty affecting future environmental quality;
- An increase in the uncertainty affecting the future GDP per capita; and
- An increase in the correlation in the two risks.

A symmetric analysis can be made for the determinants of the economic discount rate r_{1t}.

AN ANALYTICAL SOLUTION

The integral $EU_2(c_{1t}, c_{2t})$ has an analytical solution in the special case of a bivariate geometric Brownian motion for (c_{1t}, c_{2t}) and a Cobb–Douglas utility function. Suppose that

$$U(c_1, c_2) = kc_1^{1-\gamma_1} c_2^{1-\gamma_2} \tag{10.9}$$

in the domain $(c_1, c_2) \in \mathbb{R}^{+2}$. We suppose that

$$k = sign(1 - \gamma_1) = sign(1 - \gamma_2) \tag{10.10}$$

in order to guarantee that U is increasing in its two arguments. The concavity of U with respect to its two arguments requires that γ_1 and γ_2 are positive. If they are both larger than unity, it is easy to check that this utility function satisfies the assumptions made in the previous section that pairs of harms are "mutually aggravating," that the two goods are substitutes, and that the agent is (cross-)prudent in consumption and in environmental quality:

$$U_{12} < 0; \ U_{222} > 0; \ U_{122} > 0; \ U_{112} > 0; \ U_{111} > 0. \qquad (10.11)$$

In the same way as the benchmark univariate model presented in chapter 3, let us assume that $(\ln c_{1t}, \ln c_{2t})$ is normally distributed with mean $(\ln c_{10} + \mu_1 t, \ln c_{20} + \mu_2 t)$ and variance-covariance matrix $\Sigma = (\sigma_{ij} t)_{i,j=1,2}$. We have that:

$$EU_2(c_{1t}, c_{2t}) = k(1 - \gamma_2) E \exp(z_t), \qquad (10.12)$$

where $z_t = (1 - \gamma_1) \ln c_{1t} - \gamma_2 \ln c_{2t}$ is normally distributed with mean:

$$Ez_t = (1 - \gamma_1)(\ln c_{10} + \mu_1 t) - \gamma_2 (\ln c_{20} + \mu_2 t), \qquad (10.13)$$

and variance:

$$Var(z_t) = ((1 - \gamma_1)^2 \sigma_{11} + \gamma_2^2 \sigma_{22} - 2(1 - \gamma_1)\gamma_2 \sigma_{12})t. \qquad (10.14)$$

Using lemma 1 yields:

$$\frac{EU_2(c_{1t}, c_{2t})}{U_2(c_{10}, c_{20})} = \exp((1 - \gamma_1)\mu_1 - \gamma_2 \mu_2 + 0.5((1 - \gamma_1)^2 \sigma_{11}$$
$$+ \gamma_2^2 \sigma_{22} - 2(1 - \gamma_1)\gamma_2 \sigma_{12}))t. \qquad (10.15)$$

By equation (10.4), we obtain that:

$$r_{2t} = \delta + \gamma_2 \mu_2 - 0.5\gamma_2^2 \sigma_{22} - (1 - \gamma_1)\mu_1 - 0.5(1 - \gamma_1)^2 \sigma_{11}$$
$$+ (1 - \gamma_1)\gamma_2 \sigma_{12}. \qquad (10.16)$$

Finally, let $g_i = t^{-1} \ln(Ec_{it}/c_{i0}) = \mu_i + 0.5\sigma_{ii}$ be the growth rate of Ec_{it}. Equation (10.16) can thus be rewritten as:

$$r_{2t} = \delta + \gamma_2 g_2 - 0.5\gamma_2(\gamma_2 + 1)\sigma_{22} + (\gamma_1 - 1)g_1$$
$$- 0.5\gamma_1(\gamma_1 - 1)\sigma_{11} - (\gamma_1 - 1)\gamma_2 \sigma_{12}. \qquad (10.17)$$

The term structure of the ecological discount rate is flat. In such an economy, the random evolution of aggregate consumption and environmental quality does not justify the use of a smaller discount rate for benefits occurring in a more distant future.

In addition to the rate of pure time preference, the five determinants of the ecological discount rate that were described in the previous section can be recognized in the right-hand side of equality (10.17):

- $\gamma_2 g_2$ is the positive ecological growth effect, assuming an improving environmental quality;
- $-0.5\gamma_2(\gamma_2+1)\sigma_{22}$ is the negative ecological prudence effect;
- $(\gamma_1-1)g_1$ is the positive substitution effect, assuming a growing economy;
- $-0.5\gamma_1(\gamma_1-1)\sigma_{11}$ is the negative cross-prudence in consumption effect;
- $-(\gamma_1-1)\gamma_2\sigma_{12}$ is the negative correlation effect, assuming a positive correlation between the economic and ecological growth rates.

Symmetrically, we can compute the economic discount rate:

$$r_{1t} = \delta + \gamma_1 g_1 - 0.5\gamma_1(\gamma_1 + 1)\sigma_{11}$$
$$+ (\gamma_2 - 1)g_2 - 0.5\gamma_2(\gamma_2 - 1)\sigma_{22} - (\gamma_2 - 1)\gamma_1\sigma_{12}. \tag{10.18}$$

We can also determine the difference between the two discount rates:

$$r_{2t} - r_{1t} = g_2 - g_1 + (\gamma_1\sigma_{11} - \gamma_2\sigma_{22}) + (\gamma_2 - \gamma_1)\sigma_{12}. \tag{10.19}$$

Interestingly, under certainty, the difference between the two discount rates is independent of the parameters of the Cobb–Douglas utility function. This equation provides two arguments in favor of using an ecological discount rate that is smaller than the economic discount rate. First, it is often suggested that the growth rate for environmental quality is smaller than the economic growth rate ($g_2 < g_1$). Indeed, g_2 is potentially negative. Second, it seems that there is more uncertainty surrounding the evolution of environmental quality than the evolution of the economy itself ($\sigma_{22} > \sigma_{11}$). If the degrees of aversion to risk on c_1 and on c_2 are not too heterogeneous, this implies that ($\gamma_1\sigma_{11} - \gamma_2\sigma_{22}$) is negative. The last term on the right-hand side of equation (10.19) is more difficult to sign.

A CALIBRATION EXERCISE

Because of the lack of time-series data about environmental quality, calibrating the previous specification is problematic. Various authors have argued in favor of a closer link between environmental quality and economic growth. Following this idea, let us make the alternative assumption that the environmental quality is a deterministic function of economic achievement: $c_{2t} = f(c_{1t})$. Common wisdom suggests that environmental quality is a decreasing function of GDP per capita, but this is heavily debated in scientific circles. The environmental Kuznets curve hypothesis speculates that the relationship between per capita income and environmental quality has an inverted U-shape, but there is no consensus about the validity of this hypothesis (see for example Millimet, List, and Stengos 2003). From now on it is hypothesized that there is a monotone relationship by assuming that there exists $\rho \in \mathbb{R}$ such that $c_{2t} = kc_{1t}^{\rho}$, where ρ can be either positive or negative. If we assume that c_{1t} follows a geometric Brownian motion, c_{2t} also follows a geometric Brownian motion, so that an analytical solution for the discount rates can be obtained. Using the standard trick of lemma 1, it follows that:

$$r_{2t} = \delta + (\rho\gamma_2 + \gamma_1 - 1)(g_1 - 0.5(\rho\gamma_2 + \gamma_1)\sigma_{11}), \qquad (10.20)$$

and:

$$r_{1t} = \delta + (\gamma_1 + \rho(\gamma_2 - 1))(g_1 - 0.5(1 + \gamma_1 + \rho(\gamma_2 - 1))\sigma_{11}). \quad (10.21)$$

The interested reader can recover from these equations the different determinants of these two rates that were discussed earlier in the chapter.

In order to calibrate this model, let us assume that the rate of pure preference for the present δ is zero. It is also assumed, as before, that the relative aversion to risk on consumption is a constant $\gamma_1 = 2$. The parameter γ_2 for aversion to environmental risk is not easy to calibrate. Observe, however, that, if it were a tradable good, the share of total consumption expenditures that would be made up of expenditures on environmental quality is:

$$\gamma^* = \frac{\gamma_2 - 1}{\gamma_1 + \gamma_2 - 2}. \qquad (10.22)$$

Hoel and Sterner (2007) and Sterner and Persson (2008) suggested γ^* somewhere between 10% and 50%, which implies that γ_2 should be somewhere between 1.1 and 2 under our specification. We hereafter assume $\gamma^* = 0.3$, which implies that $\gamma_2 = 1.4$. Suppose also that $g_1 = 2\%$, and $\sqrt{\sigma_{11}} = 3.6\%$.

The last parameter to calibrate is the elasticity ρ of environmental quality to changes in GDP per capita. The calibration depends upon how environmental quality is defined. In order to estimate ρ, the SYS_LAN indicator contained in the Environmental Sustainability Index (ESI2005, Yale Center for Environmental Law and Policy 2005) has been used. It measures, for 146 countries in 2005, the percentage of total land area (including inland waters) having very high anthropogenic impact. Let c_1 be the 2005 GDP per capita from the World Economic Outlook Database of IMF (April 2008), and c_2 be defined as $3 + SYS\_LAN$ from ESI2005. In figure 10.1, we have represented this database and the associated OLS regression line, which is

$$\ln c_2 = 1.93 - 0.10 \ln c_1 + \varepsilon. \tag{10.23}$$

The *t-statistic* for the slope-coefficient is -4.69, whereas the $R2$ coefficient equals 0.13. Plugging $\rho = -0.10$ in equations (10.20) and (10.21) yields

$$r_{2t} = 1.6\% \quad \text{and} \quad r_{1t} = 3.5\%. \tag{10.24}$$

It is useful to provide a few comments on this result. First, the difference between the ecological rate and the economic rate comes mostly from the large expected economic growth rate $(g_1 = 2\%)$ compared to the expected environmental growth rate $(g_2 = \rho g_1 = -0.2\%)$. Second, the level of the

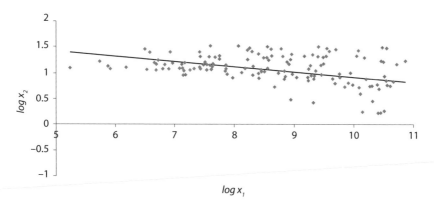

Figure 10.1. OLS regression using a panel of 146 countries in 2005, with c_1 being the GDP/cap (World Economic Outlook Database of IMF), and $c_2 = 3 + SYS\_LAN$ (Environmental Sustainability Index 2005).

ecological discount rate is mostly determined by the substitution effect. Because ρ is small in absolute value, the (negative) ecological growth effect $\gamma_2 \rho g_1 = -0.28\%$ is also small, particularly in comparison to the substitution effect $(\gamma_1 - 1)g_1 = 2\%$. Third, the effect of uncertainty (prudence, cross-prudence, and correlation effects) is marginal because of the low volatility of c_1 and c_2, and because it is assumed that shocks are not serially correlated. Finally, a comparison should be made between the economic discount rate obtained here and the one that was estimated at around 3.6% in chapter 3 (in the absence of separate treatment of environmental quality). Diminishing expectations about the quality of the environment and the associated substitution effect, $(\gamma_2 - 1)\rho g_1 = -0.08\%$, explains most of the discrepancy between the benchmark 3.6% and the 3.5% obtained here.

EXTENSION TO PARAMETRIC UNCERTAINTY

In the previous two specifications of the bivariate model, a geometric Brownian motion with known parameters was heavily relied upon. Without surprise, flat term structures were obtained under this framework. One easy extension can be made by recognizing that some of the parameters governing the stochastic economic and ecological growth are uncertain. Consider for example the model that we calibrated in the previous section, and suppose that the parameters (g_1, σ_{11}, ρ) depend upon a variable θ that is not known with certainty. Suppose as in chapter 6 that θ can take integer values 1 to n, respectively, with probabilities $q_1, \ldots, q_n$. Then, as before, it is easy to derive from equation (10.4) that

$$e^{-r_2 t} = \sum_{\theta=1}^{n} q_\theta e^{-r_2(\theta)t}, \tag{10.25}$$

where $r_2(\theta)$ is the ecological discount rate that would prevail if the true value of the unknown parameter would be θ, i.e.,

$$r_2(\theta) = \delta + (\rho(\theta)\gamma_2 + \gamma_1 - 1)(g_1(\theta) - 0.5(\rho(\theta)\gamma_2 + \gamma_1)\sigma_{11}(\theta)). \tag{10.26}$$

The reader is now accustomed to the fact that this model yields a decreasing term structure that converges to the smallest $r_2(\theta)$. A symmetric result holds for the economic discount rate.

Suppose for example that g_1 and σ_{11} are known, but the elasticity ρ of environmental quality to changes in GDP is not. Rather than assuming that $\rho = -0.1$, as was estimated in the previous section (with a small $R2$ for the OLS estimation), let us suppose that ρ is either -0.6 or $+0.4$ with equal probabilities. All other parameters remain unchanged compared to the previous section. We draw the term structure of r_{1t} and r_{2t} in the next figure. Since the economic growth follows a Brownian motion, the economic discount rate is almost independent of the time horizon. It reduces to a lower rate of 3.2% for distant cash flows, which would be the efficient economic discount rate if the elasticity ρ was -0.6. In that case, the negative substitution effect would be stronger than in the benchmark case with $\rho = -0.1$. The ecological discount rate goes from 1.6% to 0.3% when t goes from 0 to infinity, as shown in figure 10.2. The high uncertainty affecting the long-term evolution of the environment in this specification explains why the term structure of the ecological discount rate is decreasing. Another way to interpret this result is obtained by examining the worst-case scenario. In the case in which ρ would be -0.6, the large economic growth rate would have

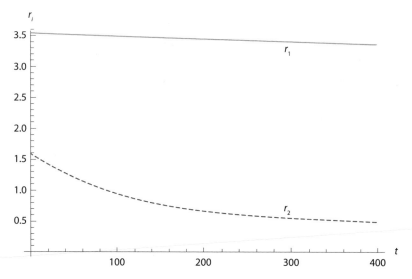

Figure 10.2. The economic and ecological discount rates with $U(c_1, c_2) = -c_1^{-1} c_2^{-0.4}$, $\delta = 0\%$, $g_1 = 2\%$, $\sqrt{\sigma_{11}} = 3.6\%$ and $c_{2t} = c_{1t}$ with $\rho \sim (-0.6, 1.2; 0.4, 1/2)$.

a strong negative impact on the quality of the environment. This would generate a strong negative ecological growth effect, $\gamma_2 \rho g_1 = -1.68\%$, which offsets most of the substitution effect $(\gamma_1 - 1)g_1 = 2\%$.

CES UTILITY FUNCTIONS

Guesnerie (2004), Hoel and Sterner (2007), Sterner and Persson (2008), and Traeger (2007) consider the case of certainty, which implies that the only determinants at play for the ecological discount rate are the ecological growth effect and the substitution effect. In exchange for this simplification, they examined a family of utility functions that are more general than the Cobb–Douglas specification. In particular, they assumed that U has constant elasticity of substitution $\sigma > 0$:

$$U(c_1,c_2) = \frac{y^{1-\alpha}}{1-\alpha} \text{ with } y = \left[(1-\gamma)c_1^{\frac{\sigma-1}{\sigma}} + \gamma c_2^{\frac{\sigma-1}{\sigma}} \right]^{\frac{\sigma}{\sigma-1}}, \quad (10.27)$$

where $\alpha > 0$ is relative aversion toward the risk on "aggregate good" y, and $\gamma \in [0,1]$ is a preference weight in favor of the environment. Parameter σ is the percentage rate at which the demand for c_2 declines when the relative price of c_2 is increased by 1%. When σ tends to unity, y tends to $c_1^{1-\gamma}c_2^{\gamma}$, so that the Cobb–Douglas specification is obtained as a special case. When $\sigma \neq 1$, the additive nature in y implies that it can never be lognormally distributed, thereby prohibiting the possibility of finding an analytical solution under uncertainty. We have that

$$U_2(c_1,c_2) = \gamma y^{\frac{1}{\sigma}-\alpha} c_2^{-\frac{1}{\sigma}}. \quad (10.28)$$

It can be checked that the two goods are substitutes if $\alpha\sigma - 1$ is positive. Under this condition, an increase in economic growth raises the ecological discount rate. Under the same condition, U_{22} is negative, so that an anticipated deterioration in the quality of the environment reduces the ecological discount rate. To make this more explicit, suppose that growth rates are constant, which means that $c_{it} = \exp(g_i t)$. The following equation is a direct rewriting of equation (10.4) under this specification:

$$r_{2t} = \delta + \frac{g_2}{\sigma} + \left(\alpha - \frac{1}{\sigma} \right)G(t), \quad (10.29)$$

with:

$$G(t) = \frac{\sigma}{\sigma - 1} \frac{1}{t} \ln\left[(1 - \gamma)e^{g_1\frac{\sigma - 1}{\sigma}t} + \gamma e^{g_2\frac{\sigma - 1}{\sigma}t}\right]. \qquad (10.30)$$

Observe that $\exp G(t)$ is the certainty equivalent of $(\exp g_1, 1 - \gamma; \exp g_2, \gamma)$ under utility function $f(G) = (\sigma/(\sigma - 1))G^{((\sigma - 1)/\sigma)t}$, it is increasing, and has an Arrow–Pratt coefficient of risk aversion which is increasing (decreasing) in t when σ is smaller (larger) than unity. This implies that the certainty equivalent $G(t)$ is decreasing (increasing) in t when σ is smaller (larger) than unity. This implies in turn that the term structure of the ecological discount rate is decreasing if $(\alpha\sigma - 1)(1 - \sigma)$ is positive. More details are given in Guesnerie (2004), Guéant, Guesnerie, and Lasry (2009), and Gollier (2010).

SUMMARY OF MAIN RESULTS

1. Most investment projects have economic and environmental impacts. Under the standard cost-benefit analysis, future environmental impacts are monetarized and discounted at the rate examined earlier in this book.

2. An alternative approach consists in discounting future environmental impacts into present equivalent environmental impact, and to transform them into current monetary value. This ecological discount rate need not be equal to the rate at which economic impacts are discounted.

3. The model examined in this chapter has a bivariate utility function. The standard marginalist approach allows us to derive two extended Ramsey rules respectively for the economic discount rate and for the ecological discount rate. In parallel to the wealth effect for the economic rate, there is an "ecological growth effect" which has a positive impact on the ecological rate if the environment improves over time and agents are averse to environmental inequalities.

4. The two Ramsey rules have six terms. For the ecological rate, we have impatience, the aversion to inequality with respect to the environment, the prudence toward environmental risks, in addition

to three other terms linked to the interactions between economic and environmental elements in the utility function. One of them is a substitution effect. If the two goods are substitutes, the economic growth reduces the future value of the environment, thereby raising the ecological rate.

REFERENCES

Bommier, A. (2007), Risk aversion, intertemporal elasticity of substitution and correlation aversion, *Economics Bulletin*, 29, 1–8.

Cropper, M. L., S. K. Aydede, and P. R. Portney (1994), Public preferences for life saving: discounting for time and age, *Journal of Risk and Uncertainty*, 8, 243–265.

Cropper, M. L., J. K. Hammitt, and L. A. Robinson (2011), *Valuing Mortality-Risk Reductions: Progress and Challenges, Annual Review of Resource Economics*, in press (also published as National Bureau of Economic Research Working Paper 16971, April 2011).

Cropper, M. L., and P. R. Portney (1990), Discounting and the evaluation of life-saving programs, *Journal of Risk and Uncertainty*, 3, 369–379.

Eeckhoudt, L., B. Rey, and H. Schlesinger (2007), A good sign for multivariate risk taking, *Management Science*, 53 (1), 117–124.

Eeckhoudt, L., and H. Schlesinger (2006), Putting risk in its proper place, *American Economic Review*, 96(1), 280–289.

Epstein, L. G., and S. M. Tanny (1980), Increasing generalized correlation: a definition and some economic consequences, *Canadian Journal of Economics*, 13, 16–34.

Gollier, C. (2010), Ecological discounting, *Journal of Economic Theory*, 145, 812–829.

Guéant, O., R. Guesnerie, and J.-M. Lasry (2009), Ecological intuition versus economic "reason," mimeo, Paris School of Economics.

Guesnerie, R. (2004), Calcul économique et développement durable, *Revue Economique*, 55, 363–382.

Hoel, M., and T. Sterner (2007), Discounting and relative prices, *Climatic Change*, DOI 10.1007/s10584-007-9255-2, March 2007.

Malinvaud, E. (1953), Capital accumulation and efficient allocation of resources, *Econometrica*, 21 (2), 233–268.

Millimet, D. L., J. A. List, and T. Stengos (2003), The environmental Kuznets curve: Real progress or misspecified models? *Review of Economics and Statistics*, 85, 1038–1047.

Richard, S. F. (1975), Multivariate risk aversion, utility independence and separable utility functions, *Management Science*, 22, 12–21.

Sterner, T., and M. Persson (2008), An Even Sterner Report: Introducing relative prices into the discounting debate, *Review of Environmental Economics and Policy*, 2 (1), 61–76.

Traeger, C. P. (2007), Sustainability, limited substitutability and non-constant social discount rates, Department of Agricultural & Resource Economics DP 1045,
Berkeley.

Weikard, H.-P., and X. Zhu (2005), Discounting and environmental quality: When
should dual rates be used? *Economic Modelling*, 22, 868–878.

Yale Center for Environmental Law and Policy (2005), *2005 Environmental Sustainability Index: Benchmarking national environmental stewardship*, Yale University.

11

Alternative Decision Criteria

The discounted expected utility (DEU) model that is used in this book is not without its critics. Since Allais (1953), many researchers have found contexts in which human behavior is incompatible with the DEU model. It is clear that the model is violated by many people, in many contexts. Some of these violations are informative about the true nature of individuals' actual preferences, whereas others are generated by errors, biased beliefs, lack of information, or a lack of time and effort spent on finding the optimal strategy. These violations imply that the DEU model is not very good for explaining, or predicting, actual behaviors under uncertainty. However, the aim of this book is not positive, it is normative. The interest is not directly in what people actually do, but instead to determine what they *should* do.

Many experiments stress the weakness of the independence axiom (IA), which is the cornerstone of the von Neumann–Morgenstern expected utility theory. The IA can be illustrated as follows. Suppose that, for tonight, you are offered tickets for the theater or a meal at a restaurant. Which do you prefer? Suppose that you prefer to go to the restaurant. Now, you are told that the theater and the restaurant are downtown. The only way to get there is to take the subway because you live in the suburbs. The problem is that there is a 10% probability that the subway will be on strike. Therefore, the actual decision choice that you face is not whether you prefer to go to the restaurant with certainty, or to go to the theater with certainty. The actual choice is whether you prefer lottery R to lottery T, where lottery R is a good dinner at the restaurant with probability 0.9, or staying at home with probability 0.1, and lottery T is a nice evening at the theater with probability 0.9, or staying at home with probability 0.1. The IA claims that it is natural to assume that the fact that there is now a 0.1 probability of staying at home, whatever choice you make, should not change your initial preference. If you prefer the restaurant to the theater in the certainty case, you should also prefer lottery R to lottery T. This is intuitive, and it is desirable that our collective preferences satisfy this axiom. Although many people violate this axiom, as cleverly shown by Allais (1953), we want to rely on this axiom to drive public decisions.

Several interesting decision criteria, which provide an alternative to the expected utility model, have blossomed over the last three decades. Most of them violate the independence axiom, and will not be examined here. The aim in this chapter is to describe a sample of the alternative decision criteria that have features which are normatively attractive.

RECURSIVE EXPECTED UTILITY

The concavity of the utility function plays two roles in the DEU model. The index $-u''/u'$ measures the aversion to consumption inequalities across time and across states of nature. The first feature yields the crucial wealth effect in the Ramsey rule, whereas the second is linked to risk aversion and to prudence. It is possible to question the logic for decreasing marginal utility of consumption generating both an aversion to risk within each period as well as an aversion to non-random fluctuations of consumption between periods. If the marginal welfare gain from k more units of consumption is less than the marginal loss owing to k units of reduction in consumption, agents will reject the opportunity to gamble on a fifty-fifty chance to gain or lose k units of consumption. For the same reason, if their current consumption plan is constant, patient consumers will reject the opportunity to exchange k units of consumption today against k units of consumption tomorrow. Kreps and Porteus (1978), Selden (1979), and Epstein and Zin (1991) claimed that there is no logical reason to impose the use of the same utility function for both of these psychological processes. They proposed an alternative model which disentangles attitudes toward consumption smoothing over time and across states. Following Gollier (2002) and

Traeger (2009), this section summarizes the application of this model to the problem of evaluating a safe investment project.

The analysis is limited to a model with two dates. As before, let c_0 and c_1 denote consumption per capita respectively in the present and in the future. Welfare at date 0 is evaluated "recursively" by backward induction, in two steps. The certainty equivalent m of future consumption, c_1, is evaluated first by using an increasing and concave von-Neumann–Morgenstern utility function v:

$$v(m) = Ev(c_1). \tag{11.1}$$

A time-aggregating utility function u is then used to evaluate intertemporal welfare W:

$$W = u(c_0) + e^{-\delta}u(m). \tag{11.2}$$

The utility function v characterizes attitudes toward risk, whereas function u characterizes attitudes toward time. The reader can easily check that the standard DEU model is recovered if the functions u and v are identical. If v is linear, it follows that $m = Ec_1$ and the agent is risk-neutral. This is compatible with a positive wealth effect in the Ramsey rule if u is concave and $Ec_1 > c_0$. In other words, one can be risk-neutral and have a preference for a reduction in consumption fluctuations over time. Symmetrically, one can be risk-averse and, at the same time, neutral toward consumption fluctuations over time. This would be the case if v is concave and u is linear. To sum up, $-v''/v'$ measures risk aversion, whereas $-u''/u'$ measures aversion to intertemporal inequality of consumption.

Consider a safe investment project that generates, at date 1, $\exp(r)$ monetary units per monetary unit invested at date 0. A marginal investment in this project has no effect on intertemporal welfare W if:

$$-u'(c_0) + e^{r-\delta}u'(m)\frac{\partial m}{\partial s}\bigg|_{s=0} = 0, \tag{11.3}$$

where $m = m(0)$ and $m(s)$ is defined as follows:

$$v(m(s)) = Ev(s + c_1). \tag{11.4}$$

It yields:

$$\frac{\partial m}{\partial s}\bigg|_{s=0} = \frac{Ev'(c_1)}{v'(m)}. \tag{11.5}$$

All this implies that the efficient discount rate equals:

$$r_1 = \delta - \ln \frac{u'(m)Ev'(c_1)}{u'(c_0)v'(m)}. \tag{11.6}$$

When $u \equiv v$, the standard pricing formula used in this book is recovered. Let us first examine the wealth effect as in chapter 2. Suppose that c_1 is safe, so that $m = c_1$. In that case, equation (11.6) simplifies to (3.16) with $t = 1$.

The analysis of the precautionary effect is more complex than in chapter 3. In the following, the condition under which adding a zero-mean risk to c_1 reduces the efficient discount rate is determined. Using (11.6), this is the case if and only if:

$$\frac{u'(m)Ev'(c_1)}{u'(c_0)v'(m)} \geq \frac{u'(Ec_1)}{u'(c_0)}, \tag{11.7}$$

or equivalently, if:

$$\frac{Ev'(c_1)}{v'(m)} \geq \frac{u'(Ec_1)}{u'(m)}. \tag{11.8}$$

Observe first that the right-hand side of this inequality is less than unity, because m is larger than Ec_1 under risk aversion. This upper bound is attained when the representative agent has a neutral attitude toward consumption inequalities over time. Thus, inequality (11.8) will surely hold if its left-hand side is greater than unity, that is, if $Ev'(c_1)$ is greater than $v'(m)$. Let $x = v(c_1)$ and $g(x) = v'(v^{-1}(x))$. With this notation, this condition can be rewritten as:

$$Eg(x) \geq g(Ex). \tag{11.9}$$

By Jensen's inequality, this is the case if and only if g is convex. Because $g(v(c)) = v'(c)$, it is obtained that:

$$-g'(v(x)) = -\frac{v''(x)}{v'(x)}, \tag{11.10}$$

This immediately implies that g is convex if and only if v exhibits decreasing absolute risk aversion (DARA).

It can be concluded that the precautionary effect on the discount rate is negative, as in the standard DEU model, if v exhibits DARA. This condition is necessary and sufficient if u is linear. It is notable that DARA is a condition that is stronger than prudence since

$$\frac{\partial}{\partial c}\left(\frac{-v''(c)}{v'(c)}\right) = \frac{v''(c)^2 - v'''(c)v'(c)}{v'(c)^2}$$

$$= \left(\frac{-v''(c)}{v'(c)}\right)\left(\left(\frac{-v''(c)}{v'(c)}\right) - \left(\frac{-v'''(c)}{v''(c)}\right)\right). \quad (11.11)$$

The implication is that DARA holds if and only if prudence is greater than risk aversion. It should not be a surprise that a more general model than the DEU model generates more demanding conditions for a specific comparative static property (precautionary saving).

This model can be calibrated using power utility functions and a lognormal distribution for c_1:

$$v'(c) = c^{-\gamma_v}, \quad u'(c) = c^{-\gamma_u}, \quad \text{and} \quad \ln c_1 \sim N(\ln c_0 + \mu, \sigma). \quad (11.12)$$

Observe that function v exhibits DARA, therefore a negative precautionary effect must be expected. Using lemma 1, it follows that:

$$\ln m = \ln c_0 + \mu + 0.5(1 - \gamma_v)\sigma^2 = \ln c_0 + g - 0.5\gamma_v\sigma^2, \quad (11.13)$$

with $g = \mu + 0.5\sigma^2$. This in turn implies that:

$$\frac{u'(m)Ev'(c_1)}{u'(c_0)v'(m)} = \frac{\exp(-\gamma_u(g - 0.5\gamma_v\sigma^2))\exp(-\gamma_v(\mu - 0.5\gamma_v\sigma^2))}{\exp(-\gamma_v(g - 0.5\gamma_v\sigma^2))}$$

$$= \exp(-\gamma_u(g - 0.5\gamma_v\sigma^2))\exp(0.5\gamma_v\sigma^2). \quad (11.14)$$

This implies that the socially efficient discount rate equals:

$$r_1 = \delta + \gamma_u g - 0.5\gamma_v(\gamma_u + 1)\sigma^2. \quad (11.15)$$

In the DEU case, with $\gamma_u = \gamma_v$, this formula is equivalent to equation (3.23). This shows that the model does not radically modify our understanding of the determinants of the efficient discount rate. In the short run, the driving force of the discount rate is the wealth effect, which is the same as in the DEU case. Because σ^2 is small, changing the precautionary effect from $0.5\gamma_u(\gamma_u + 1)\sigma^2$ to $0.5\gamma_v(\gamma_u + 1)\sigma^2$ does not affect r_1 very significantly. An appraisal of the effect of $\gamma_v \neq \gamma_u$ for the long-term discount rate remains to be made.

MAXMIN AMBIGUITY AVERSION

In chapter 6, models in which the true probability distribution of future consumption, c_1, is uncertain were examined. The DEU model was used to evaluate safe projects under this two-stage risk context, with stage 1 being the random selection of the true distribution, and stage 2 being the random draw of the realization of c_1 from this distribution. Since Ellsberg (1961), it has been known that many people do not evaluate such a two-stage risk in a way that is compatible with the DEU model.

Let us consider a simplified version of the Ellsberg game. Consider an urn that contains 100 balls, some are black, and the others are white. The two games that will be considered have the same basic structure. The player must pay an entry fee to play the game. The player bets on one of the two colors. The experimenter randomly extracts a ball from the urn, and pays 1,000 euros to the player if the color of the ball corresponds to the one on which they bet. In the first game, which is referred to as the "risky game," there are exactly 50 black balls and 50 white balls. Betting on either of the two colors yields the same lottery to win 1,000 euros with probability ½, therefore most people are indifferent as to which color they bet on. The entry fee that individuals are ready to pay is less than the expected gain of 500 euros because of risk aversion.

Consider alternatively the "ambiguous game," in which the player gets no information about the proportion of black and white balls in the urn. The closed ambiguous urn is brought in front of the player before the player selects the color to bet on. What is usually observed in this second experiment is that most people are still indifferent between betting on white or on black, but that they are ready to pay much less to play this ambiguous game than the risky game. This cannot be explained under the DEU model. Indeed, if the player is indifferent between white or black, this must mean that they believe that their chance to win by betting white is the same as by betting black. This implies that their expected probability to win is ½ because the probabilities must sum up to unity, independently to the color on which the player bets. The player therefore faces a lottery to win 1,000 euros with probability ½, which is the same lottery as in the risky game. The player should thus be ready to pay the same entry fee in the two games. The fact that most people are ready to pay much less for the ambiguous game than for the risky game tells us that people are ambiguity-averse, a psychological trait that cannot be explained by the DEU model. Ambiguity aversion just means that people prefer a lottery to win a widget with a sure probability p than another lottery to win the same widget with an ambiguous probability with mean p.

The first attempt to produce a decision criterion that produces ambiguity aversion was made by Gilboa and Schmeidler (1989). Suppose that people form an expectation about the set of plausible distributions of the random variable x that they face. A form of ambiguity aversion is obtained if we state that agents evaluate their welfare, ex ante, once their choice has been made, by the minimum expected utility over a set of plausible probability distributions. This "maxmin" criterion would explain the behavior observed in the Ellsberg game. Indeed, suppose that people form their beliefs such that the probability of a white draw is either 0.25 or 0.75. If they bet on white, people will compute their welfare by assuming that there are only 25 white balls. If they bet on black, they will do so by assuming that there are only 25 black balls. Thus, under the maxmin criterion, their welfare will be measured by the expected utility of 1,000 euros with the minimum plausible probability, which is 0.25, whether they bet on white or on black. The certainty equivalent of that lottery is indeed much smaller than in the risky game in which the probability to win is 0.5.

Let us apply this idea to the discounting problem. To retain the notation used earlier, suppose that the distribution of c_1 depends upon an unknown parameter θ that can take n possible values $\theta = 1, \ldots, n$. Let $\theta = 1$ denote the value of the parameter that yields the smallest expected utility at date 1. The efficient discount rate would then satisfy the standard pricing formula (3.16), but in which the distribution of c_1 would be $c_1 | \theta = 1$ rather than the unconditional distribution of c_1 as assumed in chapter 6. What would the consequences be for the short-term efficient discount rate r_1? Suppose that the uncertainty is about the mean growth rate. In that case, ambiguity aversion would replace the mean growth rate by the minimum growth rate in the Ramsey rule. Suppose alternatively that the uncertainty is about the volatility of the growth rate. In that case, ambiguity aversion would replace the mean volatility by the maximum volatility in the Ramsey rule. In the two cases, the problem becomes equivalent to computing the discount rate that would be efficient conditional on each realization of θ, and then selecting the smallest of these rates as the efficient discount rate r_1. Interestingly enough, in the case of a random walk, the *short-term* discount rate that is efficient under the maxmin theory is the discount rate that is efficient for the *distant future* in the DEU model examined in chapter 6.

SMOOTH AMBIGUITY AVERSION

There are difficulties using the maxmin model in order to provide normative recommendations. This is because it does not explain how to determine the set of plausible distributions that is part of the preferences of the representative agent. This is problematic because this model is very sensitive to the characteristics of the worst probability distribution, which could be arbitrarily catastrophist. Klibanoff, Marinacci, and Mukerji (KMM, 2005, 2009) have recently proposed a model that is easier to implement, and is less sensitive to the extreme plausible distribution. They define ambiguity aversion as the aversion to any mean-preserving spread in the space of probabilities. Remember that risk aversion is an aversion to any mean-preserving spread in the space of payoffs. For example, risk aversion means that one prefers to get 500 in two equally probable states, than to receive 1,000 in state 1, and 0 in state 2. Taking this risky lottery as a benchmark, ambiguity aversion means that one prefers a lottery in which the true probability of state 1 is 0.5 with certainty rather than a lottery where the probability of state 1 is either 0.25 or 0.75 with equal probabilities. The maxmin model examined earlier is an extreme version of aversion to mean-preserving spreads in the space of probability distributions.

KMM have proposed the following decision criterion under ambiguity. For each possible value of θ, the conditional expected utility $E[u(c_1)|\theta]$ is computed. In the standard DEU criterion used in chapter 6, we just take the mean of the conditional expected utilities under the subjective distribution $(q_1, \ldots, q_n)$ of θ. Rather than doing this, we take its certainty equivalent by using an increasing and concave function ϕ:

$$W = u(c_0) + e^{-\delta}M \quad \text{with} \quad \phi(M) = \sum_{\theta=1}^{n} q_\theta \phi(E[u(c_1)|\theta]). \qquad (11.16)$$

Because ϕ is concave, M is smaller than the unconditional expected utility, which means that this welfare function exhibits ambiguity aversion. It is helpful to examine two special cases. First, if function ϕ is the identity function, then this welfare function is the same as in the standard DEU case, in which agents are neutral to mean-preserving spreads in probabilities. The expected utility criterion is linear in probabilities. In fact, function $-\phi''/\phi'$ is an index of absolute ambiguity aversion. The other special case is obtained by assuming that $\phi(u) = -A_\phi^{-1} \exp(-A_\phi u)$, where the index of absolute ambiguity aversion A_ϕ tends to infinity. It was demonstrated in chapter 6 that $E\phi(u)$ tends to the minimum of u in that case, so that we get the maxmin criterion as another special case.

As usual, let us consider a safe investment project that yields $\exp(r)$ monetary units at date 1 per monetary unit invested at date 0. At the margin, this project has no effect on intertemporal welfare, W, if:

$$-u'(c_0) + e^{r-\delta} \frac{\sum_{\theta=1}^n q_\theta \phi'(E[u(c_1)|\theta])E[u'(c_1)|\theta]}{\phi'(M)} = 0. \quad (11.17)$$

This yields the following efficient discount rate:

$$r_1 = \delta - \ln \frac{\sum_{\theta=1}^n q_\theta \phi'(E[u(c_1)|\theta])E[u'(c_1)|\theta]}{u'(c_0)\phi'(M)}. \quad (11.18)$$

Gierlinger and Gollier (2011) illustrate two effects of ambiguity aversion in this model: an ambiguity prudence effect and a pessimism effect. The ambiguity prudence effect is easiest to explain if it is assumed that the representative agent is risk-neutral, that is, if u is the identity function. This switches off both the wealth effect and the precautionary effect of the standard DEU model. In that case, equation (11.18) simplifies to

$$r_1 = \delta - \ln \frac{\sum_{\theta=1}^n q_\theta \phi'(\bar{c}_{1\theta})}{\phi'(M)} \quad \text{with} \quad \phi(M) = \sum_{\theta=1}^n q_\theta \phi(\bar{c}_{1\theta}), \quad (11.19)$$

where $\bar{c}_{1\theta}$ is the conditional expected consumption at date 1. Therefore, the ambiguous distribution of economic growth reduces the efficient discount rate if:

$$\sum_{\theta=1}^n q_\theta \phi'(\bar{c}_{1\theta}) \geq \phi'(M) \quad \text{whenever} \quad \sum_{\theta=1}^n q_\theta \phi(\bar{c}_{1\theta}) = \phi(M). \quad (11.20)$$

Exactly the same technical condition was encountered in the section on recursive expected utility (see condition (11.8)), where it was shown that it requires that the ϕ function exhibits decreasing absolute aversion: $(-\phi''/\phi')' \leq 0$. We refer to this condition as "decreasing absolute ambiguity aversion" (DAAA). Duplicating this proof, define function $g(x) = \phi'(\phi^{-1}(x))$ and $x_\theta = \phi(\bar{c}_{1\theta})$. Condition (11.20) can then be rewritten as $Eg(x) \geq g(Ex)$, where x is distributed as $(x_1, q_1; \ldots; x_n, q_n)$. The proof is concluded by observing that this is the case if g is convex, which is equivalent to DAAA. This is more demanding than requiring the prudence of ϕ ($\phi'' \geq 0$). This ambiguity prudence condition guarantees that, under risk-neutrality, the existence of some ambiguity on the distribution of future consumption reduces the discount rate.

The pessimism effect is similar to the one that is obtained under the maxmin criterion. It is easiest to illustrate by switching off the ambiguity prudence effect, that is, by assuming that absolute ambiguity aversion $-\phi''/\phi'$ is constant. If it is assumed that $\phi(u) = -A_\phi \exp(-A_\phi u)$, it follows that $\phi'(M)$ equals $\Sigma_\theta q_\theta \phi'(Eu_\theta)$. This implies that equation (11.18) can be rewritten as:

$$r_1 = \delta - \ln \sum_{\theta=1}^{n} \hat{q}_\theta \frac{E[u'(c_1)|\theta]}{u'(c_0)} \quad \text{with} \quad \hat{q}_\theta = q_\theta \frac{\phi'(E[u(c_1)|\theta])}{\sum_{\tau=1}^{n} q_\tau \phi'(E[u(c_1)|\tau])}. \quad (11.21)$$

If this discount rate is compared to the one that was obtained under the standard DEU criterion, which is equation (6.2) with $t = 1$, it can be observed that the only difference is that the beliefs described by $(q_1, \ldots, q_n)$ have been distorted, becoming $(\hat{q}_1, \ldots, \hat{q}_n)$ defined in (11.21). Because ϕ' is decreasing, these distorted beliefs put more probability weight on the θ that yields a smaller conditional expected utility. This is a clear expression of pessimism, whose extreme version was illustrated by the maxmin model. If it is supposed, for example, that there is uncertainty about the expected growth rate, the probabilities will be distorted in favor of the θ with the smallest expected growth rate, for which the expected marginal utility is larger. This will tend to reduce the discount rate r_1.

To sum up, ambiguity aversion tends to reduce the discount rate. One can illustrate this intuitive idea by considering the following specification suggested in Gierlinger and Gollier (2011). Suppose as in chapter 6 that

$\ln c_t \mid \theta$ is normally distributed with mean $\ln c_0 + \mu_\theta t$ and variance $\sigma^2 t$. Suppose that the mean of the change μ_θ in the log of consumption is itself normally distributed with mean μ_0 and variance σ_0^2. Consider the case of a power utility function with constant relative risk aversion γ. This model is exactly the benchmark case that was considered in chapter 6. The only new dimension is ambiguity aversion. Suppose that ϕ exhibits constant relative ambiguity aversion $\eta = -|u|\phi''(u)/\phi'(u)$. Using lemma 1 twice, Gollier and Gierlinger (2011) obtained the following formula:

$$r_t = \delta + \gamma g - 0.5\gamma(1+\gamma)(\sigma^2 + \sigma_0^2 t) - 0.5\eta|1-\gamma^2|\sigma_0^2 t, \quad (11.22)$$

where $g = \mu_0 + 0.5(\sigma^2 + \sigma_0^2 t)$ is the growth rate of expected consumption. This equation should be compared to equation (6.13), which is a special case of (11.22) with $\eta = 0$. This observation allows us to conclude that ambiguity aversion yields a new determinant to the discount rate, which, under the specification considered here, is negative and linear with the time horizon. This is because, with an uncertain trend in economic growth, the degree of ambiguity is magnified by the time horizon in this framework.

It is noteworthy that Gierlinger and Gollier (2011) show that the introduction of ambiguity aversion does not always reduce the discount rate, even under decreasing absolute ambiguity aversion.

INTERGENERATIONAL HABIT FORMATION

Although the current generation consumes considerably more goods and services than their parents, they are not really happier. This is a paradox. The indices of happiness do not parallel those of GDP per capita (see for example Layard 2005). One possible explanation is that people evaluate their well-being in relative rather than in absolute terms. In particular, their felicity at date t is not a function of their consumption at date t alone. In the literature on external habit formation, it is assumed that the agent's felicity at date t is a function of c_t and of a weighted average of past consumption $(c_{t-1}, c_{t-2}, \ldots)$. This breaks down the time-additivity property of the DEU model. Constantinides (1990) has argued for a positive effect of past consumption on today's marginal utility of consumption, which is a simple definition of a consumption habit. A large consumption level in the past raises the marginal utility of current consumption, thereby creating some form of addiction to consumption.

A simple specification is the multiplicative habit in which the felicity at date t is measured by $u(c_t/c_{t-1}^\alpha)$, for some positive constant $\alpha \leq 1$. A special case is $\alpha = 1$, in which case the felicity is a function of the growth rate of consumption rather than of the level of consumption. For example, if the growth rate of consumption is a positive constant, the felicity will remain constant over time in this model. Under these preferences, at any time, a temporary increase in consumption above its historical trend is beneficial in the short run, but generates a negative externality for future welfare because of the consumption habit that this transitory increase generates. When α is less than unity, this negative externality is reduced. Therefore, α is a measure of the degree of habit formation.

To keep the model simple, let us assume that $u(x) = x^{1-\gamma}/(1-\gamma)$ with $\gamma > 1$. Suppose also that the growth rate of consumption is a positive constant g. Observe now that

$$u\left(\frac{c_t}{c_{t-1}^\alpha}\right) = \frac{1}{1-\gamma} c_t^{(1-\alpha)(1-\gamma)} e^{\alpha g(1-\gamma)} = kc_t^{1-\gamma'}, \qquad (11.23)$$

with $\gamma' = \alpha + (1-\alpha)\gamma$. This shows that the existence of a multiplicative internal consumption habit transforms the intertemporal welfare function in a very simple way. First, it multiplies the felicity by a common positive constant $e^{\alpha g(1-\gamma)}$. Second, it modifies the degree of relative risk aversion from γ to γ', which is the mean of γ and 1, weighted respectively by $(1-\alpha)$ and α. Since it is usually assumed that γ is larger than unity, this model of habit formation just reduces the degree of concavity of the felicity function. The Ramsey rule (2.12) therefore still holds, but with γ being replaced by the smaller γ':

$$r_t = \delta + \gamma' g. \qquad (11.24)$$

Owing to a consumption habit downsizing the wealth effect, it yields a smaller discount rate. The intuition is that investing for the future is a good way to impose self-control on today's level of consumption, thereby limiting the formation of consumption habits that have adverse effects on future welfare. Gollier, Johansson-Stenman, and Sterner (2010) extend this result to the case of uncertainty.

The internal habit formation model briefly described earlier has some interesting features with which to explain observed human behaviors. For example, it can contribute to solving the equity premium puzzle (Constantinides 1990). However, it is still an open question whether or not this model should be used for normative analysis of public policies spanning several generations. It is clear that parents transfer consumption habits to their children, so that habit formation is not strictly speaking an intra-individual feature. But is it enough to justify more sacrifices from the current generation?

Many other models alternative to DEU could have been considered for inclusion in this chapter, but to be concise, decisions had to be made. Other models that could have been discussed include, for example, the cumulative prospect theory introduced by Tversky and Kahneman (1992). This model shares with the habit formation model the idea that future consumption will be evaluated in relation to some reference point that may be related to past consumption. But prospect theory also has other features, such as the assumption that agents are risk-lovers over a range of losses below the reference point. It is also assumed that they distort the distribution function by using some specific nonlinear function that plays a role symmetric to the utility function that transforms payoffs into utility in a nonlinear way. This transformation raises the subjective probability of extreme events, which has the effect of raising the precautionary term in the extended Ramsey rule, thereby reducing the discount rate. It is still too early to determine which of these innovations will survive the rigors of the scientific validation process over the longer term.

SUMMARY OF MAIN RESULTS

1. A standard critique made to the discounted expected utility model is that the concavity of the utility function expresses at the same time the aversion to inequalities and the aversion to risk. Moreover, it does not take account the possibility of an aversion to ambiguity on probabilities, or the formation of consumption habits.

2. Recursive preferences à la Kreps-Porteus-Epstein-Zin allows for disentangling the aversion to intertemporal inequalities and the

aversion to risk. The extended Ramsey rule is easily adapted to this generalization of the DEU model.

3. Ambiguity about the distribution of future economic growth was introduced in chapter 6 with uncertainty about the parameter of the stochastic process. Ambiguity aversion has two effects on the term structure of discount rate. First, it implies pessimism about the trend or about the volatility, thereby reducing the level of the term structure. Second, because ambiguity is increasing with maturity, it makes the term structure more downward sloping.

4. Habit formation is introduced in the DEU model by making instantaneous felicity a function of past consumption. It weakens the wealth effect, thereby reducing the discount rate.

REFERENCES

Allais, M. (1953), Le comportement de l'homme rationnel devant le risque, Critique des postulats et axiomes de l'école américaine, *Econometrica*, 21, 503–546.

Constantinides, G. (1990), Habit formation: a resolution of the equity premium puzzle, *Journal of Political Economy*, 98, 519–543.

Ellsberg, D. (1961), Risk, ambiguity, and the Savage axioms, *Quarterly Journal of Economics*, 75, 643–669.

Epstein, L. G., and S. Zin (1991), Substitution, risk aversion and the temporal behavior of consumption and asset returns: An empirical framework, *Journal of Political Economy*, 99, 263–286.

Gierlinger, J., and C. Gollier (2011), Socially efficient discounting under ambiguity aversion, mimeo, Toulouse School of Economics.

Gilboa, I., and D. Schmeidler (1989), Maxmin expected utility with a non-unique prior, *Journal of Mathematical Economics*, 18, 141–153.

Gollier, C. (2002), Discounting an uncertain future, *Journal of Public Economics*, 85, 149–166.

Gollier, C., O. Johansson-Stenman, and Th. Sterner (2010), Ramsey discounting when relative consumption matters, mimeo, Toulouse School of Economics.

Klibanoff, P., M. Marinacci, and S. Mukerji (2005), A smooth model of decision making under ambiguity, *Econometrica*, 73(6), 1849–1892.

Klibanoff, P., M. Marinacci, and S. Mukerji (2009), Recursive smooth ambiguity preferences, *Journal of Economic Theory*, 144, 930–976.

Kreps, D. M., and E. L. Porteus (1978), Temporal resolution of uncertainty and dynamic choice theory, *Econometrica*, 46, 185–200.

Layard, Richard (2005), *Happiness: Lessons from a New Science*, London and New York: Penguin Press.

Selden, L. (1979), An OCE analysis of the effect of uncertainty on saving under risk independence, *Review of Economic Studies*, 46, 73–82.

Traeger, C. P. (2009), Recent developments in the intertemporal modeling of uncertainty, *Annual Review of Resource Economics*, 1, 261–286.

Tversky, A., and D. Kahneman (1992), Advances in prospect theory—Cumulative representation of uncertainty, *Journal of Risk and Uncertainty*, 5, 297–323.

PART IV

———◀◦▶———

EVALUATION OF RISKY
AND UNCERTAIN PROJECTS

12

◀◉▶

Evaluation of Risky Projects

This book is mostly devoted to the evaluation of safe investment projects. However, most real projects are not safe, and indeed many of them are very risky. This is particularly the case for those yielding cash flows in the distant future. For example, the size of the damages associated with climate change is vastly uncertain. How should this affect the way in which we discount the reduction of these damages obtained from our green investments? In a highly uncertain distant future, how do we value R&D yielding uncertain distant benefits and costs, as is the case for genetically manipulated organisms, or for space exploration? In a less abstract fashion, how do we compare merits of various investment projets that differ not only in their maturities but also in their degrees of riskiness? For example, should we invest in fighting malaria, whose benefits are immediate and almost certain, or in new education and transportation infrastructures in developing countries, whose benefits are more distant and more uncertain?

The last part of this book is devoted to exploring adaptations to the rules presented earlier in the book to the problem of risky and uncertain projects. The evaluation of risky projects and of risky assets has been the Holy Grail of the theory of asset pricing, which is an important branch of the modern theory of finance. This chapter provides a short overview of the main concepts, ideas, and tools that have been produced by more than fifty years of research in that field.

THE EQUITY PREMIUM

It is easy to make a crude estimate of the effect of risk on the value of projects or assets in the economy. Investors in financial markets have the opportunity to invest in a large set of projects. Their optimal asset allocation is such that they are indifferent at the margin to a transfer of wealth from one asset to any other one. This is why two safe assets with the same maturity must have the same return. By risk aversion, if an asset has a cash flow that correlates positively with aggregate risk in the economy, its equilibrium price is smaller than the corresponding safe asset with the same expected payoff at the same maturity. In other words, the expected return of the risky asset is greater than the return on the safe asset. This means that investors discount the expected cash flows of the risky asset at a higher rate. This "equity premium" tells us something important about our collective preferences: Risky projects should be undertaken only if their expected internal rate of social return is large enough to compensate for the increased risk that it yields for the stakeholders. The social planner should do the same to evaluate risky public investments. This chapter is devoted to the analysis of the risk premium for risky projects that should be added to the discount rate for safe projects.

Dimson, Marsh, and Staunton (2002) have computed the annualized return on bonds and equities for different countries during the twentieth century. Using extended data from the same authors over the period 1900–2006, the main facts are summarized in table 12.1. In the United States, the return on T-bills, which are probably the safest assets in the world, gave a real return of around 1.0%, whereas 10-year Treasury bonds and equities delivered an average real return of respectively 1.9% and 6.6% per year. This implies an equity premium of around 5.6%. The real return of these three asset classes varies significantly across different countries during the period. In particular, the real return of fixed-income assets was negative in countries that fought a world war on their own soil, including Japan, France, and Italy. Observe also that the equity premium varies across countries within the range of 3–7%.

In table 12.2, the same exercise has been repeated over the shorter time period of 1971–2006. It is notable that the safe return on government bonds was much larger in this period than over the century as a whole, whereas the return on equities has remained stable. A possible explanation for this

TABLE 12.1.
Annualized real returns of equity and bonds, 1900– 2006

	Bill	Bond	Equity
Australia	0.6%	1.3%	7.8%
Canada	1.6%	2.0%	6.3%
Denmark	2.3%	3.0%	5.4%
France	−2.9%	−0.3%	3.7%
Italy	−3.8%	−1.8%	2.6%
Japan	−2.0%	−1.3%	4.5%
Netherlands	0.7%	1.3%	5.4%
United Kingdom	1.0%	1.3%	5.6%
Sweden	1.9%	2.4%	7.9%
Switzerland	0.8%	2.1%	5.3%
USA	1.0%	1.9%	6.6%

Sources: Morningstar; and Dimson, Marsh, and Staunton (2002)

TABLE 12.2.
Annualized real returns of equity and bonds, 1971– 2006

	Bill	Bond	Equity
Australia	2.5%	2.8%	6.3%
Canada	2.7%	4.5%	5.8%
Denmark	3.5%	7.0%	9.0%
France	1.2%	6.6%	7.8%
Italy	−0.3%	2.8%	3.0%
Japan	0.4%	3.9%	5.0%
Netherlands	1.8%	3.9%	8.5%
United Kingdom	1.9%	3.9%	7.1%
Sweden	2.4%	4.2%	11.0%
Switzerland	0.4%	2.8%	6.1%
USA	1.3%	4.0%	6.6%

Sources: Morningstar; and Dimson, Marsh, and Staunton (2002)

is the successful fight against inflation by central banks in recent years. The data set also exhibits a smaller equity premium for the shorter period. For example, in the United States, the annualized real return on T-bills has been 1.3%, whereas the annualized real return on equity has been 6.6%, implying an equity premium of 5.3%.

By the standard arbitrage argument, these numbers justify a discount rate of only 1.3% to evaluate safe short-term projects in the United States. At the same time, if the project under scrutiny has a risk profile similar to that of U.S. equities, a discount rate of 6.6% should be used. This is not far from the 7% that is recommended by the OMB in 1992. However, it would be inefficient to use that discount rate to evaluate a safe project. These numbers give us some sense of the scale of the effect of risk on the evaluation of risky projects.

CERTAINTY EQUIVALENT AND RISK PREMIUM

Consider a representative agent with utility function u and a (risky) consumption plan $(c_0, c_1, \ldots)$. Let us also consider an investment project that yields B_t monetary units per capita at date t per monetary unit invested today. B_t is allowed to be random and potentially correlated with consumption c_t. Investing ε in the project yields the following intertemporal welfare:

$$W(\varepsilon) = u(c_0 - \varepsilon) + e^{-\delta t} Eu(c_t + \varepsilon B_t). \tag{12.1}$$

A marginal investment in that project has a positive effect on intertemporal welfare if:

$$-u'(c_0) + e^{-\delta t} EB_t u'(c_t) \geq 0. \tag{12.2}$$

This can be rewritten as:

$$-1 + e^{-\delta t} \frac{Eu'(c_t)}{u'(c_0)} \frac{EB_t u'(c_t)}{Eu'(c_t)} \geq 0. \tag{12.3}$$

It is easier to write this condition as:

$$NPV = -1 + e^{-r_t t} F_t \geq 0, \tag{12.4}$$

with:

$$r_t = \delta - \frac{1}{t} \ln \frac{Eu'(c_t)}{u'(c_0)}, \tag{12.5}$$

and:

$$F_t = \frac{EB_t u'(c_t)}{Eu'(c_t)}. \tag{12.6}$$

When the future cash flow is uncertain, its evaluation requires a two-step procedure. First, the risky cash flow B_t is replaced by its certainty equivalent, F_t, defined by (12.6). This first operation simplifies the problem to the one of valuing a safe project. Therefore, the second step is obvious: this certainty equivalent must be discounted by using the discount rate r_t defined by (12.5), which the reader will recognize as the rate that is efficient for safe projects that has been described throughout this book. The project should be implemented if and only if its net present value computed with this two-step procedure is positive. This procedure is very useful, because it shows us that what has been done so far in this book to characterize the efficient discount rate can also be used to evaluate risky projects.

The only new element to be examined in this chapter is the transformation of a risky cash flow B_t into its certainty equivalent F_t. If this project can be traded on frictionless financial markets, its equilibrium forward price should be equal to F_t. Equation (12.6) is in fact the classical equilibrium asset pricing formula that can be found in most textbooks on the theory of finance. It happens to be the case that F_t is a weighted mean of the different possible realizations of B_t. For example, if B_t is certain, then $F_t = B_t$. If it is risky, let us define the "risk-neutral expectation" operator E^* as in chapter 7:

$$E^* f(b) = \frac{Ef(b)u'(c_t)}{Eu'(c_t)}. \tag{12.7}$$

This corresponds to the notion of the "risk-neutral probability" of a state, which is the true probability of a state multiplied by the marginal utility of consumption in that state, and divided by $Eu'(c_t)$ in order to guarantee that the risk-neutral probabilities sum up to one. It therefore follows that $F_t = E^* B_t$. The certainty equivalent of a cash flow is equal to its risk-neutral expectation. Hereafter the implications of this observation are described. It is natural to define the risk premium for the valuation of the cash flow B_t as the difference between the expected cash flow EB_t and its certainty equivalent $F_t = E^* B_t$.

THE ARROW–LIND THEOREM

The simplest case arises when the cash flow B_t is risky, but this risk is independent of the systematic risk corresponding to c_t. In that case, applying equation (12.6) immediately implies that $F_t = EB_t$. The equilibrium price—and the efficient valuation—of the asset is actuarially fair, in the sense that the risk premium vanishes. There is no risk premium associated with idiosyncratic risk. This result is usually referred to as the Arrow–Lind Theorem in the public economics literature (Arrow and Lind 1970).

It is important to get the intuition for this result. To put it simply, risks that are uncorrelated with the aggregate risk are in fact fully diversified away in the portfolio of the representative agent. At the margin, adding this risk to the portfolio does not increase the portfolio riskiness. This is due to the fact that the risk premium for small risk is proportional to its variance. This comes from the Arrow–Pratt approximation (3.3). Thus, when the size k of the risk goes to zero, its risk premium goes to zero as k^2, whereas its expected value goes to zero as k. This means that when the size of the risk is small, only the mean matters when valuing it. Following Segal and Spivak (1990), in the DEU model, risk aversion is a second-order phenomenon. This is not the case for many other decision criteria under uncertainty, as for example with prospect theory.

Of course, the Arrow–Lind theorem has its own limitations beyond the assumption of independence between B_t and c_t. In particular, as explained in chapter 9, the existence of a representative agent requires that risk be efficiently shared in the economy. This means in particular that the cash flows of the project need to be efficiently disseminated among all agents in the economy. In theory, this will be the case if markets are complete and frictionless. Profits are disseminated in the economy through well-diversified portfolios. Risk associated with employment or consumer safety will be efficiently covered through insurance. But in reality, different stakeholders in the project will bear specific risks linked to it, and they will not be able to transfer them to other agents because of various agency problems. In that case, the second-order nature of risk aversion cannot be used to abstract the evaluator to independent risks that are small at the aggregate level, but that are large at the level of some uninsured stakeholders. The cost-benefit analysis requires in this context to estimate the certainty equivalent benefits of each category of stakeholders (see chapter 14).

THE CONSUMPTION-BASED CAPITAL ASSET PRICING MODEL

Suppose alternatively that the cash flow of the project and the GDP per capita are positively stochastically dependent. To be more precise, suppose that B_t and c_t are more concordant than when assuming independence as in the previous section, in the sense of Tchen (1980). In crude words, this means that when the economy is growing faster, the conditional distribution of the cash flow of the investment is improved in the sense of first-degree stochastic dominance. Using lemma 2 in chapter 8, this statistical dependence of (B_t, c_t) raises the value F_t of the cash flow if $h(B_t, c_t) = B_t u'(c_t)$ is supermodular. That is, if u is concave. In other words, the risk premium is positive if the cash flow is positively statistically related to the systemic or macroeconomic risk, and the risk premium is negative if they are negatively statistically related. The Arrow–Lind theorem is obtained in the limit case of independence. In case of a negative correlation, implementing the project reduces the global risk. It therefore has an insurance value, which takes the form of a negative risk premium.

Suppose that $(\ln B_t, \ln c_t)$ follows an arithmetic Brownian motion. Their trends and volatilities are denoted respectively (μ_B, μ_c) and (σ_B, σ_c). Their index of correlation is denoted ρ. It implies that $(\ln B_t, \ln c_t)$ are jointly normal. Suppose that $u'(c) = c^{-\gamma}$. Lemma 1 can then be used twice to compute the two expectations in (12.6):

$$Eu'(c_t) = \exp(-\gamma(\ln c_0 + \mu_c t - 0.5\gamma\sigma_c^2 t)). \tag{12.8}$$

$$\begin{aligned} EB_t u'(c_t) &= E(\exp(\ln B_t - \gamma \ln c_t)) \\ &= \exp(\ln B_0 - \gamma \ln c_0 + \mu_B t - \gamma\mu_c t \\ &\quad + 0.5t(\sigma_B^2 + \gamma^2\sigma_c^2 - 2\gamma\sigma_B\sigma_c\rho)). \end{aligned} \tag{12.9}$$

Using (12.6), it follows that:

$$F_t = B_0 \exp t(\mu_B + 0.5(\sigma_B^2 - 2\gamma\sigma_B\sigma_c\rho)). \tag{12.10}$$

Now, observe that $EB_t = B_0 \exp t(\mu_B + 0.5\sigma_B^2)$, so that equation (12.10) can finally be rewritten as:

$$F_t = (EB_t)e^{-\gamma\beta\sigma_c^2 t} = (EB_t)e^{-\pi(\beta)t}, \tag{12.11}$$

where the "consumption β" of the project is defined as:

$$\beta = \frac{\rho\sigma_B}{\sigma_c} = \frac{\text{cov}(\ln B_t/B_{t-1}, \ln c_t/c_{t-1})}{\sigma_c^2}, \tag{12.12}$$

and where $\pi(\beta) = \gamma\beta\sigma_c^2$ is defined as the risk premium of the project. The consumption β of an investment project can be interpreted as the expected percentage increase in its net social benefit when aggregate consumption increases by 1%. It is noteworthy that the β of the project is constant in this context of a joint arithmetic Brownian motion for $(\ln B_t, \ln c_t)$. Equation (12.11) confirms that the signs of the risk premium and of the covariance of $(\ln B_t, \ln c_t)$ are the same. Under this specification, the certainty equivalent of the cash flow at maturity t increases (or decreases) exponentially with t. There are two reasons for that. First, the expected cash flows increase exponentially. Second, the effect of risk on the certainty equivalent also increases exponentially.

Computing the risk premium therefore requires information about the volatility σ_B of the cash flows and about their correlation ρ with the growth of GDP per capita. If similar investment projects have been implemented in the past, one can use these observations to estimate these parameters by using standard regression methods. If suitable data are not available, the Monte Carlo methodology is a good alternative. It remains important, however, to keep in mind that the idiosyncratic risk of the project has no value, because agents diversify it away. As stated by the Arrow–Lind Theorem, only the correlation with the macroeconomic risk is relevant.

RISK PREMIUM AND THE RISK-ADJUSTED DISCOUNT RATE

In this chapter, the reader has been advised to disentangle the problem of time (discounting) and the problem of risk (certainty equivalence). However, under the joint lognormal specification, considered in this section, a nice simplification occurs. Observe from equation (12.11) that the certainty equivalent of a cash flow expressed as a fraction of its expected value varies exponentially with time. Therefore, taking into account this treatment of risk is equivalent to adapting the discount rate to the riskiness of the project in the following way. As explained in chapter 4, the discount rate for safe projects is constant when the logarithm of consumption follows an arithmetic Brownian motion. In that case, the discount rate obtained from equation (12.5) equals $r_f = \delta + \gamma \mu_c - 0.5 \gamma^2 \sigma_c^2$. Combining equations (12.4) and (12.11) yields:

$$NPV = -1 + e^{-r_f t} F_t = -1 + e^{-r(\beta)t} EB_t, \qquad (12.13)$$

with:

$$r(\beta) = r_f + \gamma\beta\sigma_c^2 = r_f + \pi(\beta). \qquad (12.14)$$

Equation (12.13) tells us that the two-step evaluation procedure that was presented earlier in this chapter is equivalent to an alternative procedure in which one discounts the expected cash flows at a rate that takes into account the riskiness of the project. This risk-adjusted rate r, defined by equation (12.14), is the sum of the risk-free discount rate r_f examined in this book and a risk premium $\pi(\beta) = \gamma\beta\sigma_c^2$. This risk-adjusted discount rate $r(\beta)$, which can be interpreted as the minimum expected rate of return of an investment project with risk profile β, is specific to each project through the estimation of each project's β. Equation (12.14) is usually referred to as the "consumption-based capital asset pricing" formula (CCAPM) first developed by Lucas (1978).

This alternative evaluation procedure is very specific to the joint lognormal specification considered earlier. In general, the certainty equivalent cash flows are not proportional to their expected values, and when they are, they do not vary exponentially with time, as in (12.11). Consider, for example, the case of the nuclear sector. The life cycle for the costs of producing electricity with nuclear technology passes through different phases, each yielding very different levels of risk. During the construction phase, risks on cash flows come mostly from uncertainty surrounding costs of labor and physical inputs. During the long production period, when the plant is generating electricity, the uncertainty is mostly about the price of electricity on the market. In the decommissioning phase, the uncertainty is about the cost of recycling or storing nuclear waste. Clearly, the correlations of these cash flows with the macroeconomic risk differ greatly between the three phases, and this alternative evaluation procedure needs to be adapted. This can be done by estimating the β of the cash flows in each phase separately, and by using different discount rates for them according to the CCAPM formula (12.14).

VALUATION OF THE MACROECONOMIC RISK AND THE EQUITY PREMIUM

In this section, an investment project whose risk profile exactly duplicates the macroeconomic risk is examined. This project has a cash flow that duplicates the GDP per capita. When c_t increases or decreases by 1%, so does B_t. This project has a consumption β equaling 1. If one recognizes that the GDP is formed by the sum of the revenues generated by all (physical and human) investments in the economy, an investment project with a consumption β equaling 1 should be considered as representative of the "average" project in the economy. Under the geometric Brownian specification, the riskiness of such a project should be taken into account by raising the discount rate above r_f by $\gamma \sigma_c^2$. Earlier in this book, risk aversion γ was estimated to be around 2, whereas the volatility of the growth of GDP per capita, σ_c, was estimated at around 3.6%. Therefore, a macroeconomic risk premium of around $\pi_m = \pi(1) = 0.26\%$ is obtained. This means that one should discount such an investment project with a discount rate of 3.86%, because the safe discount rate, r_f, was estimated at 3.6%.

Suppose alternatively that there is a project whose cash flows increase by $\beta\%$ when GDP per capita increases by 1%. Observe that this implies that $\text{cov}(\ln B_t / B_{t-1}, \ln c_t / c_{t-1})/\sigma_c^2 = \beta$, so that we are indeed referring here to the consumption β. Following the CCAPM equation (12.14), such a project should be evaluated by using the following discount rate:

$$r(\beta) = r_f + \beta\pi_m = 3.6\% + \beta \times 0.26\%. \tag{12.15}$$

Suppose that this investment corresponds to a traded asset. At equilibrium, agents should be indifferent to a marginal increase in their investment in this asset, so that its price must be such that the NPV of buying the asset is zero. This is the case if the equilibrium expected return of this asset is $r(\beta)$.

Let us now consider an asset that duplicates the equity market. Kocherlakota (1996) used annual data from the Standard & Poor 500 for the U.S. equity market over the period 1889–1978. He obtained a consumption β for this equity portfolio of approximately $\beta_{SP500} = 1.72$. This beta larger than one demonstrates the leveraged nature of equity. Applying equation (12.15) implies that the expected excess return of the S&P 500 should be around $1.72 \times 0.26\% = 0.44\%$. However, as shown earlier in this chapter, the excess return of equity in the United States during the twentieth century was in fact around 5.6% per year. This large discrepancy between the observed equity premium and the prediction of the CCAPM is called the equity premium puzzle.

Weil (1989) reinforces the puzzle by observing that the real risk-free rate observed in the United States over the same period is much smaller than predicted by the same model. The CCAPM formula for the risk-free rate is nothing other than the extended Ramsey rule examined in chapter 3, which corresponds to around 3.6%. This is indeed much larger than either the 1.0% documented earlier in this chapter for the period 1900–2006. It is noteworthy that this "risk-free rate puzzle" can be solved by reducing the index of risk aversion, whereas the equity premium requires an increase in the index of risk aversion to be solved.

This puzzle has attracted much attention in the economics profession. In all, hundreds of papers have been published to try to solve it. The main difficulty comes from the low level of the macroeconomic risk premium $\pi_m = \gamma \sigma_c^2$, and the low volatility of the growth of individual consumption that lies behind it. As seen earlier in this book, there are reasons to believe that this latter risk is underestimated. A possible explanation is the absence of efficient risk-sharing, so that the representative agent approach is not valid. To solve this problem, the method that led to equation (12.15) can be reversed to evaluate the efficient risk-adjusted discount rate. Suppose that markets estimate correctly the macroeconomic risk and the consumption β for equities ($\beta_{SP500} = 1.72$). The average real return of the equity market in the United States has been $r_{SP500} = 6.6\%$. Combining this with an observed short risk-free rate of $r_f = 1.0\%$ yields an estimate of the macroeconomic risk premium $\pi_m = \gamma \sigma_c^2$ by using equation (12.14):

$$\pi_m = \frac{r_{SP500} - r_f}{\beta_{SP500}} = \frac{6.6\% - 1.0\%}{1.72} = 3.26\%. \tag{12.16}$$

This implies the following alternative formula for the risk-adjusted discount rate:

$$r(\beta) = 1.0\% + \beta \times 3.26\%. \tag{12.17}$$

For example, a project whose risk profile duplicates the macroeconomic risk ($\beta = 1$) should be discounted at a rate of 4.26%. An investment whose risk profile is similar to the riskiness of the SP500 ($\beta = 1.72$) should be discounted at 6.6%.

The CCAPM discount rate r defined by (12.17) is linked to the "weighted average cost of capital" (WACC) used by firms to evaluate the NPV of their investment projects. At equilibrium, the cost of capital of a corporation with a portfolio of investments each with different β must be the capital-weighted average of the discount rates $r(\beta)$ of these investments. However, each new project should be evaluated with its own $r(\beta)$ rather than with the firm's WACC. As explained by Krüger, Landier, and Thesmar (2011), if firms use a company-wide WACC as the unique discount rate, they over-invest (respectively, underinvest) in divisions with a market beta higher (respectively, lower) than the firm's core industry beta. This "WACC fallacy" can also be found in the public sector, when a single discount rate that includes an "average" risk premium is used to evaluate public policies. To our knowledge, France is the first country to recommend using a risk-sensitive discount rate, in a report of the Centre d'Analyse Stratégique that we submitted to the French government in July 2011 (Gollier 2011). In this report, we recommend to use formula $\pi(\beta) = \beta \times 3\%$.

A SOLUTION TO THE EQUITY PREMIUM PUZZLE

At this stage, an important question arises about the pricing of risky investment projects. Which of the two rules (12.15) and (12.17) should be used for the risk-adjusted discount rate? Compared to observed prices on the market, the calibration of the CCAPM suggests a larger risk-free rate (3.6% vs. 1.0%) and a smaller macroeconomic risk premium (0.26% vs. 3.26 %). These two discrepancies can be explained by the hypothesis that the markets assume a larger macroeconomic risk, σ_c, than there is evidence for in the data. Indeed, a larger uncertainty over economic growth reduces the risk-free rate because of the magnified precautionary effect, in particular in the long run. Part II discussed various arguments for why the macroeconomic risk could be underestimated in the long term, and it was shown that reducing the interest rate from 4% to 2% is within the range of reasonable values. In addition, observe that raising the perceived macroeconomic risk, σ_c, also raises the macroeconomic risk premium $\pi_m = \gamma \sigma_c^2$. Therefore, what was done in part II may be helpful in solving the equity premium puzzle.

One possible path is to recognize that our calibration can be affected by the peso problem that was illustrated in chapter 6. It may just be the case that the data set does not contain the deep potential recessions and economic catastrophes that investors have in mind when determining their asset allocations. Barro (2006) shows that this could solve the puzzle. Weitzman (2007) proposes an alternative explanation based on the presence of uncertainty surrounding the stochastic dynamics of the economy. Let us briefly describe the idea, which follows the line of argument developed in chapter 6.

Suppose that the growth process of the economy is lognormal with parameters (μ_c, σ_c), but the true values of these parameters are uncertain. As usual, let us describe this parametric uncertainty by assuming that they are functions of parameter θ, which can take integer values 1 to n, with probability q_1 to q_n, respectively. Let us reconsider the macroeconomic risk premium $\pi_m = \pi(1)$, i.e., the premium associated to an asset whose cash flows duplicate the GDP/cap. Without parametric uncertainty, by using equations (12.6) and (12.11), it is equal to:

$$\pi_m = -\frac{1}{t}\ln\frac{F_t}{Ec_t} = -\frac{1}{t}\ln\frac{Ec_t u'(c_t)}{Ec_t\,Eu'(c_t)}. \tag{12.18}$$

With the parametric uncertainty described previously, this equation must be rewritten as follows:

$$\pi_m = -\frac{1}{t}\ln\frac{\sum\limits_{\theta=1}^{n} q_\theta E[c_t u'(c_t)\,|\,\theta]}{\left(\sum\limits_{\theta=1}^{n} q_\theta E[c_t\,|\,\theta]\right)\left(\sum\limits_{\theta=1}^{n} q_\theta E[u'(c_t)\,|\,\theta]\right)}. \tag{12.19}$$

Assume constant relative risk aversion γ. Using lemma 1, this can be rewritten in the following way:

$$\pi_m = -\frac{1}{t}\ln\frac{\sum\limits_{\theta=1}^{n} q_\theta e^{(1-\gamma)(\mu_c + 0.5(1-\gamma)\sigma_c^2)t}}{\left(\sum\limits_{\theta=1}^{n} q_\theta e^{(\mu_c + 0.5\sigma_c^2)t}\right)\left(\sum\limits_{\theta=1}^{n} q_\theta e^{-\gamma(\mu_c - 0.5\gamma\sigma_c^2)t}\right)}. \tag{12.20}$$

In the special case of no parametric uncertainty, this simplifies to $\pi_m = \gamma\sigma_c^2$. Otherwise, when (μ_c, σ_c) depends upon θ, it can be shown that the macroeconomic risk premium is increasing with the time horizon. Weitzman (2007) shows that if the uncertainty is about σ_c^2, whose inverse is distributed according to a gamma distribution as described in chapter 6,

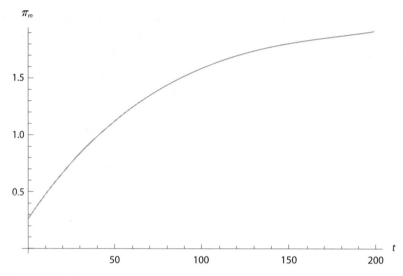

Figure 12.1. The term structure of the macroeconomic risk premium with $\delta = 0\%$, $\gamma = 2$, $\sigma_c = 3.6\%$, and $\mu_c \sim (1\%, 1/2; 3\%, 1/2)$.

then π_m becomes infinite. This therefore reverses the equity premium puzzle. As an alternative, consider a model in which $\sigma_c = 3.6\%$ is known, but the growth of log consumption is either 1% or 3% with equal probabilities (as in our simple calibration exercise in chapter 6). Taking $\gamma = 2$ as usual, a term structure for the macroeconomic risk premium is obtained, which is shown graphically in figure 12.1. The parametric uncertainty magnifies the long-term risk, raising the equilibrium risk premium. The long-term risk premium enters into the range of the equity premium observed in financial markets over the last century.

A simple picture emerges from this analysis. For short horizons, the safe discount rate should be relatively large, and the risk premium should be relatively small. However, for longer horizons, one should use a smaller safe discount rate r_f following the methods that were developed in part II. At the same time, a larger macroeconomic risk premium π_m should be used, as justified by arguments like the one developed here. This is in line with the intuition that if the macroeconomic risk increases with time at a faster rate than the one assumed by the standard Brownian motion model used in finance, then one should do two things. First, more effort should be made for the future in general (implying a reduction of the discount rate). Second, it should bias our investment toward safer projects.

THE CAPITAL ASSET PRICING MODEL

In chapter 9, the use of a representative agent was justified through the existence of efficient risk-sharing schemes in the economy. Real people may have very different von Neumann–Morgenstern preferences, and very heterogeneous income risks or investment projects. Still, if insurance markets are complete, one can assume the existence of a representative agent who consumes the income per capita in the economy, and who gets a fair share of the cash flows of the investment project under consideration. The efficiency of the allocation of risk in the economy implies that all agents will value collective investment projects in the same way. They use the same discount rates, and the same risk premia. People will unanimously accept or reject marginal investment projects. This property of competitive and complete markets has been used systematically throughout this manuscript.

Since Townsend (1994), economists have tested the efficiency of risk-sharing in our economies. The general tone of the results obtained in this literature is that risks are not shared efficiently, even in small rural villages in developing countries where stronger informal incentive devices exist to control risk transfers. As already observed in chapter 9, this implies that different people who are exposed to different risks will value collective investments differently. Consider for example an investor who is fully invested in a diversified portfolio of risky assets, and has no other source of income than this investment. Therefore, the income of this investor is the return of that stock's portfolio, which is denoted r_t^p. This could be taken to represent the community of large investors on financial markets. From their specific point of view, how will they value an investment project? Their intertemporal welfare can be written as:

$$W^p(\varepsilon) = u(r_0^p - \varepsilon) + e^{-\delta t} Eu(r_1^p + \varepsilon B_1), \qquad (12.21)$$

where the investment project consists of investing ε today for a risky payoff εB_1 at date 1. The same methodology as shown here can be used to get a symmetric result. These investors will use a risk-adjusted discount rate:

$$r(\beta^p) = r_f + \beta^p \pi^p, \tag{12.22}$$

where

$$\beta^p = \frac{\text{cov}(\ln B_t/B_{t-1}, \ln r_t^p/r_{t-1}^p)}{\sigma^{p2}} \tag{12.23}$$

measures the sensitivity of the return of the project with the investor's portfolio rather than with the macroeconomic risk, and $\pi^p = \gamma \sigma^{p2}$ is the risk premium associated with that portfolio.

The capital asset pricing model developed in the 1960s used the capital market as the representative portfolio of investors to price assets. Other reference portfolios or income profiles could be used. The fact that people facing different risks will evaluate collective investment projects in different ways presents collective decision makers with a difficult challenge. This tells us that the process of valuing an investment project cannot in general be disentangled from the question of who will bear the risk.

VALUING THE REDUCTION OF INEQUALITIES

Another application of the analysis presented in this chapter is to the evaluation of projects that reduce (or increase) inequalities in our society. Suppose that the economy is composed of N agents, indexed by $i = 1, \ldots, N$. Let q_i be the Pareto weight of agent i in the social welfare function, with $\Sigma_i q_i = 1$, and let c_{it} denote his consumption at date t. Consider an investment project whose sure payoffs are not distributed homogeneously in the population, yielding potentially an increase or a reduction of income inequalities. Let B_{it} be the benefit accruing to agent i at date t. One can define an inequality-neutral payoff F_t, following Dalton–Atkinson, as:

$$\sum_{i=1}^{N} q_i u(c_{it} + \varepsilon B_{it}) = \sum_{i=1}^{N} q_i u(c_{it} + \varepsilon F_t). \tag{12.24}$$

For a marginal investment:

$$F_t = \frac{\sum_{i=1}^{N} q_i B_{it} u'(c_{it})}{\sum_{i=1}^{N} q_i u'(c_{it})} = \frac{EB_t u'(c_t)}{Eu'(c_t)}, \tag{12.25}$$

where the expectation operator is with respect to (B, c) which, under a "veil of ignorance," takes value (B_{it}, c_{it}) with probability q_i. Equation (12.25) is formally equivalent to (12.6), and the same methodology that was developed to evaluate the risk premium can be used to evaluate the "inequality premium." In particular, if (B, c) exhibits more concordance, that is, if the project raises income inequality at date t, the inequality-neutral payoff will be smaller than the Pareto-weighted average payoff, under risk aversion. This is a direct consequence of lemma 2.

CONCLUSION

1. Valuing risky projects introduces a new dimension to the theory of investment. We have shown that this new dimension can be treated by transforming each future cash flow into its certainty equivalent. By doing this, one is back to the problem of evaluating a safe project, and the discount rates discussed in this book can be used.

2. Arrow–Lind theorem: An important result is that marginal projects whose risks can be diversified away in individual portfolios do not get any risk premium. They are actuarially priced, i.e., they should be implemented as soon as the discounted value of their expected cash flows is non-negative. This is because risk aversion is second order (compared to the expected value) in the DEU model.

3. Consumption-based Capital Asset Pricing theory: In a very particular case with a joint Brownian motion for the cash flows of the project and aggregate consumption, this methodology is equivalent to an increase in the discount rate by a risk premium which is proportional to the beta of the project. The beta measures the expected percentage increase in the net social benefit of the project when aggregate consumption increases by 1%.

4. The predictive power of the CCAPM is weak. It underestimates risk premia ("equity premium puzzle"), and it overestimates the interest rate ("risk-free rate puzzle"). These puzzles are linked to the low volatility of aggregate consumption, which may hide a much higher individual risk when risk-sharing markets do not work properly.

5. The CCAPM remains useful for a normative analysis. Risky projects should be evaluated by computing the NPV of expected cash flows using a discount rate equaling the risk-free rate examined earlier in this book plus a risk premium equaling $\beta \times 3\%$. If there is some parametric uncertainty, the systematic risk premium of 3% should be made increasing with respect to maturity. If some stakeholders bear a sizeable share of risk at some specific maturities, a specific risk premium should be substracted from the expected net benefit in the numerator of the NPV formula.

REFERENCES

Arrow, K. J., and R. C. Lind (1970), Uncertainty and the evaluation of public investment decision, *American Economic Review*, 60, 364–378.

Barro, R. J. (2006), Rare disasters and asset markets in the twentieth century," *Quarterly Journal of Economics*, 121, 823–866.

Dimson, E., P. Marsh, and M. Staunton (2002), *Triumph of the Optimists: 101 Years of Global Investment Returns*, Princeton: Princeton University Press.

Gollier, C. (2011), *Le calcul du risque dans les investissements publics*, Centre d'Analyse Stratégique, Rapports & Documents no. 36, La Documentation Française.

Kocherlakota, N. R. (1996), The equity premium: it's still a puzzle, *Journal of Economic Literature*, 34, 42–71.

Krüger, Ph., A. Landier, and D. Thesmar (2011), The WACC Fallacy: The Real Effects of Using a Unique Discount Rate, TSE Working Paper no. 11-222.

Lucas, R. (1978), Asset prices in an exchange economy, *Econometrica*, 46, 1429–1446.

Segal, U. and A. Spivak (1990), First order versus second order risk aversion, *Journal of Economic Theory*, 51, 111–125.

Tchen, A. H. (1980), Inequalities for distributions with given marginals, *Annals of Probability*, 8, 814–827.

Townsend, R. M. (1994), Risk and insurance in village India, *Econometrica*, 62, 539–592.

Weil, P. (1989), The equity premium puzzle and the risk free rate puzzle, *Journal of Monetary Economics*, 24, 401–421.

Weitzman, M. L. (2007), Subjective expectations and asset-return puzzle, *American Economic Review*, 97, 1102–1130.

13

—◄○►—

The Option Value of Uncertain Projects

Up to now in this book, an investment project was described by its flow of costs and benefits. When we introduced uncertain cash flows in the previous chapter, we did not allow the decision maker to react to the potential new information that could arise about the profitability of the project. The only decision was whether or not to invest in the project. This is quite counterintuitive. Indeed, the most basic idea of risk management is that flexibility is crucial to behaving efficiently in an uncertain world. According to this idea, an investment project is not univocally characterized by its cash flow. Rather, it is described by an oft complex and intricate dynamic decision process, where decisions must be made at different points in time. When a country decides to invest in a civil nuclear program, it must first decide to start the program, with a research and development phase that is followed by the decision to build a first prototype electricity plant. If it is successful, the decision must be made to implement the construction of several power plants in the country. Afterward, the country has the option to expand the program, or to use the accumulated experience to start a second-generation program. Similarly, when one considers the possibility of creating a high-speed railway between New York and Philadelphia, one should include in the evaluation of this investment project the option value that this first investment generates to extend the line to Boston, or to Washington. When initiating a program of abatement of greenhouse gases, one can start with a slow reduction rate with the idea that one will have the option to strengthen the program in the future if the economic and technological environment becomes more favorable.

If no new information is made available between different decision dates, the standard NPV approach remains valid to evaluate this kind of project. One just needs to make sure that all components of the project with a positive incremental NPV are included in the project from the beginning. But in most applications, new information is revealed over time about variables that may affect the profitability of the investment project and its extensions. During the implementation phase of the nuclear program, one can get new information about costs and safety, about the competitiveness of alternative technologies to produce electricity, or about the evolution of the demand for electricity. A similar observation can be made for the illustration about the high-speed train. Concerning the climate change application, the U.S. government has often justified its low-key position to fight climate change on the basis that it is better to wait for better information about the intensity of the problem, and about the cost of green technologies. Thus, the full characterization of an investment project can be an intricate combination of decisions and information revelations scattered along the time line. In some circumstances, the flow of information depends upon past decisions (such as R&D and experimentation).

In this context, the standard NPV approach is not adapted, since the cash flows to be discounted depend upon decisions to be made in the future that themselves depend upon information not yet available today. The method to be used in this context is based on backward induction, in which the standard NPV is used in each decision date, starting from the last one, and contingent to each possible signal observable at that date. In each decision date but the last one, the information-dependent optimal choices that will be made in the future are used to compute the risk-adjusted NPV that drives the decision at that date. By construction, these net present values include a positive option value coming from the possibility to flexibly react to future information. These observations were first made independently by Henry (1974) and Arrow and Fisher (1974). Since then, an important literature on option value has been developed, which is nicely summarized by Dixit and Pindyck (1994).

In the remainder of this chapter, I first illustrate the notion of an option value with a simple numerical example. I then examine a more sophisticated application with a Poisson two-armed bandit. In the first case, there is an option value to wait. In the second case, there is an option value to experiment. Applications are very wide in spectrum, from finance to climate change through corporate governance, R&D strategy, public health policy, or the extraction of natural resources.

A SIMPLE NUMERICAL EXAMPLE

Consider a simple investment project. For the next ten years, it yields a sure annual payoff that is normalized to unity. The annual payoff beyond this time horizon is uncertain. With equal probabilities, it will be either 1.6 forever or 0.4 forever. We assume that these events are not correlated to other macroeconomic variables, as economic growth. There is an irreversible sunk cost to implement the project which is equal to 20, independent of the date at which the project is implemented. We assume that the risk-free discount rate is 4%, and is constant over time. Should one invest in this project? Because the project is small and uncorrelated with aggregate growth, risk neutrality can be assumed.

Because the annual payoffs are independent with respect to the growth of aggregate consumption, the beta of the project is zero, and one can use the risk-free rate to discount the expected cash flows. If one invests today, one gets

$$NPV = \int_0^\infty e^{-0.04t} \, dt - 20 = \frac{1}{0.04} - 20 = 5. \qquad (13.1)$$

Because the expected net present value of the strategy to invest today is positive, this suggests that investing today is optimal. If the project is financed by a perpetuity, the investor will have to pay an annual interest of 0.8. The net cash flow of the project is thus equal to 0.2 over the first ten years. It is afterward equal to 0.8 in the good state of nature, or -0.4 in the bad state of nature. In that state of nature, the investor will feel regret about the initial decision to invest.

This strategy would indeed be optimal if investing today or never investing were the only two options. In reality, the right question today is whether to invest today, or to postpone that decision to the future. As is often the case in investment decisions, the problem is dynamic in nature, because the decision to invest can be postponed to get more information.

Of course, postponing the investment decision by one year has no interest. It would save one year of interest payment on the perpetuity associated with the financing of the investment cost, but the investor would give up the first annual cash flow. The net benefit of this equals $20 \times 0.04 - 1 = -0.02$, which is negative. Waiting to invest has a cost expressed by the difference between the unearned annual cash flows and the saved cost of capital.

The only benefit to postponing the decision would be to learn the state of nature about the long-term profitability of the project, and this would require waiting ten years. If one does this, one must separately consider the two alternative scenarios. In the bad state of nature, it is obvious that not investing is optimal, because the value of the perpetuity of 0.4 is not enough to compensate for the sunk cost ($10 < 20$). In the good state of nature, it is optimal to invest in the project for the symmetric argument. Evaluated at that time and in that state of nature, the NPV of investing in the project equals $(1.6/0.04) - 20 = 20$, which is positive. One is now confronted with two alternative strategies. The first strategy consists of investing today, with an expected NPV of 5. The second strategy consists of investing in ten years only in the good state of nature. In short, it yields a single cash flow of 20 with probability 50% in ten years. Evaluated from today, the expected present value of this alternative project equals $0.5 \times 20 \times e^{-0.04 \times 10} = 6.7$. This is larger than the expected NPV from investing today. In spite of the fact that investing today has a positive expected NPV, postponing the decision to invest in ten years is optimal. The value of information obtained from waiting is larger than the cost to wait coming from giving up ten years of positive cash flows net of the cost of capital.

The literature on real option values relies heavily on this methodology based on backward induction. When there exist traded assets whose prices are correlated with the payoff of the project, the option value can be evaluated by using techniques of pricing by arbitrage, as in the financial literature on options initiated by Black and Scholes (1973). McDonald and Siegel (1986) evaluate by arbitrage the option value to wait in the context of a cash flow governed by a geometric Brownian motion. Describing the resolution of the decision problem in this context would require using more sophisticated methods based on the Ito's Lemma, which is beyond the scope of this book.

LEARNING IN THE POISSON BANDIT PROBLEM

In this section, we consider a more sophisticated investment problem with two mutually exclusive projects. In order to obtain an analytical solution to this problem, we depart from the standard discrete time approach used in this book to consider a continuous time framework. The first project is safe and yields a constant cash flow s. Its NPV equals

$$\int_0^\infty se^{-rt}\,dt = \frac{s}{r}. \tag{13.2}$$

The other project is uncertain. It entails payoffs at random dates in the future, with an uncertain frequency. More specifically, the uncertain project distributes a lump-sum payoff h at random dates according to a Poisson process with parameter λ. This means that, when dt is small, there is a probability λdt to get a cash flow h in any time interval $[t, t + dt]$. The problem is that parameter λ is unknown. It can take two possible values, λ_0 and $\lambda_1 \geq \lambda_0$. At any date t, the beliefs of the decision maker are summarized by the probability p_t that the true value of λ is the good one λ_1. The expected Poisson parameter at date t is thus $\lambda(p_t)$ with

$$\lambda(p) = p\lambda_1 + (1 - p)\lambda_0. \tag{13.3}$$

Suppose that the subjective belief at date 0 about facing a good project with $\lambda = \lambda_1$ is p_0. Suppose also that the decision maker is risk-neutral, for example because the uncertain project is fully diversifiable.

Consider first a rigid context in which the take-it-or-leave-it decision to invest must be made at date 0, and is irreversible. In such a context, it is efficient to invest in the uncertain project if and only if its subjective discounted expected payoff, $\lambda(p_0)h/r$, is larger than s/r, the sure discounted payoff of the safe project, where r denotes the discount rate. This is the case if and only if the probability of facing a good investment project is larger than $p^m = (s/h - \lambda_0)/(\lambda_1 - \lambda_0)$. In order to make the problem interesting, we hereafter assume that the safe project is preferred to the bad risky project ($s > \lambda_0 h$), but is dominated by the good one ($s < \lambda_1 h$). This implies that $p^m \in [0, 1]$.

The evaluation problem becomes more complex if we relax the irreversibility assumption. Let us alternatively assume that the decision maker can switch from one project to the other at any time. The problem of evaluating the uncertain project and of describing the associated optimal investment strategy is referred to in the literature as the "two-armed bandit" problem, with one safe arm, and one uncertain arm. Rothschild (1974) and Bolton and Harris (1999, 2000) are the classical references cited in this field.

When the decision maker is on the safe project, he is unable to get any information about the uncertain project. In this alternative context, it may be desirable to first invest in the uncertain project even when $p_0 < p^m$, because of the value of learning the true value of λ by doing so. In a word, it may be optimal to experiment to learn about the true value of λ. If the observed frequency of Poisson events is too low, that would signal a bad project, and the agent should switch to the safe investment sooner or later. In the remainder of the chapter, we determine the option value generated by investing in the uncertain project.

We first examine the intensity of learning in an interval of time $[t, t + dt]$, as described in figure 13.1. Suppose that p_t is the probability of facing a good project, as evaluated at date t. If no payoff is observed in this interval, the probability of facing a good project will be lowered. Otherwise, this

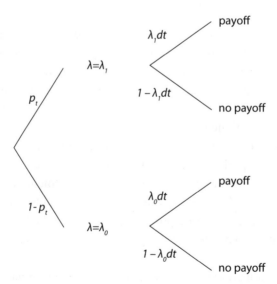

Figure 13.1. Scenarios of learning in the two-armed Poisson bandit problem.

posterior probability will be increased. In order to quantify the dynamics of beliefs, we use Bayes' rule under the following probabilistic scenarios in the interval of time $[t, t + dt]$:

Suppose that no payoff is observed during this interval of time. In that case, the beliefs at date $t + dt$ must equal

$$p_{t+dt} = \frac{p_t(1 - \lambda_1\, dt)}{p_t(1 - \lambda_1\, dt) + (1 - p_t)(1 - \lambda_0\, dt)}$$

$$= p_t - p_t(1 - p_t)(\lambda_1 - \lambda_0)\, dt + o(dt^2). \tag{13.4}$$

It implies that when no payoff is observed, the probability to face a good project decreases smoothly at rate $(1 - p_t)(\lambda_1 - \lambda_0)$ per unit of time. On the contrary, if a payoff is observed during the interval of time $[t, t + dt]$, the beliefs at time $t + dt$ must satisfy

$$p_{t+dt} = \frac{p_t \lambda_1\, dt}{p_t \lambda_1\, dt + (1 - p_t)\lambda_0\, dt} = \frac{p_t \lambda_1}{\lambda(p_t)} > p_t. \tag{13.5}$$

Thus, when a payoff is obtained in $[t, t + dt]$, the probability of a good project has an upward jump from p_t to $j(p_t) = p_t \lambda_1 / \lambda(p_t)$. The intensity of the upward jump goes to zero when p_t tends to unity. Observe that $p = 1$ is an absorbing state.

Of course, the stochastic process of the beliefs p_t is a martingale in the sense that $E p_{t+dt} = p_t$. One can compute the rate of reduction in the subjective probability of facing a good project conditional to actually facing a bad project $(\lambda = \lambda_0)$. We have that

$$E[dp_t \mid \lambda = \lambda_0] = \lambda_0\, dt(j(p_t) - p_t) - (1 - \lambda_0\, dt)p_t(1 - p_t)(\lambda_1 - \lambda_0)\, dt$$

$$= -\frac{p_t^2(1 - p_t)(\lambda_1 - \lambda_0)^2}{\lambda(p_t)}\, dt + o(dt^2). \tag{13.6}$$

In this context, the expected value of the Poisson parameter λ declines in expectation:

$$E\left[\frac{d\lambda_t}{dt} \mid \lambda = \lambda_0\right] = (\lambda_1 - \lambda_0)E\left[\frac{dp_t}{dt} \mid \lambda = \lambda_0\right] = -\frac{p_t^2(1 - p_t)(\lambda_1 - \lambda_0)^3}{\lambda(p_t)}. \tag{13.7}$$

A symmetric result is obtained conditional to the good project.

OPTIMAL INVESTMENT STRATEGY IN THE POISSON BANDIT PROBLEM

Thus, investing in the uncertain project conveys information about its quality. Because we assume that the agent can switch to the safe project if the uncertain one has a low subjective expected return, this learning process has a value that should be taken into account in the evaluation process. Let k_t denote the strategy at date t, where $k_t = 1$ means that the agent invests in the uncertain project at date t, and $k_t = 0$ means that the agent invests in the safe project at that date. We focus on Markov strategies, that is, strategies that only depend upon current beliefs: $k_t = k(p_t)$. We are looking for the Markov strategy that maximizes the discounted expected cash flow extracted from the investment:

$$U = E\left[\int_0^\infty (s(1 - k_t) + \lambda_t hk_t)e^{-rt} dt \right], \tag{13.8}$$

where the expectation operator is over the stochastic processes of p_t and k_t.

We hereafter follow the resolution strategy proposed by Keller and Rady (2010). The Bellman equation for this problem can be written as

$$U(p) = \max_{k \in \{0,1\}} ((1 - k)s + k\lambda(p)h)dt + e^{-rdt} EU(p + dp). \tag{13.9}$$

Because dt is small, this can be rewritten as

$$\begin{aligned} U(p) = \ &\max_{k \in \{0,1\}} ((1 - k)s + k\lambda(p)h)dt \\ &+ (1 - rdt)(U(p) + kdt(\lambda(p)(U(j(p)) - U(p)) \\ &- (\lambda_1 - \lambda_0)p(1 - p)U'(p))). \end{aligned} \tag{13.10}$$

Indeed, if the agent does not experiment ($k = 0$), there is no learning and $dp = 0$. If she experiments, dp will be adapted according to the Bayes rule as described earlier, and $U(p + dp)$ will differ from $U(p)$ according to the second line of equation (13.10). After eliminating $U(p)$ in both sides of this equality, it is rewritten as follows:

$$\begin{aligned} rU(p) = \ &\max_{k \in \{0,1\}} (1 - k)s + k\lambda(p)h \\ &+ k(\lambda(p)\Delta U(p) - p(1 - p)U'(p)\Delta\lambda), \end{aligned} \tag{13.11}$$

where $\Delta U(p) = U(j(p)) - U(p)$ and $\Delta\lambda = \lambda_1 - \lambda_0$. The objective to maximize in the right-hand side of this equation is the sum of the expected payoff and of the value of information. Conditional to the current belief p, it is optimal to experiment if

$$s < \lambda(p)h + \lambda(p)\Delta U(p) - p(1-p)U'(p)\Delta\lambda. \qquad (13.12)$$

In that case, the discounted expected value of the uncertain project satisfies the following ordinary differential-difference equation:

$$rU(p) = \lambda(p)h + \lambda(p)\Delta U(p) - p(1-p)U'(p)\Delta\lambda. \qquad (13.13)$$

It can be shown that the solution of this equation is

$$U(p) = \frac{\lambda(p)h}{r} + C(1-p)\left(\frac{1-p}{p}\right)^{\mu}, \qquad (13.14)$$

where C is a constant of integration and μ is the unique positive root of the following equation:

$$r + \lambda_0 - \mu(\lambda_1 - \lambda_0) = \lambda_0\left(\frac{\lambda_0}{\lambda_1}\right)^{\mu}. \qquad (13.15)$$

It can be shown that μ is increasing in the discount rate r. Equation (13.14) shows that in the continuation region (where experimenting is optimal), the discounted expected payoff of the uncertain project equals the subjective expected value of its cash flow ($\lambda h/r$) plus an option value V of switching to the safe project.

Of course, investing in the safe strategy is an absorbing state, with $U(p) = s/r$. Investing in the safe project is optimal if the probability of facing the good project is below a threshold p^* that is obtained jointly with the constant of integration C by solving the joint value-matching condition $U(p^*) = s/r$ and the smooth-pasting condition $U'(p^*) = 0$. Following Keller and Rady (2010), the solution of this system of two equations with two unknown is

$$p^* = \frac{\mu(s - \lambda_0 h)}{\mu(s - \lambda_0 h) + (\mu + 1)(\lambda_1 h - s)}, \qquad (13.16)$$

and

$$C = \frac{s - \lambda(p^*)h}{r(1-p^*)\left(\dfrac{1-p^*}{p^*}\right)^{\mu}} > 0. \qquad (13.17)$$

It is easy to see that the critical probability p^* is smaller than the myopic threshold $p^m = (s/h - \lambda_0)/(\lambda_1 - \lambda_0)$. This expresses the fact that it may be optimal to experiment when the expected return of the uncertain project is below the sure return of the safe project.

Because C is positive, the option value $V(p)$ to switch to the safe project is positive in the continuation region $p > p^*$. It takes the following form:

$$V(p) = \frac{s - \lambda(p^*)h}{r} \frac{(1-p)\left(\dfrac{1-p}{p}\right)^{\mu}}{(1-p^*)\left(\dfrac{1-p^*}{p^*}\right)^{\mu}}. \tag{13.18}$$

It is not surprising, then, that, at $p = p^*$, the option value $V(p^*) = (s - \lambda(p^*)h)/r$ just compensates for the difference between the discounted expected cash flows of the two projects.

Let us illustrate the problem with the following numerical example. Suppose that the safe asset yields a constant payoff $s = 1$ per unit of time. The uncertain project generates a payoff $h = 10$ ten times larger, but only at random dates, with a frequency that equals either $\lambda_0 = 5\%$ or $\lambda_1 = 15\%$. It yields the myopic strategy to invest in the uncertain project if the subjective probability of facing a good project is larger than $p^m = 50\%$. Suppose also that the discount rate is $r = 4\%$. Equation (13.15) exhibits solution $\mu = 0.657$. We also get from equation (13.16) that the critical subjective probability of the good project presented previously which it is optimal to invest in the uncertain project is $p^* = 28.4\%$. We finally have that $C = 4.1$, so that in the continuation region $p > p^*$, the discounted expected payoff of the optimal investment strategy equals

$$U(p) = \frac{\lambda(p)h}{r} + 4.10 \times (1-p)\left(\frac{1-p}{p}\right)^{\mu}. \tag{13.19}$$

This function is depicted in figure 13.2. The option value can be quite large. For example, if the subjective belief is $p = 50\%$, the option value is $V(0.5) = 2.05$, or 7.6% of the total value of the project $U(0.5) = 27.05$.

As seen from this analysis, option values add an important degree of complexity to the evaluation analysis. Defining an efficient dynamic risk management strategy is inescapably difficult when the current uncertainty is subject to further revision due to the arrival of new information. The

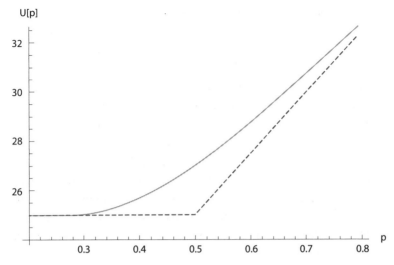

Figure 13.2. The discounted expected payoff of the optimal investment strategy, with $s = 1$, $h = 10$, $\lambda_0 = 5\%$, $\lambda_1 = 15\%$, and $r = 4\%$. The dashed curve is the value of the project when using the myopic strategy.

citizen, the judge, the politician, and the entrepreneur may have a hard time determining this strategy. How many vaccines should one purchase against a possible epidemic of unknown severity? How much effort to abate greenhouse gases whose effects on the environment are still imperfectly known? Should we impose a moratorium on some new biotechnologies yielding genetic manipulations whose long-term ecological impacts are uncertain? The precautionary principle that emerged at the Rio conference in 1992 is aimed at providing a cautious decision principle in the context of evolving uncertainties. My interpretation of this principle is that the theory of real option values should be considered seriously for the evaluation of public policies (Gollier and Treich 2003).

SUMMARY OF MAIN RESULTS

1. In an uncertain world, flexibility is crucial. Irreversible decisions have a hidden cost coming from the subsequent inability to use information that will emerge in the future.

2. The theory of real option value has the objective to adjust the standard cost-benefit methodology, which is static by nature, in order to integrate these dynamic aspects of the evaluation problem.

3. The computation of option values must be done by backward induction. At each node of the decision tree, the optimal decision is made by taking into account the optimal decisions in the subsequent nodes of that part of the tree.

4. In the case of the two-armed Poisson bandit problem, an optimal stopping-time strategy can be analytically derived. It is optimal to experiment with the uncertain project as long as the continuously updated probability of facing a good project is large enough. The computation of the minimum probability and of the associated NPV of the uncertain project takes into account an option value of learning.

REFERENCES

Arrow, K. J., and A. C. Fisher (1974), Environmental preservation, uncertainty and irreversibility, *Quarterly Journal of Economics*, 88, 312–319.

Black, F., and M. Scholes (1973), The pricing of options and corporate liabilities, *Journal of Political Economy*, 81 (3), 637–654.

Bolton, P., and C. Harris (1999), Strategic experimentation, *Econometrica*, 67, 349–374.

Bolton, P., and C. Harris (2000), Strategic experimentation: the undiscounted case, in P. J. Hammond and G. D. Myles (eds.), *Incentives, Organizations and Public Economics—Papers in Honour of Sir James Mirrlees*, Oxford: Oxford University Press.

Dixit, A. K., and R. S. Pindyck (1994), *Investment under Uncertainty*, Princeton: Princeton University Press.

Gollier, C., and N. Treich (2003), Decision-making under scientific uncertainty: The economics of the Precautionary Principle, *Journal of Risk and Uncertainty*, 27, 77–103.

Henry, C. (1974), Investment decisions under uncertainty: the irreversibility effect, *American Economic Review*, 64, 1006–1012.

Keller, G., and S. Rady (2010), Strategic experimentation with Poisson bandits, *Theoretical Economics*, 5(2), 275–311.

McDonald, R., and D. Siegel,(1986), The value of waiting to invest, *Quarterly Journal of Economics*, 101, 707–728.

Rothschild, M. (1974), A two-armed bandit theory of market pricing, *Journal of Economic Theory*, 9, 185–202.

14

———◀○▶———

Evaluation of Non-marginal Projects

The beauty and usefulness of cost-benefit analysis is that it relies on a few numbers, which represent the social value of the different dimensions of costs and benefits: the value of life, the value of environmental assets, the discount rate, or the risk premium for example. Once these values are determined, the evaluator is just required to estimate the flows of these multi-dimensional impacts, and to value them according to these prices. We show in this chapter that this simple toolbox can be used only if the actions under scrutiny are marginal, that is, if implementing them has no macroeconomic effects. Otherwise, one needs to go back to the basics of public economics to evaluate these actions. Alternative non-marginal strategies need to be compared through their impact on the social welfare function, whose description may raise new questions and new challenges in the public debate.

In this book we used the classical marginalist approach to value investments and assets. Under this approach, prices and values express marginal rates of intertemporal substitution. We obtained the ubiquitous pricing formula for the discount rate by considering a marginal transfer of consumption through time. For the risk premium, we evaluated a marginal introduction of the investment risk on welfare. This approach makes sense to express prices that sustain equilibrium with divisible goods, but this requires knowing the allocation at equilibrium. This approach also makes sense when one normatively evaluates a marginal action along the current equilibrium consumption path. It does not make sense when one evaluates non-marginal projects. Non-marginal projects are those which have an impact on the consumption path, so that they affect equilibrium prices and normative values. Discount rates and risk premiums become endogenous in that case.

Following Gollier (2011), let us illustrate this point with two examples. The first one is provided by Dietz and Hepburn (2010), and is about a large infrastructure project in Laos. The Nam Theun II hydropower dam project has a generation capacity of 1 giga-watt from a 350 meter-difference in elevation between the reservoir and the power station. The construction cost was US$ 1.3 billion, to be compared to gross consumption of the country, which is around US$2.5 billion. The construction started in 2005, and was completed in the spring of 2010. The export of electricity is expected to yield an annual benefit of US$250 million. From these figures, it is clear that the implementation of the project does affect the growth rate of the economy, and the willingness to invest for the future. Therefore, the choice of the discount rate to evaluate the project and to optimize its size must be endogenously determined.

The second example is in the context of climate change. In Dietz, Hope, and Patmore (2007), the expected damages due to climate change in the business-as-usual "high-climate" scenario are evaluated to 13.8% of world GWP in 2200. The 5–95% confidence interval spans a range from 2.9% to 35.2% of GWP. Consider a strategy that would eliminate these damages at some non-marginal cost. If we use the classical approach of discounting, should we use the extended Ramsey rule with a reduced growth rate to take into account the increasing damages, and with an increased uncertainty on growth coming from the uncertainty about these damages? This is problematic if the aim of the policy is precisely to reduce the intensity and the uncertainty of climate change!

When comparing different non-marginal policies, one needs to go back to the basic principles of public economics. If option A yields a consumption path $\{c_t^A\}_{t=0,1,...}$ and if option B yields a consumption path $\{c_t^B\}_{t=0,1,...}$, option A dominates option B if and only if it yields a larger discounted expected utility:

$$\sum_{t=0} e^{-\delta t} Eu(c_t^A) \geq \sum_{t=0} e^{-\delta t} Eu(c_t^B). \tag{14.1}$$

This approach is rarely used in cost-benefit analyses, probably because of the complexity of the problem. Indeed, it requires a full description of the utility function, of the rate of pure preference for the present, and of the joint probability distribution of the status-quo consumption and of the pay-off of the action. In spite of these challenges, this approach to the evaluation of non-marginal projects was undertaken by Nordhaus and Boyer (2000), Stern (2007), and Nordhaus (2008). Tol (2005), who reviewed the empiri-cal literature on the estimation of the shadow value of emission abatement, showed that 62 of the 103 estimations of shadow value of carbon ignored the non-marginal nature of the impacts of climate change and of our global strategy to limit them.

Following Dietz and Hepburn (2010), we hereafter examine the error that one makes by following the classical discounting approach when eval-uating non-marginal projects.

EVALUATION ERROR FOR THE DISCOUNT RATE

Suppose that we use the classical discounting approach to evaluate a project that has a non-marginal impact on the growth of consumption. What is the sign and the size of the error that one makes on the true value of the project? Concerning the sign of the effect, the intuition is quite simple. If the proj-ect is standard, with a cost incurred today for a sure benefit in the future, investing in the project will raise the expected growth rate of consumption. It will increase the discount rate through the wealth effect. Thus, the classi-cal discounting approach will rely on a too small discount rate. Therefore, since it underestimates the discount rate, it overestimates the social value of the project. Consider a project that reduces current consumption by k today, and that increases consumption by a sure amount x at some specific date t. What is the maximum cost k that one is ready to incur today to get x at date t? In other words, what is the present value of increasing consumption by x at date t? Earlier in this book, we addressed this question in the special case with x being small, and we obtained that $k_t = xe^{-r_t t}$, where r_t is the discount rate. Suppose now that x is not small. The maximum cost that one is ready to incur today to get x at date t is a function $k_t(x)$ whose properties are explored in this section. This function is defined as follows:

$$u(c_0 - k_t(x)) + e^{-\delta t} Eu(c_t + x) = u(c_0) + e^{-\delta t} Eu(c_t), \qquad (14.2)$$

where c_0 and c_t are consumption levels in the status-quo scenario respectively at dates 0 and t. If the maximum cost is incurred, investing has no effect on the intertemporal utility of the agent. This means that $k_t(x)$ is the value of x. Our aim here is to compare $k_t(x)$ to $k_t = xe^{-r_t t}$. Of course, we have that $k(0) = 0$. What about $k'(0)$?

Differentiating equation (14.2) with respect to x yields

$$k_t'(x) = \frac{e^{-\delta t} Eu'(c_t + x)}{u'(c_0 - k_t(x))},$$

(14.3)

which is positive. Using pricing formula (4.1) yields

$$k_t'(0) = e^{-r_t t}.$$

(14.4)

Not surprisingly, this result just states that the linear extrapolation $k_t(x) \simeq xe^{-r_t t}$ is exact for marginal projects. Differentiating once again, equation (14.3) yields in turn

$$k_t''(x) = \frac{k_t'(x)^2 u''(c_0 - k_t) + e^{-\delta t} Eu''(c_t + x)}{u'(c_0 - k_t)}.$$

(14.5)

This is unambiguously uniformly negative. Thus, the valuation function $k_t(x)$ is increasing and concave. It implies that the extrapolation formula $k_t = xe^{-r_t t}$ which is systematically used in cost-benefit analyses overestimates the true social value of all projects with positive future cash flows.

One can estimate the order of magnitude of the valuation error by considering the following numerical example. Normalize current consumption to unity. Suppose that the growth rate of consumption is a safe 2%, that relative risk aversion is a constant equaling 2, and that the rate of impatience is zero. In this framework, the discount rate is 4%. The true present valuation function $k_t(x)$ is depicted in figure 14.1 for a project with a one-year time horizon ($t = 1$). It appears that it is very quickly different from $xe^{-0.04}$. For example, for a benefit that represents 10% of current consumption, the true present value is $k_t(0.1) = 8\%$, which should be compared to the traditional valuation $0.1e^{-0.04} = 9.6\%$. The (over-)estimation error represents one-fifth of the true present value.

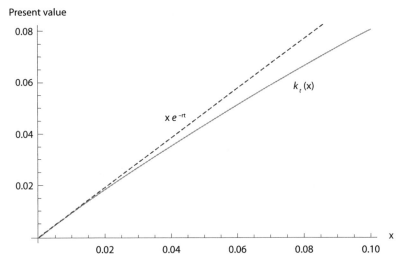

Figure 14.1. The true present valuation function as a function of the size x of the future benefit. We assume that $t = 1$, $c_0 = 1$, $c_1 = 1.02$, $\delta = 0$, and $u'(c) = c^{-2}$. The dashed line corresponds to the present value extrapolated from the Ramsey rule ($r = 4\%$).

THE SIZE-ADJUSTED EFFICIENT DISCOUNT RATE

The use of an explicit welfare function to evaluate a non-marginal project may be cumbersome for practioners. We hereafter elaborate an alternative approach in which we preserve the basic discounting approach, but in which we adapt the discount rate to take into account the size of the project. This may be done by defining the size-adjusted discount rate $r_t(x)$ by the following condition:

$$k_t(x) = xe^{-r_t(x)t}, \tag{14.6}$$

where $k_t(x)$ is defined by condition (14.2). If the cost of the project is less (larger) than its present value defined by (14.6), its implementation will obviously raise (reduce) the intertemporal welfare, so that $r_t(x)$ can indeed be interpreted as a size-adjusted discount rate. It can be rewritten explicitly as

$$r_t(x) = -\frac{1}{t}\ln\frac{k_t(x)}{x}. \tag{14.7}$$

Using L'Hospital's rule, we obtain the standard formula for marginal projects:

$$r_t(0) = -\frac{1}{t}\ln k'(0) = \delta - \frac{1}{t}\ln\frac{Eu'(c_t)}{u'(c_0)}, \tag{14.8}$$

where the second equality is obtained from (14.3). We are interested in measuring the sensitivity of the discount rate in the neighborhood of small benefits. By condition (14.7), we have that

$$r_t'(x) = -\frac{1}{t}\frac{k_t'(x)x - k_t(x)}{xk_t(x)}. \tag{14.9}$$

Using L'Hospital's rule twice, we obtain:

$$r_t'(0) = -\frac{1}{t}\lim_{x\to 0}\frac{k_t''(x)x}{k_t(x) + xk_t'(x)} = -\frac{1}{t}\lim_{x\to 0}\frac{k_t'''(x)x + k_t''(x)}{2k_t'(x) + xk_t''(x)} = -\frac{k_t''(0)}{2tk_t'(0)}. \tag{14.10}$$

From equations (14.4) and (14.5), we have that

$$-\frac{k_t''(0)}{k_t'(0)} = -\frac{k_t'(0)^2 u''(c_0) + e^{-\delta t}Eu''(c_t)}{u'(c_0)k_t'(0)}$$

$$= k_t'(0)\left(-\frac{u''(c_0)}{u'(c_0)}\right) + \frac{e^{-\delta t}Eu'(c_t)}{u'(c_0)k_t'(0)}\left(-\frac{Eu''(c_t)}{Eu'(c_t)}\right) \tag{14.11}$$

$$= e^{-r_t(0)t}\frac{R_0}{c_0} + \frac{R_t}{Ec_t}.$$

where $R_0 = -c_0u''(c_0)/u'(c_0)$ is the index of relative risk aversion evaluated at c_0, and $R_t = -Ec_t Eu''(c_t)/Eu'(c_t)$ is the risk-adjusted relative risk aversion at date t. Combining equations (14.10) and (14.11) yields

$$r_t'(0)Ec_t = \frac{e^{(\mu_t - r_t(0))t}R_0 + R_t}{2t}, \tag{14.12}$$

where $e^{\mu_t t} = Ec_t/c_0$ is the annualized growth rate of expected consumption between dates 0 and t. Notice that the left-hand side of equation (14.12) is the quasi-elasticity of the discount rate relative to the size of the cash flow in the neighborhood of $x = 0$. It measures the percentage increase in

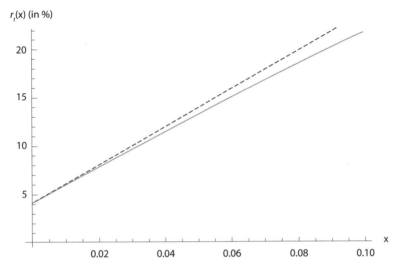

Figure 14.2. The size-adjusted discount rate as a function of the size x of the future benefit. We assume that $t = 1$, $c_0 = 1$, $c_1 = 1.02$, $\delta = 0$, and $u'(c) = c^{-2}$. The dashed line corresponds to size-adjusted rate from the first-order Taylor approximation $r_t(x) \simeq r_t(0) + r'_t(0)x$.

the efficient discount rate when the cash flow at date t increases by 1% of expected consumption. When t is normalized to unity, the right-hand side of this equality is close to the average of relative risk aversion evaluated at dates 0 and t.

Let us reconsider the numerical example of the previous section, with $t = 1$, $c_0 = 1$, $c_1 = 1.02$, $\delta = 0$, and $u'(c) = c^{-2}$. It yields $R_0 = R_1 = 2$ and $Exp(\mu_1 - r_1(0)) = 0.98$. Consider a benefit that represents 1% of consumption at date 1. Adjusting for the size of this benefit would require increasing the discount rate from 4% to $4\% + 1\% \times (0.98 \times 2 + 2)/2 = 5.98\%$. In figure 14.2, we draw function $r_t(x)$ for benefits x up to 10% of future GDP.

EVALUATION ERROR FOR THE RISK PREMIUM

The risk premium presented in chapter 12, and the standard asset prices from the classical theory of finance, are also valid only for marginal risks.

Let us for example re-examine the theorem of Arrow and Lind (1970) that states that the risk premium should be zero if the cash flows are risky but independent of the risk on aggregate consumption. We noticed in chapter 12 that this result is justified by the observation that risk aversion is of the second order on the certainty equivalent. When a risk tends to zero, its risk premium tends to zero as the square of its size. Consider a risky cash flow $\mu + xy$ at date t, where y is a zero-mean risk, x is a scalar that characterizes the size of the risk on the cash flow, and μ is the expected cash flow. Let us consider the compensating risk premium $\pi_c(x)$ which is implicitly defined by the following equality:

$$Eu(c_t + \mu + xy + \pi_c(x)) = Eu(c_t + \mu). \tag{14.13}$$

The compensating risk premium is the amount to pay to the risk bearer to compensate her for the risk. In general, it differs from the standard risk premium, which is the equivalent sure reduction in consumption that has the same effect on expected utility as the risk under consideration. But for small risks, the classical risk premium and the compensated risk premium are equal.

Of course, $\pi_c(0) = 0$. Differentiating equation (14.13) with respect to x yields

$$E(y + \pi_c'(x))u'(c_t + \mu + xy + \pi_c(x)) = 0. \tag{14.14}$$

It implies that

$$\pi_c'(x) = -\frac{Ey\, u'(c_t + \mu + xy + \pi_c(x))}{Eu'(c_t + \mu + xy + \pi_c(x))}. \tag{14.15}$$

The right-hand side of this equality is non-negative, since y and u' are negatively correlated when x is positive. By the covariance rule, it implies that $Eyu' \leq EyEu' = 0$. However, when x tends to zero, we have that $\pi_c'(0) = 0$. This is the Arrow–Lind theorem. Marginal risks that are uncorrelated to the economy have no social cost. But what can we say about non-marginal independent risks? Differentiating equation (14.14) again implies that

$$E(y + \pi_c'(x))^2 u''(c_t + \mu + xy + \pi_c(x)) = -\pi_c''(x)\, Eu'(c_t + \mu + xy + \pi_c(x)). \tag{14.16}$$

Observe that the left-hand side of this equality is uniformly negative under risk aversion. It implies that the compensating risk premium is an increasing and convex function of the size of risk. This result does not hold for the classical risk premium, as shown by a counter-example presented in Eeckhoudt and Gollier (2001).

One can evaluate the error when estimating the risk premium by using the Arrow–Lind theorem. Using equation (14.16) around $x = 0$ and assuming $\mu = 0$ for the sake of a simple notation, we obtain that

$$\pi_c''(0) = -\frac{Ey^2 Eu''(c_t)}{Eu'(c_t)} = \frac{Ey^2 R_t}{Ec_t}, \tag{14.17}$$

where $R_t = -Ec_t Eu''(c_t)/Eu'(c_t)$ is the risk-adjusted relative degree of risk aversion at date t. The second-order Taylor approximation of the compensated risk premium around $x = 0$ implies that

$$\frac{\pi_c(x)}{Ec_t} \simeq 0.5 \, Var\left(\frac{xy}{Ec_t}\right) R_2, \tag{14.18}$$

which is the Arrow–Pratt approximation. This means that the risk premium expressed as a percentage of initial expected consumption is approximately equal to half times the product of the variance of the relative change in consumption by the risk-adjusted relative risk aversion. For example, if the standard deviation of the cash flow of the project equals 5% of aggregate consumption, and relative risk aversion equals 2, the risk premium is approximately equal to one-fourth of a percent of aggregate consumption. As explained earlier in this book, this approximation is exact when y is log normally distributed, c_t is constant, and the utility function belongs to the CRRA family.

SUMMARY OF MAIN RESULTS

1. Cost-benefit analysis is based on the marginalist approach. It can be used only if the investment project under evaluation is marginal, i.e., if its implementation does not affect equilibrium prices in the economy. The evaluation of non-marginal projects must be done by measuring their impact on the social welfare function.

2. A non-marginal investment project with positive future cash flows will have an impact on welfare that is smaller than when estimated by using the standard discounting method. This is because

implementing the project will increase economic growth. This will in turn increase the discount rate through the wealth effect.

3. The risk premium associated with a risky non-marginal project will be larger than by using the CCAPM approach. This is because the (compensated) risk premium is convex in the size of risk.

REFERENCES

Arrow, K. J., and R. C. Lind (1970), Uncertainty and the evaluation of public invest-ment decision, *American Economic Review*, 60, 364–378.

Dietz, S., and C. Hepburn (2010), On non-marginal cost-benefit analysis, Grantham Research Institute on Climate Change and the Environment, WP18.

Dietz S., C. Hope, and N. Patmore (2007), Some economics of "dangerous" cli-mate change: reflections on the Stern Review, *Global Environmental Change*, 17, 311–325.

Eeckhoudt, L., and C. Gollier (2001), Which shape for the cost curve of risk? *Journal of Risk and Insurance*, 68, 387–402.

Gollier, C. (2011), Discounting and risk adjusting non-marginal investment projects, *European Review of Agricultural Economics*, 38 (3), 297–324.

Nordhaus, W. D. (2008), *A Question of Balance: Weighing the Options on Global Warming Policies*, New Haven, CT: Yale University Press.

Nordhaus, W. D., and J. Boyer (2000), *Warming the World: Economic Models of Global Warming*, Cambridge, MA: MIT Press.

Stern, N. (2007), *Stern Review: The Economics of Climate Change*, Cambridge: Cam-bridge University Press.

Tol, R.S.J. (2005), The marginal damage costs of carbon dioxide emissions: an assess-ment of the uncertainties, *Energy Policy*, 33 (16), 2064–2074.

Global Conclusion

The discount rate is a key parameter in economics because it determines how our societies value their future. The aim of this book was to help build a consensus on the social discount rate to use in the NPV decision rule: to find the discount rate which gives a positive NPV only for those projects that raise the sum of present and future generations' felicity. In this book, I advocated the following set of principles:

1. The driving force of discounting is the collective aversion to (intertemporal) inequalities which in the models in this book is represented by a concave relation between consumption and felicity. The relative aversion to inequality has been set to 2. This is normative and implies that one should be ready to give up as much as 4 euros of consumption from individual A to increase the consumption level of individual B by 1 euro, when A consumes twice as much as B.
2. Following the Ramsey rule, safe real cash flows maturing within the next 5–10 years should be discounted at a rate that is two times the real growth rate of the economy. Assuming an expected growth rate of the economy around 2% per year, this yields a discount rate of 4% for short horizons.
3. Because of large uncertainties about the evolution of our economies in the distant future, the long branch of the term structure of real discount rates should be decreasing. This is perfectly compatible with the time consistency of collective decisions. Given this uncertainty, the real discount rate for safe projects should converge to somewhere between 1% and 2% for distant maturities.
4. Uncertain projects should be evaluated using the same discount rates, but to discount the certainty equivalents of their cash flows.

In the special case in which these cash flows follow a geometric Brownian process as does aggregate consumption, this is equivalent to discount the expected cash flows at a rate adjusted for risk. This risk premium should be equal to 3% of the project's beta, which measures the expected percentage increase in its net social benefit when aggregate consumption increases by 1%.

5. The adaptability of projects should be valued by estimating option values.

Index

additive model, 42, 45
additive time preferences, 28–29
Allais, M., 24, 43, 168–69
Allais' paradox, 43
ambiguity aversion: maxmin, 173–75; smooth, 175–78
ambiguity prudence effect, 176–77
anticipatory feelings, 28–29
Arrow, K. J., 31, 190, 204, 222
Arrow-Debreu securities, 132–33, 135
Arrow-Lind theorem, 190–92, 222
Arrow-Pratt approximation, 44, 57–58, 190, 223
Asheim, G. B., 32–33n
asset pricing: capital asset pricing model (CAPM), 11, 200; classical equilibrium formula for, 189; consumption-based capital asset pricing model (CCAPM), 190–96, 201–2; evaluation of risky projects, 185 (*see also* risky projects/risk premium)
autoregressive model, 68
Aydede, S. K., 151

bandit problem, 210
Bansal, R., 67, 71
Barro, R. J., 75–76, 197
Baumol, William, vii
Baumstark, Luc, 9
Bayes rule, 87, 90, 92, 96, 209
Bernoulli-von Neumann-Morgenstern expected utility theory, 42–43. *See also* von Neumann-Morgenstern expected utility theory
Black, F., 206
Bolton, P., 208
Bommier, A., 155
Boyer, J., 217
Broome, J., 31
Brownian motion, discrete version of, 67
business cycles, economic growth and, 64

cake-sharing rule, 135–37
capital: continuously compounded rate of return on, 23; opportunity cost of, 5, 98; rate of return on marginal productive, 25; rate of return on risk-free, 98
capital asset pricing model (CAPM), 11, 200
CBA. *See* cost-benefit analysis
CCAPM. *See* consumption-based capital asset pricing model
Cecchetti, S. G., 79
certainty equivalent, 151–52, 189
China, 51–52, 77
Clark, G., 1, 74, 145
climate change: concerns regarding, 1–2; discount rate applied to, 6; global inequality and, 131; non-marginal project, example of, 216; precautionary principle at the Rio conference, 213; risk assessment and, 12
Club of Rome, 1
Cochrane, J. H., 114
compensating risk premium, 222–23
concordance and supermodularity, 121–23
Constantinides, G., 178
consumption: accounting for optimal under the Weitzman argument, 104–5; estimating the growth rate of, 41–42; intergenerational habit formation and, 178–80; uncertainty about in the distant future, 101–2
consumption-based capital asset pricing model (CCAPM), 190–96, 201–2
consumption habits, 28–29
continuously compounded rates, 23
Copenhagen Consensus, 7
correlation aversion, 155
correlation effect, 156, 159
cost-benefit analysis (CBA), 4–5, 149, 215
Cox, J., 114
Cropper, M. L., 151